Inspiration and of the Bible

An Historical and Exegetical Study

First Prizewinner
Zondervan's Third Christian Textbook Contest

by
R. LAIRD HARRIS

Professor of Old Testament, Covenant Theological Seminary, St. Louis, Mo.

ZONDERVAN PUBLISHING HOUSE OF THE ZONDERVAN CORPORATION GRAND RAPIDS, MICHIGAN 49506

INSPIRATION AND CANONICITY OF THE BIBLE
Copyright 1957, 1969 by
Zondervan Publishing House
Grand Rapids, Michigan

Library of Congress Catalog Card Number: 78-81044

Enlarged and revised "Contemporary
Evangelical Perspectives" edition

ISBN 0-310-25891-X

Printed in the United States of America

83   84   85   86   87   88 — 20   19   18   17   16

To My Wife
*with greatest appreciation of
our union in the things
of the Word*

ACKNOWLEDGMENTS

Acknowledgment is gratefully given to the following publishers and owners of copyrighted material for permission to use brief extracts from their books:

The Christian Doctrine of God by Emil Brunner, published by the Westminster Press, Philadelphia.

Christianity and Liberalism by J. Gresham Machen, Macmillan, permission by the copyright owners, Westminster Theological Seminary, Philadelphia.

The Doctrine of the Word of God (Volume I, Part I), by Karl Barth, published by T. & T. Clark, Edinburgh.

Faith and History by Reinhold Niebuhr, published by Charles Scribner's Sons, New York.

The Faith of Modernism by Shailer Mathews, Macmillan, permission by the copyright owner, Robert E. Mathews, Columbus, Ohio.

The Mishna tr. by H. Danby, published by the Clarendon Press, Oxford.

Nature and Destiny of Man by Reinhold Niebuhr, published by Charles Scribner's Sons, New York.

Philosophy of the Christian Revelation by Edwin Lewis, published by Harper and Brothers, New York.

A Preface to Bible Study by Alan Richardson, copyright, 1944, The Westminster Press, Philadelphia.

The Christian Answer, ed. by H. P. van Dusen, published by Charles Scribner's Sons, New York.

PREFACE

Inspiration is a much-treated subject. It is, however, one of perennial importance. Somewhat strangely, it seems to the author, the question of inspiration is often considered without giving proper attention to the question of canonicity. It would seem that the second matter is corollary to the first, for to know what is inspired is as vital as to know the nature of inspiration. Therefore in the present study, the canonicity of both the Old Testament and the New is treated with the doctrine of inspiration, and attention is also given to the other question, subsidiary to that of inspiration, the transmission of the Biblical text through the centuries.

The author has not tried to be novel. His view of inspiration is in full accord with the historic Christian position. Likewise, his views of the transmission of the sacred text and of the canon are not novel, although several differing views concerning the principle of determination of the canon — views not necessarily mutually exclusive — have been held through the centuries, and there is more room for divergent views on this point. An abundance of new information on the subject of both the text transmission and the canon of the Old Testament may be obtained from the Dead Sea Scrolls. It is hoped that the following pages will assist Christians in evaluating this angle of study of the scrolls, whose discovery was so unexpected and which shed such surprising and welcome light upon the history of the Old Testament. It may be helpful to add that the new scrolls have not altered any point already held for years by conservative Old Testament scholars such as Robert Dick Wilson, etc. Several of the positions of extreme critics have been disproved by the new finds, as the following pages indicate, though the scrolls are not

7

early enough to render a final verdict in many of the critical-conservative discussions. An attempt has been made to assess them for what they are worth and not to push their witness beyond the available evidence.

More than a hundred years ago S. R. L. Gaussen, of Geneva, wrote his book *Theopneusty — or the Plenary Inspiration of the Holy Scriptures*. It has been a standard. But during the last century the four winds of the heavens have blown with hurricane force upon Gaussen's edifice. Can the historic Christian view still be sustained? In the late nineteenth century higher criticism grew to such colossal proportions that the Biblical scholarship of Europe was almost totally captured. Today it is taught as certain fact in by far the largest number of theological seminaries of Europe and America. During the same period the teaching of evolution so captured the scientific world that the view is abroad that science has flatly demolished any strict and fair interpretation of the early chapters of Genesis. Books have appeared in large numbers on such themes as *What Can We Still Believe?* Many have attempted a strategic withdrawal before these two powerful antagonists of the doctrine that the Bible is actually true in its history and science as well as in spiritual matters.

The author is one of those who believes the Book. He believes that higher criticism — constructed, as it plainly was, in an era when virtually nothing was known about ancient times as a result of archeological investigation — has not measured up to the new information and must be greatly modified or totally rejected. Likewise, there is indication, touched upon in the following chapters, that evolution has no known mechanism of operation and that its explanation, at least of human origins, has already been so modified that we may say the evidence for the crossing over from one group of life forms to another, and specifically from brute to human forms, is simply lacking. There is considerable evidence for variation within the human species, but for evolutionary development, none. It is possibly time for Christians to become aware of these new facts and, in boldness, to reaffirm the historic Christian position. This position has been held all these years by countless millions of humble believers. They have based their faith on evidence of a different kind — the witness of their Lord. But in the light of the new evidence and studies, the humble faith can perhaps be shown to be the best-supported science and history as well. This is the author's conviction.

Great issues hang on the consequences of our position. It is all too often held that verbal inspiration (which, carefully defined, is the historic Christian view) is an elective in Christian theology which may be accepted or omitted. It is hoped that the present study will convincingly show that the humble Christian believer has been right in his instinctive judgment that one must accept all the Bible or have no certainty regarding any of it. A textbook on physics may be 99 per cent right and 1 per cent wrong. The part that is right we believe because it is inherently true and provable. The remainder we are at liberty to reject. But he who believes the Bible piecemeal has already denied that it is to be believed at all upon authority. For the same Lord that authenticates the Psalms also authenticates Genesis 3 and the authorship of Daniel. When a Christian denies Biblical facts and history, he doubts his Lord. Here arises the earnestness of all Christian inquiry into matters of Biblical authority. It is still true that if "ye believed Moses, ye would have believed me: for he wrote of me." Biblical questions are still basic. It is hoped that they have received fair and careful treatment in these pages. May this study stimulate others in the same field.

It is a pleasant duty to acknowledge a deep indebtedness to others — to the great men who have gone before, but also to several friends of today.

The view here presented that the original division of the Old Testament canon did not consist of three definite sections, but was somewhat fluid, and that certain books were sometimes in the second division and sometimes in the third, is not original with the author. It apparently was held in former days, but the view of a threefold development gained credence among critical scholars in the last century. Then, among conservatives, the prestige of the name of William Henry Green carried the day for the theory of a tripartite canon. Robert Dick Wilson, approaching the evidence afresh, taught the view here espoused of a fluid threefold classification of the books. It was passed on to the author by his teacher, Wilson's pupil, Dr. Allan A. MacRae. It is a pleasure to acknowledge this debt.

In the survey of the evidence from the early Christian centuries as to why our present New Testament books were chosen, the author has been greatly assisted by a younger colleague and friend, Mr. William A. Sanderson. Mr. Sanderson first approached the evidence while pursuing a master's thesis under the author. Another of the author's students, Mr. Carl Cassel, who did similar master's thesis work at Wheaton College, came to the same conclusion. Both of these theses have been used for reference to the material, though the material has been constantly checked. It is perhaps of interest that when these students began their research, both had a different view of the test of canonicity held by the Early Church. Examination of the evidence led them also to the views here espoused.

Finally, thanks are due to patient students who, in year after year of classes, have offered incentive and encouragement in the study of God's Word. The author's thanks to students who have taught him!

R. Laird Harris

Covenant College and Theological Seminary
St. Louis, Missouri

CONTENTS

BIBLIOGRAPHY

Allegro, John M., *The Dead Sea Scrolls* (London: Penguin Books, 1956).

Audet, J. P., "Affinités littéraires et dpctroma; es di 'Manuel de Discipline' " in *Revue biblique*, 1952, pp. 219-38; 1953, pp. 41-82.

Bardtke, H., *Die Handschriftenfunde am Toten Meer* (Berlin: Evangelische Haupt-Bibelgesellschaft, 1952).

Bauchet, J. M. P., "The Newly Discovered Scrolls of the Judean Desert" in *Catholic Biblical Quarterly*, 1949, pp. 308ff.

Baumgarten, J. M., "Sacrifice and Worship Among the Jewish Sectarians of the Dead Sea (Qumran) Scrolls" in *Harvard Theological Review*, 1953, pp. 141ff.

Baumgartner, W., "Die Bedeutung der Hohlenfunde aus Palastina fur die Theologie" in *Schweizerische Theologische Umschau*, 1954, pp. 49ff.

Birnbaum, S. A., "The Date of the Habakkuk Cave Scroll" in *Journal of Biblical Literature*, 1949, pp. 161ff.

————, "Notes on the Internal and Archaeological Evidence Concerning the Cave Scrolls" in *Journal of Biblical Literature*, 1951, pp. 227-32.

Brownlee, W. H., "The Jerusalem Habakkuk Scroll" in *Bulletin of the American Schools of Oriental Research*, December, 1948, pp. 8-18.

————, "A Comparison of the Covenanters of the Dead Sea Scrolls with Pre-Christian Jewish Sects" in *Biblical Archaeologist*, 1950, pp. 50-72.

————, "The Cross of Christ in the Light of Ancient Scrolls" in *The United Presbyterian*, November 20, 1953, pp. 6-11; December 7, p. 11.

Crowfoot, G. M., "Linen Textiles from the Cave of Ain Feshkha in the Jordan Valley" in *Palestine Exploration Quarterly*, 1951, pp. 5-31.

Davies, W. D., " 'Knowledge' in the Dead Sea Scrolls and Matthew 11:25-30" in *Harvard Theological Review*, 1953, pp. 113-39.

Eissfeldt, O., "Die Bedeutung der 1947 in Palastina aufgefundeded alten hebraischen und aramaischen Handschriften" in *Forschungen und Fortschritte*, 1949, pp. 196-200.

Gaster, Theofor H., *The Dead Sea Scriptures* (New York: Doubleday and Company, 1956).

Guillaume, A., "Mt. 27, 46 in the Light of the Dead Sea Scrolls" in *Palestine Exploration Quarterly*, 1951, pp. 78-80.

Guindon, W. G., "Radio-active Carbon and the Dead Sea Scrolls" in *Catholic Biblical Quarterly*, 1951, pp. 268-75.

Johnson, S. E., "The Dead Sea Manual of Discipline and the Jerusalem Church of Acts" in *Zeitschrift fur die alttestamentliche Wissenschaft*, 1954, pp. 106-20.

Lieberman, S., "Light on the Cave Scrolls from Rabbinic Sources" in *Proceedings of the American Academy for Jewish Research*, 1951, pp. 395-404.

Mowry, L., "The Dead Sea Scrolls and the Gospel of John" in *Biblical Archaeologist*, 1954, pp. 78-97.

Rabin, C., "Notes on the Habakkuk Scroll and the Zadokite Documents" in *Vetus Testamentum*, 1955, pp. 148-62.

Rabinowitz, I., "Sequence and Dates of the Extra-Biblical Dead Sea Scroll Texts and 'Damascus Fragments' " in *Vetus Testamentum*, 1953, pp. 175-85.

Roberts, B. J., "The Dead Sea Scrolls and the Old Testament Scriptures" in *Bulletin of the John Rylands Library,* 1953, pp. 75-96.

Sukenik, E. L., *mgylwt gnwzwt* (Jerusalem: Bialik Foundation, I, 1948; II, 1950).

Teicher, J. L., "The Damascus Fragments and the Origin of the Jewish Christian Sect" in *Journal of Jewish Studies,* 1951, pp. 115-43.

————, "Jesus in the Habakkuk Scroll" in *Journal of Jewish Studies,* 1952, pp. 53-55.

————, "The Teaching of the Pre-Pauline Church in the Dead Sea Scrolls" in *Journal of Jewish Studies,* 1952, pp. 11-18.

————, "Jesus' Sayings in the Dead Sea Scrolls" in *Journal of Jewish Studies,* 1954, p. 38.

Zeitlin, S., "The Essenes and Messianic Expectations" in *Jewish Quarterly Review,* 1954, pp. 83-119.

ABBREVIATIONS

BA   —*The Biblical Archaeologist*
BASOR— *Bulletin of the American Schools of Oriental Research*
JBL   — *Journal of Biblical Literature*
ANF   — *The Ante-Nicene Fathers,* ed. by Robertson and Donaldson
DSD   — The Dead Sea Scroll, Manual of Discipline
DSIsª — The Dead Sea Scroll of Isaiah, the First
CDC   — The Covenant of the Damascus Covenanters (Zadokite Fragments)
DSM   — Dead Sea Manual of Discipline

PART I — INSPIRATION

CHAPTER 1

INTRODUCTION

In our country and throughout Western civilization the great majority of men give high honor to the Bible. It may not be read as faithfully as it might be. In many a home it may be left to gather dust on the hall table. But doubtless the majority of American homes have Bibles and reverence the Word of God at least in theory. In the homes and hearts of millions it is reverenced in fact as well as in theory, and the blessings of its ennobling doctrine still enrich many lives as they have blessed the lives and the homes of our forefathers.

The Bible was the first book printed. A portion of the Bible, the *Bay Psalm Book,* was the first book printed in this country. The Bible is still far and away the best-selling book in our land. When the Revised Standard Version was published, its sale — in spite of numerous defects which many believe mar that new translation — exceeded all expectations of friends and opponents alike. The Bible has been translated into many more languages than any other book and blesses its devoted readers in more than a thousand languages. Its power in our English culture is not the result of the especially beautiful style of the King James Version of 1611. Indeed, it is fair to say that the King James Version was the product of those who loved the Bible rather than that it was the cause of such love. Several previous versions had made the English people know and love the Bible as God's Word in whatever dress it appeared. On the Continent the great movement of revival called the Protestant Reformation had been sparked by a renewed emphasis upon the Bible. The two great principles of the Reformation were justification by faith alone and the supreme authority of the Bible. In Germany one of the most enduring fruits of the work of the great Reformer was Luther's translation of the Bible, a translation which, four centuries later, is still loved by many a German. It is usually recognized that Luther's choice of a dialect for his version is the thing that assured that dialect a place of supremacy so that it is to this day the nation's language. So mightily grew the Word of God and prevailed.

The question has been repeatedly asked: What is it about the Bible that has caused it to receive such tremendous recognition — world-wide and enduring — from people of various temperaments and civilizations, and to beget in its adherents a devotion to the extent of martyrdom itself? What is the secret of the Bible's appeal? In itself it is a strange phenomenon that a history of the struggles and the sins of the kings and the priests of an ancient and feeble nation should have a compelling fascination even for the children of our day. And men ask themselves what possible meaning the story of a religious Teacher of Jewry and His little band of twelve fishermen can have for our day. If the Bible were merely a collection of ancient tales, not to say legends, the imposing structure of the Christian Church, with all its beneficent enterprises, would rest upon a foundation of sand. If the Bible were merely a classic, it could be of interest, but there would be no explanation of its power over the hearts of men. That the Bible is a Book of interest and of beauty and of moral force, few would care to deny. But that it is more than this seems abundantly self-evident.

The fact is that the Bible has had its influence in the world and in the hearts of men in those places where it has been received as nothing less than God's Book, a revelation of life and light and immortality. There, its beauty is seen to be the beauty of truth. Its stories are the records of actual divine intervention in history. Its characters are men to whom and through whom God has spoken. And its central figure is the incarnate God. This, as we shall see, is what the Bible claims to be — a Book inspired by the Spirit of God, bringing a message of salvation to despairing and helpless men.

Several definitions are necessary as we approach a subject so much discussed as inspiration of the Bible. The word "inspiration" is used in a variety of senses. When the flag is being lowered at retreat, military music on the parade ground may be called deeply inspiring. Elevated poetry, or art, or a rhetorical appeal for action in a good cause may be said to be inspiring. But the Bible is said to be inspired in the old sense of the word. The term "inspire," of course, implies that there is a spirit within. We say music is inspiring because it elevates the spirit within us. But the older use of the word with regard to the Bible comes from the reference in II Timothy 3:16, "All scripture is inspired of God," meaning that the Holy Spirit of God had worked in the production of the Bible. The Spirit of God was within the authors who produced it. To put it simply, the Christian Church has believed through the centuries that the Bible was produced of God. It is God's Word. It is inspired by God. But because the word "inspiration" is used in different senses even in theological circles, it has become necessary now to qualify the term to indicate specifically what is meant when a man affirms belief in the "inspiration" of the Bible. In a former generation the word "plenary," meaning "full," was used as the qualifying adjective to indicate one's belief that the Bible was "fully inspired." This is the terminology used by Charles Hodge in his well-known *Systematic Theology*. He means by this that the Bible is all from God; it is the Word of God *in toto,* and there is no admixture of human error in its production.[1] The same fact is now often expressed in other ways because Hodge's phrase has sometimes been taken to mean merely that all parts of the Bible from Genesis to Revelation were in some way produced by God's help, but are not all necessarily of absolute divine truth. To preserve the older concept, the phrase "verbal inspiration" or "verbal plenary inspiration" is now often used to declare that God superintended the very choice of words in the Holy Volume so that it may be truly said to be entirely God's Word without admixture of human error. This may also be expressed by insisting that the Bible is "true throughout" or by specifying that it is without error in fact, doctrine, or judgment.

The idea of "verbal inspiration" has been rejected by a great many theologians in the last half-century. It is, of course, the privilege of any man to reject any truth. There are very few teachings which have been denied by no one! But it seems exceedingly unfortunate that the doctrine of verbal inspiration has not only been rejected in recent days but misunderstood, then caricatured, maligned, and held up to attack as if to kill it were to do God service. At present all we wish to do is to define the doctrine. The support of it must come later.

Some caricature the doctrine by saying that they cannot believe so rigid and mechanical a "dictation theory." Now, rigid the doctrine may be; but it is not mechanical, unless it be held that the Spirit of God has no ways to work except mechanical ways. According to the Bible the Spirit of God took the king of Assyria on a great expedition against Israel and Judah without the king's knowing at all that he was accomplishing the purposes of Jehovah, the God of Israel (Isa. 10:5f.). The Lord is equally able, according to our doctrine, to use and supervise King David's willing mouth to speak what is God's truth and only the truth (II Sam. 23:2) without his thereby having his own natural powers of rhetoric and song suspended. Of course, there are parts of the Bible that were dictated. God not only spoke the Ten Commandments, but Scripture says they "were the work of God, and the writing was the writing of God" (Ex. 32:16). Many of the words of the glorified Christ to John on the Isle of Patmos were written from dictation. But in general the claim of the prophets and apostles is that their words were the words of God because these men were "moved by the Holy Ghost" (II Pet. 1:21), not because their writings were dictated word for word.

No creed of any consequence in the Christian Church has taught the dictation theory, though, as we shall see, the creeds are full of assertions that there are no contradictions in Scripture, that all of it is to be believed, that God is the Author of the whole, etc. And there are few if any theological authors of importance who have held to the dictation theory, even though the usual view through the history of the Christian Church has been that the Scriptures are true to the smallest detail. Perhaps the only creed that might be charged with teaching dictation is the Roman Catholic declaration written by the Council of Trent in 1546. The statement here is that the Scriptures were *Spiritu Sancto dictatas*.[2] But we should doubtless simply translate these words "Spoken by the Spirit of God." The method of God's giving His Word to the human author is probably not specified in the Tridentine statement, and the Roman Catholic Church today does not hold to a mechanical dictation theory, though it does hold strictly to the full inspiration of the words. The statement of the Vatican Council of 1870 was that the Bible (including the Apocrypha) "contains revelation with no admixture of error."[3] In holding to the doctrine of verbal inspiration the Protestant creeds and the Roman Church are and have always been in agreement. This was not the point at issue in the days of the Reformation.

It should be unnecessary, but may perhaps be wise, to insert a protest against the equation of verbal inspiration and mechanical dictation. The protest of Machen[4] is still worth reprinting: "The Spirit, it is said, is represented in this doctrine as dictating the Bible to writers who were really little more than stenographers. But of course all such caricatures are without basis in fact, and it is rather surprising that intelligent men should be so blinded by prejudice about this matter as not even to examine for themselves the perfectly accessible treatises in which the doctrine of plenary inspiration is set forth. It is usually considered good practice to examine a thing for one's self before echoing the vulgar ridicule of it. But in connection with the Bible, such scholarly restraints are somehow regarded as out of place. It is so much easier to content one's self with a few opprobrious adjectives such as 'mechanical,' or the like. Why engage in serious criticism when the people prefer ridicule? Why attack a real opponent when it is easier to knock down a man of straw?" Engelder quotes A. H. Strong, T. A. Kantonen, E. E. Flack, A. Deissmann, G. T. Ladd, W. Sanday, and others who make this fatal confusion (he could also have cited Karl Barth). He also quotes Quenstedt of the Lutheran Reformation, Epiphanius and other ancients, Graebner, F. Pieper, Warfield, and other moderns as definitely not holding a mechanical theory, but advocating verbal inspiration none the less.[5] Warfield enters a protest like Machen's against the caricature.[6]

This doctrine of verbal inspiration, even rightly understood, has now been widely abandoned. The Bible has withstood many attacks through the centuries from enemies of all sorts. But in the last century it has been called upon to withstand repeated attacks in the house of its friends. The Bible is now freely doubted by the preachers in the pulpits and the teachers in the seminary classrooms of our land.

It is difficult for the laymen of our churches to believe that our ministers in many, if not the majority, of the pulpits of our larger denominations no longer believe the Bible to be true throughout, as our forefathers did. The facts come as so unwelcome a shock that they are either disbelieved or, as more usually happens, they are not faced. But such attitudes will not do. The evidence is too overwhelming to be denied. And the subject is too crucial to be neglected. The Church has lost ground — though not numbers — in the last half century. Is it not striking, to say the least, that the period of growing apathy of the Church, retrenchment of its missions, failure of its moral influence, and loss of its evangelistic zeal parallels almost exactly the period of the spread of disbelief in the Bible and the central doctrines contained therein? The question of the full truthfulness of the Bible must be faced by intelligent Christians. Like the even more basic question "What think ye of Christ?" it cannot be shrugged aside.

THE RISE OF HIGHER CRITICISM

To understand this change in attitude toward the Bible a brief historical sketch is necessary. For centuries the Church had believed what lies upon the face of the Biblical evidence, that the various books of the Bible were written by the authors whose names they bear and were contemporary more or less with the events they narrate, just as they claim to be. The unity of the various books was not questioned, except, perhaps, by an occasional ancient and extreme heretic like Celsus. These views were not seriously challenged until the late eighteenth century. During the nineteenth century quite opposite views came to the fore which have popularly become known by the name "higher criticism."

It is not necessary to give more than the briefest review of the development of this movement. Jean Astruc (1753) is credited with first having noticed the variation of the divine names in Genesis and having concluded from this that part of Genesis was a combination of different sources. He held in orthodox-enough manner that Moses had used two ancient historical sources, one using the Hebrew name of God, *YHWH*, or "Jehovah," and the other the Hebrew word *Elohim*, meaning "God." It was later writers who extended this hypothesis of documentary sources to the entire Pentateuch and even to later writings also. They declared that the Pentateuch was not the work of Moses but a composite of historical pieces written by other and unknown hands. The hypothesis was advanced by a German, Eichorn (1823), modified by Hupfeld (1853), then again modified by Karl H. Graf, whose views were popularized by Julius Wellhausen (1878). The new theories were spread in England especially by Robertson Smith, editor of the *Encyclopedia Brittanica* in his day.

The theory now held took shape in 1865 when Graf decided that the document using the word *Elohim* was itself actually composed of two sources, the one rather early and the other the work of men of priestly emphasis. Thus two documents, as it was at first held, became four, for Deuteronomy had been assigned to the days of Josiah. These four documents have been called "J," from the original idea that it used the name "Jehovah," "E," from its use of the word *Elohim* for God, "D," from the large proportion of Deuteronomy in it, and "P," from the priestly characteristics found in this document. So the basis of higher criticism as we have had it now for many years is the division of the first five or seven books of the Bible into the J, E, D, and P Documents.[7]

It should not be supposed that anyone who knows Hebrew can pick up his Bible and read a few verses in Genesis and know for sure that these verses belong to this or that document. The alleged differences of style are not so sharp as that. Indeed, there is the widest divergence of opinion among critics as to exactly what belongs in the various documents. And the criteria giving a basis for division fail so often and are so confusing to the picture that no end of subordinate documents and sub-editors or "redactors" are brought in to help sustain the theory. In the hands of extreme critics the situation has become almost ludicrous. For instance, in the volume on Genesis in the *International Critical Commentary*, Skinner, a competent scholar, would divide Genesis 21:1 into two parts. The first half, "And the LORD visited Sarah as he had said," is J: notice the use of the name Jehovah. The second half, "And the LORD did unto Sarah as he had spoken," is E: of course, "Jehovah" is used in this half also, but doubtless it is a gloss (a later substitution) for *Elohim,* which must have stood here in the original document. Strong critical spectacles must be worn if one is to divide verses in this manner by the use of criteria that are not there! One is reminded of the episode in *Alice in Wonderland* when Alice, looking up the path, said, "I see nothing." "Such marvelous eyesight," commented the Queen, "to be able to see nothing, and at this distance, too!" It may be feared that the tendency of the critical hypothesis is to enable at least the extreme critics to see nothing, but to divide the documents nevertheless. Our purpose at present, however, is not so much to consider higher criticism as to show its relation to the question of belief in the Bible.

A further point must be stressed. The orthodox objection to higher criticism is not simply the analysis of the Pentateuch into sources but to the dates assigned to those sources. It is quite possible, even probable, that Moses used sources for his histories in Genesis. There is nothing in this position which is inconsistent with the doctrine of verbal inspiration. Luke in his prologue assures us that he had carefully used every source he could consult. The use of written sources by Moses in the remainder of the Pentateuch would be harder to accept, as he himself was the best source for all those histories. But the great departure of higher criticism from the old view is the date ascribed to these documents. The claim is that they were written centuries, even a thousand years, after Moses. They maintain that the P Document is in style and outlook very similar to that of the Book of Ezekiel and may therefore very safely be dated to the period of the disruptions during and after the Exile — about 450 B.C. The J Document is said to have affinities with the great prophetic movements in the days of the monarchy and is therefore dated to about 850 B.C. (now often put a bit earlier). The E Document shows a further development and is said to be about 750 B.C. The D Document is confidently asserted to have been the scroll of the Law which Hilkiah the priest maintained he had found in the rubbish of the Temple during the days of Josiah, and whose discovery made such a stir in the kingdom. Actually, they say, Hilkiah did not discover a long-lost book; he simply brought to the king a book that had been recently written and palmed it off on the unsuspecting monarch as the production of Moses, the great lawgiver of bygone days. Its date would thus be about 625 B.C. The entire Pentateuch would have been patched together about 400 B.C.

From this sketch of the documentary hypothesis it is easy to see why those who have always believed in the integrity of the Bible, and especially in the truth of the words of Christ, are greatly concerned. It is unmistakably clear that the Pentateuch claims to be a unit; that the other books of the Old Testament refer to it as the law of Moses; that Christ declares it to be true and to be the work of Moses, who spoke in prophecy of Himself. It is quite apparent that the widespread denials of the full truthfulness of the entire Bible, including the New Testament, are in close connection with this view of higher criticism which has grown so tremendously in the last century. It must be admitted that Jesus Christ was not a higher critic.[8] His view of the authorship of the various books was the usual one of past centuries. It has become therefore a choice between Christ and criticism. The effect of higher criticism has been to deny Christ or to reduce Him to purely human proportions. He was, it is said, a child of His time, subject to the mistakes and limitations of the knowledge of His day. It is the problem of modern theology, having achieved this result, to make His revelation and His work relevant to our day. And it seems indeed to be a great problem, almost akin to retaining a flow of current after one has thrown a monkey wrench in the generator!

But still the situation is not all before us. Postdating the Pentateuch in the manner described necessitated re-examination of the rest of the books. It is said that the theology of the J Document is primitive and that traces of the old idolatry shine through. For instance, because of the scene in which Aaron worshiped the golden calf it is said that all Israel once worshiped a golden calf — bull worship.[9] And the similar worship of golden calves by Jeroboam in North Israel in about 920 B.C. is also typical of old Israelite practice. But the reformers of the J Document at about 850 tried to eradicate all that and pictured Aaron and Jeroboam as introducing a new idolatry, apostatizing from the worship of Jehovah. And after the men of the J Document had elevated Jehovah to the position of supremacy in Israel, the men of the E Document went further and declared that the God of Israel was supreme in all the world. Thus Israel's religion evolved from the low stage of polytheism and idolatry to henotheism (one God for each nation), and, finally, the eighth-century prophets discovered monotheism. This evolution of Israel's faith, which critical writers ascribe to the Hebrew nation's genius for religion, has been part and parcel of the documentary view. Indeed, it has had a large part in the judgment of critics in selecting the different portions for the documents concerned.

Now, it is abundantly plain that if monotheism were the invention of the eighth century B.C., then David did not write the Psalms, Solomon did not write Proverbs, Job was a later creation, and the early parts of Samuel and Chronicles are largely fiction. These all must be postdated. With this view of Israel's religion, of course, there is no room for specific supernatural prediction. Naturally, the prophets may still be called "seers" and their shrewd guesses as to what may happen on the political scene may have brought them quite a reputation, but it is unthinkable that Abraham was told by God that his children would spend four centuries in bondage (Gen. 15) or that David could predict the resurrection of Jesus Christ (Ps. 16) or that Isaiah could predict Cyrus' coming two centuries before the time (Isa. 44 and 45) or that Daniel could predict three great world empires to follow Babylon (Dan. 7 and 8). But the simple expedient of postdating solves all these difficulties for the critics. They therefore urge that Isaiah was not written by one man in about 700 B.C., but by two men; others say three, and still others say many more than three. Deutero-Isaiah, who wrote the Cyrus prophecy, worked during the Exile, and far from being a prophecy, it is a beautiful rewrite of current events.[10] Trito-Isaiah wrote still later. As to Daniel, the usual view is that the book was written about 168 B.C., during the heroic times of the Maccabees, who led the Jews in a glorious revolt from the domination of Antiochus Epiphanes, the king of Syria, who had desecrated the Temple and persecuted the Jews. It is past history presented as a prophecy that the Jews might take courage in the fact that God rules and would surely deliver them.

Now, as a matter of fact as well as logic, these various points in the higher critical view hang together. It is impossible to find an author who believes in the higher criticism of the Pentateuch and yet believes that David wrote all or nearly all the Psalms ascribed to him. One who believes in the partition of Isaiah also believes in the late date of Daniel, etc. And, most important for our study, one who believes in these things has nothing but scorn for the doctrine of verbal inspiration. It is mechanical; it is outmoded; it smacks of dead orthodoxy; its believers are obscurantist; they lack love in their expression of a hard creedalism; they are an inconsequential minority.

It may unfortunately be true that those who hold to verbal inspiration are a minority in places of theological learning today.[11] It may be doubted, however, whether the percentage would be so small were one to poll the people who sit in the pews. Many church members who realize that they do not read their Bibles as much as they should would nevertheless claim to believe it and would be the most surprised people in town if their minister were to acknowledge in the pulpit some Sunday morning what he really believed about the Bible! One must question the candor of the thousands of ministers in our pulpits who adroitly keep hidden from their parishioners what they believe. The prophetic spirit seems in such places to have departed from Israel. It is small wonder that the people remain confused and uncertain.

We should, perhaps, hasten to add that the documentary hypothesis in very recent years is bending somewhat under the weight of recent archaeological discoveries. The entire hypothesis was developed at a time when very little was known about ancient Semitic languages and even less about ancient history. It involves the view that the Pentateuch is largely legendary, that David and his empire are somewhat fictional, that the Aramaic expressions and forms observable in various places of the Old Testament — largely the poetic passages — are quite late in the history of Semitic literature. All of these views are now shown to have been total misconceptions. New discoveries in Nuzi and Mari give such a wealth of background to patriarchal family customs and laws that all must now admit that the accounts of the patriarchs in Genesis are correct even to small details. It is preposterous to hold that they are the legendary retrospections of authors living a thousand years after the events described.[12] The accuracies of Genesis bespeak sources contemporary with the events. It would even be almost too remarkable for Moses himself to have written with such accuracy unless the material had been fully revealed to him as in a dream or unless he had consulted documents which he used under God as historical sources of his work. And the discoveries of the buildings of Solomon at Megiddo and of his copper refineries at Ezion Geber[13] throw such a revealing light on the time of the united monarchy that David can no longer be thought of as a rude border chieftain incapable of writing his Psalms. Indeed, it is now becoming common to have portions of the Pentateuch declared authentic[14] and to have David given the credit that is his due as the Sweet Singer of Israel. If, however, this is done, if Moses was a monotheist,[15] then much of the structure of the higher critical view of the evolution of Israel's religion must be re-thought. Further, the argument that words of Aramaic affinity present in Psalms and poems of the Old Testament imply a post-exilic date has been totally abandoned in advanced circles. Rather, many of these forms are now recognized for what they were: archaic poetic features bespeaking, rather, an early origin for the pieces concerned.

In short, the higher critical theories of a former generation are still with us, but are due for an overhauling at the hands of modern archaeology, which has come of age only since the First World War and which has had many surprises for us.[16] Many, of course, will say that the new discoveries do not all support the Bible and still make the doctrine of verbal inspiration difficult to hold. There may be problems raised by the new discoveries, it is true. But the flood of light now brought to play upon the Old Testament records shows a very large proportion of clear historical accuracy. Probably the most unfriendly critic would point to less than half a dozen instances in the Old Testament where the Biblical record is in flat contradiction to facts so far alleged from archaeological investigation — and there have been, as we shall see, some notable instances where such contradictions have been solved by fuller archaeological light.[17]

EVOLUTION AND THE BIBLE

There is another place where verbal inspiration is heavily attacked today. This attack affects only a small portion of the Biblical record, but it is an important one. We refer to the subject of evolution and the Bible. It is hardly necessary to speak of science and the Bible, because science as a whole touches the Bible very little. There are few places where chemistry, physics, mathematics, etc., bear upon the Scriptures, much less contradict them. It is true that much is sometimes made of these few places, but actually they are not of much significance. For instance, some ridicule the Bible, for they declare that it gives a value of 3 for pi, instead of 3.1416. It is true that in II Chronicles 4:2 and also in I Kings 7:23 the dimensions of Solomon's great brass laver are given as thirty cubits around and ten cubits across, but what does this really prove? Three is the value of pi to the first significant figure, and though the value of pi has been worked out to the 707th decimal place, its exact value is not yet known! We are not told the preciseness of the measurements given, nor are we sure that Solomon's laver was exactly round. There is nothing here to disturb the faith of any man, nor any grounds to say that the

Scriptures are wrong in their mathematics. And so it is
with many other minor objections. Of course, it is un-
scientific to believe that Joshua's day was forty-eight hours
long, but it is equally absurd to believe that an iron axe-
head could float, or that a virgin could bear a child, or that
Christ could walk upon the water. All miracles, great or
small, are impossible with men and are an interruption
of those regular laws of nature which form the basis of
science. That is why they are miracles, and that is why
God gave them to man: to prove that there is a God in
heaven more powerful than any who is dreamed of in
many a Horatio's philosophy. But these are not conflicts
between science and the Bible. In the field of the direct
miraculous intervention of God, science cannot properly
interpose an objection.

But it is thought by many that the new concept of
evolution makes it impossible to hold to the first chapters
of Genesis. On this, many different views are held. It is
doubtless true that new discoveries have made it impossible to hold to the dates determined by Ussher in the
seventeenth century and often appearing in the margins
of our Bibles. According to these, the creation of the
world was in 4004 B.C. Needless to say, these dates are
not inspired, they do not appear in any Christian creed,
and they involve certain assumptions which Ussher ought
never to have made.[18] Also, it need not be held that the
six creative days of Genesis were each twenty-four hours
long. This, too, would be an inference from Scripture
which has been common enough in some times but is
by no means declared in the Bible. Long ago Augustine
had held that the days were periods of indefinite length,[19]
as indeed seems probable from the fact that their reckoning begins before the sun and the moon appear. Also this
indefinite use of the word "day" is evidenced by the very
next chapter (2:4), where the entire work of creation is
said to have been done in a "day." So this conclusion of
the new science that the world is ancient does not really

touch the doctrine of the Bible's truth, but only the infer-
ences that some have drawn from the Bible.

An approach fashionable in some quarters is to try to
solve the problem of evolution by speaking of a "theistic
evolution." According to this view the Bible is said to
declare the fact of creation; new scientific views merely
give us the method of His creation, which was by evolution. This idea is attractive enough, but there are some
fixed points in the Biblical record which, it seems, must
be held, and these very points are what most evolutionary
scientists apparently seek to deny. It is often said that the
emphasis of the Genesis record is that God directly inter-
vened in the creation of matter, of life, and of man. It
seems hard not to insert in the series that God also inter-
vened in the creation of certain great divisions within life.
Now, the scientists' problem with the creation of matter
is perhaps less than it once was inasmuch as matter is
now seen to be more volatile than a previous stage of
science conceived. It appears to be nothing but a com-
pact variety of energy and is convertible into energy with
catastrophic consequences. Einstein's fateful equation helps
explain creation by opening tragic possibilities of destruction! As to the creation of life, science has no more the
answer to what life is than it had some years ago. Many
a biochemist has fond hopes that by some new synthesis
of protein molecules he may be able to create living matter,
but no success has ever been achieved in this direction.
The vital processes are indeed being better understood,
and we should be thankful for this, but we have no reason
to think that the creation of life will be duplicated by man.
That it occurred by chance in some primeval slime is
pure assumption.[20]

As to the creation of man, the Bible makes it quite explicit that God did not choose a pair of the higher simians
and adopt them as His children, giving them an upward
urge to draw paintings on their cave homes and at last
to become aware of a Higher Power. Scripture says that
God created Adam first and then from his body created

Eve and set the pair sinless in the Garden of Eden, from whence they fell. Now, the theory of evolution could conceivably allow for such a sudden miraculous intervention, but no evolutionary scientist admits any such occurrence in the upward progress of man from brute ancestry. The argument is that animal life became more diversified and complex as indicated by the rock record, issuing finally in the mammals and then in a strange little arboreal animal who became the ancestor of monkeys, apes, and the big animals called men. It is regarded as the mark of an ignoramus to say that evolution now teaches that man came from monkeys. No one holds that view. Evolutionists have now advanced to the position that both monkeys and men came from the same ancestor. We are no longer grandsons of monkeys — only their distant cousins. So be it. The distinction is doubtless of importance biologically. Theologically, and, we venture to think, practically, there is no great difference. The idea of a continuous physical gradation from the brute to man cannot be squared with the Genesis record.

But neither can it be proved from the scientific facts. The mechanism of evolution which Darwin thought he had found in an infinite variation in all directions with the survival of the fittest has been abandoned completely as it is simply contradicted by all that we know about genetics. No amount of experimentation has been able to sustain the Lamarckian view of the inheritance of acquired characteristics. During the postwar period a Russian scientist, T. D. Lysenko, maintained he had found such evidence, though outside of Russia hardly anyone agreed with him. Unfortunately his notions were widely circulated in Japan and believed by many who would wish to see them proved true. In 1954, at least Lysenko seemed to be *persona non grata* in Russia also.[21] To replace these views many now tacitly assume that mutations occur in infinite variety and that the survival of the fittest of these is the mechanism of evolution. This theory, while attractive, is far from proved. One of our foremost geneticists, Richard Goldschmidt, insists that these small mutations never proceed in a straight line, but always cluster around a fixed center within each species.[22] His own view is that occasionally large mutations occur which make the transition from one species to another in one jump. This, he says, has never been observed and is not likely to be observed because it would happen only once in millions of times. And, truly, it would be a rare wonder for a chicken to lay an egg and have it hatch out a duck. But though this sort of thing is unobserved and unobservable, it is to be accepted none the less on faith. Perhaps we may be pardoned if we think that it is equally reasonable to believe that God had His own ways of forming the species during His great creative days and that thereafter things procreated according to their kind, which is all that has ever been observed in the most detailed experiments.

But what shall we say of the record of the rocks? Do not these clearly indicate that man came from simian ancestors? The answer that can be given at this time is definitely "No." For years it was thought that very early human remains showed an extremely undeveloped physique, bones that were of intermediate age showed the Neanderthal cave-man characteristics, and recent bones showed a high development. This neat series has been upset in fairly recent times, and many do not realize it. First, more careful study of the early remains of the Java man shows a great and still unbridged gap between his cranial capacity and that of the highest apes. His cousin, the Peking man, can not be fully studied just now because of the troublous times but also is definitely human. Second, there was discovered the skull of the Swanscombe man, who apparently was very early according to the usual dating yet had a very high cranial capacity approaching the brain size of modern man. Finally, the finds in the caves of Mount Carmel in Palestine in 1929-34 show several well-preserved skeletons which are from a time reputedly earlier than that of the usual Neanderthal remains, yet which have some features quite like those of modern man. The discovery shows that at least 100,000 years ago, according to the usual dating, mankind included races and features very much like those we know today, though he also included some other features—all definitely human—which appear to have died out. The conclusion has forced itself upon anthropologists like Weidenreich[23] that in the so-called Glacial Period, covering, perhaps, the last 500,000 years, there has been very little development in the physical structure of man. The beginnings of human evolution, they now say, must be sought for in the preceding or Pliocene Age. This is convenient, for no human remains or semihuman remains are so far known from this age. There is, therefore, plenty of room for speculation. But of geological facts proving an ascent of man from physically inferior origins there are none. The oldest men found anywhere are truly men, both mentally and physically. It may even be pointed out that though these early remains are confidently assigned to eras of 100,000 to 500,000 years ago, there are no independent and really reliable methods of dating them. The carbon 14[24] method of dating has yielded very interesting results for the later periods — indeed, it has resulted in cutting down the dates formerly set for the end of the last glaciation from 25,000 to 10,000 years ago — but no comparable method is yet available for the dating of these older human bones. Such developments we shall await with interest. In the meantime we must record it as a fact that both the method and the record of human evolution have not yet been found. Until these are found there seems to be no necessity to adopt the view of theistic evolution, which seems to please neither scientists nor theologians.

It is remarkable, none the less, that these two panzer attacks upon the full truthfulness of the Bible — higher criticism and evolution — have won their victories during the twentieth century. Is it not possible, some ask, that all attempted answers to them are wishful thinking, that such answers are the death gasp of an outmoded orthodoxy? Must we still believe the Bible? The Bible has resisted many other attacks; perhaps this modern one will be successful. Some may think so. But we need not think that every modern idea is necessarily the right one simply because it is modern. It can be shown that higher criticism is, in its development, very closely allied with the Hegelian philosophy of history, which pictured man as almost necessarily developing through new stages of progress. The evolution of Israel's religion and the evolutionary development of species were but grand illustrations of the German philosophy.

Now, it is natural that there should be some progress in the arts and sciences as the experience and wisdom of men accumulate. But that there is an inherent and necessary progress of all things toward newer and better syntheses, we are, in the late decades, beginning to doubt. To quote from Emil Brunner, who is no friend to the doctrine of verbal inspiration, "The belief in progress has played out its fatally dazzling role . . ."[25] The twentieth century is not all gold, though it is largely all glitter! And the ideas of higher criticism and evolution which have clearly been robbed of their original basic arguments may be continuing to live on borrowed time. They may not be solid truth but enchanting Lorelei which attract us to our own destruction. At the very least, there is no need for those who have found in the Word of God, the Bible, their hope and comfort in a confused age, to surrender their belief in this Book, which has brought nothing but blessing wherever it has been believed and followed and still promises heavenly hope for men's sorrows and threatens divine retribution for human brutality.

THE SPREAD OF MODERN DISBELIEF

But how far has the disbelief in the Bible spread among our churchmen? It is well known that in many quarters, especially among our intelligentsia, it is fashionable to regard the Bible as a piece of dated literature not meaningful for our times. Our institutions of higher learning were in large majority founded by those who believed the Bible. They have greatly changed. Having let go of the Bible, they have, in some instances, become centers of atheistic philosophy and of strange social theory, appearing in milder form as socialistic and in more radical form as outright communistic ideas. Our intelligentsia in America have largely moved away from belief in the Bible and the record of God's dealings with men which it contains. No large and important university exists in our whole country, except those of the Roman Catholic faith, which bases instruction upon the truth of the Bible. What a strange situation has arisen in the land of the Pilgrims; and most of the changes have transpired in the last seventy-five or hundred years.

But how about the Church itself? Surely the leaders of our great Protestant denominations have resisted the "acids of modernity." Unfortunately, it is not so. Painful it is to have to relate how our church leaders have for the most part felt that they could neutralize these acids simply by diluting them slightly. The effort has been not to meet the attack head on but to appease the gathering unbelief at every point and meanwhile to try to salvage some shreds of faith from the general ruin. The result has been a preaching without conviction, a religion without authority, a Christ of human proportions. And in a world sick unto death the Church has turned to the panacea of ecumenicalism to present to the world a united front — united in unbelief.

In 1893 an event of considerable moment occurred which showed the trend of the times theologically in this country. A professor at Union Theological Seminary of New York by the name of Charles A. Briggs was brought to trial for heresy by his presbytery of the Presbyterian Church in the U.S.A. Briggs' views were well known, and he made no attempt to hide them. He had accepted the teachings of higher criticism and had clearly denied the full truthfulness of Scripture. His chief antagonist in the trial was Francis L. Patton, president of Princeton Seminary. Briggs was convicted and put out of the church. In protest, Union Seminary disassociated itself from the Presbyterian Church in the U.S.A. and has since been known in this country as a leader in Modernist theology. But graduates of Union Seminary, infected with the new views, continued to enter the Presbyterian Church in the U.S.A., as well as many other communions. Other seminaries, such as McCormick in Chicago, were likewise veering toward the new beliefs.

In the early 1900's the new views already had an imposing literature. One of the most important books on higher criticism, widely used in successive editions to this day, was S. R. Driver's *Introduction to the Literature of the Old Testament,* published in 1891 in the *International Theological Library* series under the editorship of Briggs and Salmond. Then came the *International Critical Commentary* series which has been used ever since by thousands of ministers in study and sermon preparation. It is an extensive series, many volumes of which are indeed deep and valuable in their scholarship, but almost all of which are written from the viewpoint of higher criticism. Briggs and Driver were the editors for the Old Testament in the early years. A few volumes are still being added to the set.

Higher criticism was gaining strength. We next may note the rise of a popular and gifted preacher of the new thought. The name of Harry Emerson Fosdick has become known far and wide as a symbol. He has often been called the high priest of Modernism. In the 1920's he, though a Baptist, was preaching in the pulpit of the First Presbyterian Church of New York, the pastor of which was William P. Merrill. Fosdick was openly denying the plain facts of Scripture — such as the virgin birth of Christ — and his preaching was causing a considerable reaction from orthodox sources. Feeling the strength of the new theology, Fosdick in 1922 preached a memorable sermon "Shall the Fundamentalists Win?" His negative answer became prophetic for the course of the orthodox party in the following decades. But first the Presbyterian Church in the U.S.A., by action of its General Assembly, put Fosdick out of its pulpit. He has since extended his influence in the Rockefeller-financed Riverside Baptist Church of New York, only recently retiring from that pulpit.

The action against Fosdick, which included a declaration

by the Presbyterians that it was essential for their ministers to believe in the inerrancy of Scripture, the virgin birth of Christ, His actual miracles, substitutionary atonement, and bodily resurrection, occasioned a strong reaction. A committee of 150 ministers was formed, spearheaded by men of Auburn Seminary (which has closed its doors and transferred its assets to Union Seminary), who issued the so-called "Auburn Affirmation." This document declared that "the doctrine of inerrancy (of Scripture), intended to enhance the authority of the Scriptures, in fact impairs their supreme authority for faith and life."[26] It further declared that the five doctrines declared as essential by the Assembly were only "theories" concerning the inspiration of the Bible, and the incarnation, the atonement, the resurrection, and the continuing life and supernatural power of our Lord Jesus Christ. They insisted that verbal inspiration, the virgin birth, the true miracles, the substitutionary atonement, and the bodily resurrection "are not the only theories allowed by the Scriptures and our standards."

The significance of the Auburn Affirmation is that it was one of the first challenges formally raised in our American denominations against the orthodox theology and in favor of a loose view including all shades of unbelief of the Bible and its central teachings. It was signed by 1,293 Presbyterian ministers — about 10 per cent of the total — and it was not effectively challenged by any trial for heresy in any of the courts of the denomination. Two feeble efforts were made, but they died aborning. We cannot understand the widespread unbelief of the Bible in our times without realizing that higher criticism has been doing its work for at least fifty years in our country and has not been challenged as an heretical opinion for a quarter of a century in the councils of our larger denominations.

An interesting measure of the progress of Modernism in the 1920's is provided in a little book by George H. Betts, *The Beliefs of 700 Ministers*.[27] Betts sent a questionnaire to about fifteen hundred Protestant ministers and received replies from five hundred ministers and two hundred theological students. The active ministers represented chiefly the Baptist, Congregational, Episcopal, Evangelical, Lutheran, Methodist, and Presbyterian denominations and all were in the area of Chicago. The poll is by no means complete, but it is indicative and very instructive. Of the fifty-six questions we are mainly concerned with the fifteenth: "Do you believe that the Bible was written by men chosen and supernaturally endowed by God for that purpose, and by Him given the exact message they were to write?" Forty-three per cent answered "No." It would seem that the attack upon the Bible had made tremendous progress. Of the Methodists who replied 66 per cent answered "No." Perhaps even more significant were the replies received from two hundred theological students who were studying in three large widely separated denominational seminaries. To this question on the full truthfulness of the Bible 91 per cent of the seminarians answered "No." Apparently unbelief was just twice as rampant in the schools of advanced ministerial training as it was in our pulpits. It seems that one should go to seminary to learn how to attack the Bible!

Has the situation changed since 1929? Unfortunately, no. Higher criticism, though somewhat strained under the weight of new discoveries, is held as tenaciously as ever — almost as an item of faith. Those who were under attack as Modernists in the 1920's turned the tables, and in the 1930's they put out of their pulpits and unfrocked their former attackers. This was done in the case of Dr. J. Gresham Machen, Dr. J. Oliver Buswell, Dr. Carl McIntire, and others in the Presbyterian Church in the U.S.A. In the case of the Northern Baptist denomination, more than six hundred congregations have withdrawn because of these tendencies. The Methodist Church in 1938 united the Northern, Southern, and Methodist Protestant branches into the largest Protestant denomination in America in which the voice of Fundamentalist protest is well-nigh stilled. Their leading light, Dr. G. Bromley Oxnam, has actually, in his writings, called the God of the Old Testament "a dirty bully."[28] This may help to account for the fact that the united Methodist

Church is smaller than the sum of its three parts and that it is the lowest denomination in America in point of per capita giving. The glory seems to have departed.

Those who still believe the Old Book are not alone in their claim that our larger American denominations no longer hold to the Bible as without error. The Modernist leaders boast of the fact. A few representative quotations must suffice. E. G. Homrighausen, of Princeton Theological Seminary, wrote that the view that the Bible is infallible has largely died out among informed Protestants.[29] Edwin Lewis, of Drew Theological Seminary, now retired, agrees, "To say that the Old Testament in its totality is inspired is to create almost insuperable difficulties for our minds."[30] The trend of the times is adequately illustrated by a recent article in the popular *Look* magazine.[31] This article was written by Dr. John Sutherland Bonnell, a prominent Presbyterian minister in New York City. The whole thrust of Bonnell's article is that one does not have to believe the Bible or its main doctrines to be a Presbyterian. He would distinguish the Fundamentalists, who are somewhat looked down upon, from the conservatives, who are considered to be the nonradical type. A conservative would be just a bit right of center. "Conservative" in Bonnell's vocabulary no longer means one who holds strictly to the historic Christian faith. For instance, he says, "Except for a minority, Presbyterians do not believe in the literal inerrancy of the Scriptures." Again, "Except in minor Presbyterian groups, the doctrine of the virgin birth is not used as a test of orthodoxy in receiving new members or in ordaining ministers and elders." "With a few exceptions, Presbyterians do not interpret the phrase in the Apostles' Creed 'the resurrection of the body' as meaning the physical body."

Unfortunately, we fear Dr. Bonnell is substantially correct in his estimate of the opinions of ministers in the Presbyterian Church in the U.S.A., and the same may surely be said of the Methodist Church and most of the other large bodies. The laymen are likely more inclined to the old beliefs, but eventually many more of these, too, will follow their leaders, even though their leaders may be blind guides like those in Jesus' day. The sobering fact about Bonnell's article is that it accurately portrays the course of events in the American churches in the past quarter-century. In 1908, 1910, and again in 1923, the General Assembly of the Presbyterian Church in the U.S.A. declared that belief in such doctrines as the inerrancy of Scripture, the virgin birth of Christ, and the bodily resurrection of our Lord was essential for ordination to the ministry. Now a leading spokesman in that denomination declares that only a minority hold to these doctrines or require them for ordination. We agree with his statements of fact, but we should be moved to tears to see so rapid and so widespread a defection from precious doctrines held for centuries — indeed, from the beginning, as we hope to show — by all branches of Christendom. These facts perhaps underline the need for constant study of the subject of inspiration from all angles.

Other men in leading positions in our modern churches are as ready to deny the Bible. Reinhold Niebuhr, a professor at Union Theological Seminary in New York — the largest Seminary in the Eastern United States — is widely acclaimed as the leading Protestant theologian of today. That he is so regarded is itself a sad commentary on the situation in our land, for his denials of the Bible are as pervasive and dangerous as any that have been mentioned. His books show a full acquiescence in the views of higher criticism — which, however, he seems to accept at second hand, not himself being a student of the details of the Hebrew Old Testament. He refers approvingly to the J, E, D, and P Documents.[32] Second Isaiah is said to have been written during the Exile and to consist of only a small part of the book: "The Second Isaiah is the first prophet to be particularly concerned to reinforce the concept of the divine sovereignty over historical destiny with the idea of the majesty of the divine Creator of the world (Isa. 40-45)."[33] This idea that a real monotheism and doctrine of creation arose late in Israel's religious history may be held, of course, only by adopting the whole higher critical postdating of the Pentateuch, the Psalms, the Proverbs of Solomon, etc. Further, Niebuhr speaks of "Isaiah's error"[34] and even Jesus' "error," in which he says Jesus was followed by Paul.[35] In an extensive quotation he contradicts the Biblical statements on creation, Christ's second coming, the fall of man, etc.

> The idea of a divine creation of the world . . . is frequently corrupted into a theory of secondary causation and thereby comes in conflict with a valid scientific account of causation on the natural level. This corruption of religion into a bad science has aroused the justified protest of a scientific age . . .
>
> Theological externalism also corrupts the difficult eschatological symbols of the Christian faith. . . . If they are regarded as descriptions of a particular end in time, the real point of the eschatological symbol is lost . . .
>
> In the same manner a symbolic historical event such as the "fall" of man loses its real meaning when taken as literal history.
>
> In a similar fashion . . . the Jesus of history, who is known as the Christ by faith, is interpreted as an inhuman and incredible personality . . .
>
> These errors of a literalistic orthodoxy tend to obscure the real issues. . . . The Christian truth is presented as a "dated" bit of religious fantasy which is credible only to the credulous and which may be easily dismissed by modern man.[36]

Similar quotations from many American scholars may be multiplied. Wilhelm Pauck, of the Chicago Theological Seminary, says, "It is a fact that the supernatural authority of old theology is dead. The miracles of God's personal appearance in Jesus Christ and of the divine inspiration of the Bible are dead."[37] Further, "The theory that the claim of the prophets must be recognized as true is arbitrary. Why not also the testimony of other prophets and founders of religion?"[38] Paul Tillich, of Union Seminary in New York, speaks in similar vein: "Historical criticism of the Bible has liberated Christian truth from legendary, superstitious, and mythical elements in the historic tradition."[39] Shailer Mathews, long a spokesman for the new theology in this country, sums up the conviction of these scholars that belief in the Bible is simply impossible for a modern man: "For nearly a century the Bible has been studied scientifically. . . . But no sooner do men thus study the Bible than facts appear which make belief in its verbal inerrancy untenable."[40]

It is not our purpose to catalogue all the modern churchmen who deny the full truthfulness of the Bible. Many and prominent names could be cited. The importance of the foregoing quotations from men of varying theological backgrounds is that they all agree that nobody of any consequence can any longer believe the Bible. If truth goes with the majority, we may as well conclude our book with this chapter, making the first chapter the last. But it is one of the convictions of mankind that truth may be, indeed often is, crushed to earth and yet it will rise again. And the Christian faith, always associated with belief in the Bible, has been again and again well-nigh extinguished only to rise in new and grander power. It is possible that this time, too, the assailants of God's Word will be proved wrong, for God's people have a conviction of the truth of the Bible that is not touched by the change of cultures and the passing of the centuries. The Christian cannot forget that the Lord Jesus Christ believed the Bible and bade us also to believe it. Unless Christ be proved an impostor and His teaching worthless, we shall have to continue to hold to the Old Book until the very last ditch. This positive basis for our position we must now examine.

CHAPTER 2

WHY WE BELIEVE THE BIBLE

It is a matter of constant surprise to the author that most Christians when asked why they believe the Bible reply by quoting II Timothy 3:16. To quote this verse is not wrong. The verse is plain: "All scripture is given by inspiration of God, and is profitable . . ." But such a quotation allows the charge of circular reasoning: "You prove the Bible by quoting the Bible." Even more serious is the charge freely made in critical circles that II Timothy is not genuine and thus should not be considered the basis for so important a doctrine.

In any case, both the famous text in II Timothy and II Peter 1:21 are none the less valuable. Suppose they were not genuine, but were only the work of some second-century successor of the apostles whose books the Church appropriated. In that event these texts would at least prove that this doctrine of verbal inspiration was the teaching of the Early Church. Many factors combine to assure us that this is so. The Early Church placed the Bible, both the Old Testament and the New Testament, in a class totally by itself because Christians were fully persuaded it was the truth of God.

But need we allow this claim of the critics? Must we reason in a circle? Surely a doctrine so universally held as this one of verbal inspiration has a better basis. That basis is found simply in the teaching of the Lord Jesus Christ. Suppose we approach the New Testament, for the sake of the argument, merely as an exceedingly old and

obviously worth-while source book for the history of early
Christianity and the teachings of Jesus. What do we find?
We find pervading the sources, the doctrine of verbal
inspiration, and this from the lips of Jesus Himself.[1] Scattered
throughout the Gospel record in every Gospel and in every
type of record — parable, history, Passion record, etc. —
from first to last, is the assurance in the teaching of Jesus
that the Scriptures of the Old Testament, to which He
referred so frequently are true. He makes no distinction
in veracity between the religious and the practical. All
the teachings of Scripture were alike true for Christ; He
believed them all.

THE TEACHING OF JESUS

Perhaps the first passage to attract our attention is
Matthew 5:17, 18: "One jot or one tittle shall in no wise
pass from the law, till all be fulfilled." As the previous
verse shows, Christ is here referring to a book. The characteristic name for this book in the New Testament is the
usual Jewish phrase "the Law and the Prophets." This
title or a similar one like "Moses and the Prophets" is used
a dozen times in the New Testament. Once the sacred
volume is called "the law of Moses . . . the prophets, and
. . . the psalms" (Luke 24:44). At other times the entire
Old Testament is referred to simply as "the law." For
instance, Jesus quotes a verse outside of the Pentateuch
as the "law" (John 10:34). Thus in Matthew 5:18 Christ
is clearly referring to the sacred writings of the Jews as
a unit and a well-defined sacred unit, too. But He says
very positively that this Book is perfect to the smallest
detail. It is not merely verbal inspiration that He teaches
here, but inspiration of the very letters! The jot was the
Hebrew *Yodh*, the smallest letter in the Hebrew alphabet.
Just what is meant by the tittle is less clear. Most take
it to refer to the small parts of Hebrew letters which distinguish one from the other, like our dot over the *i* and
cross of the *t*. Others think it may refer to the Hebrew
letter *Waw*, which often served only to distinguish a long

from a short vowel. In any case, the main point is clear. Jesus declared that the Scriptures were letter perfect.

It is worth noting that Jesus was not necessarily referring to the perfection of written copies. This can be shown by His use of similar language referring to His own words. In Matthew 24:35 He declares that His own words are as enduring as the heaven and earth — not in written copies, obviously, for His own words were not then written at all except possibly in snatches, and in any case we have a very small proportion of His teaching. What He is referring to is the eternal force and sublime truth of His words. But notice that by these expressions He puts His own words and those of the Old Testament on a par. Some Christians cherish a New Testament in which the words of Jesus are printed in red. Observe, however, that as far as their divine authority and truth is concerned, Jesus Christ would have all the words of Scripture equally emphasized. They are all true.

But some may object that we build too heavily upon Matthew 5:17f. Possibly these are not the very words of Jesus but are only attributed to Him by some later disciple who was himself an exponent of this doctrine. Such a view is difficult to hold. First of all, it is to be noted that these verses are found in the Sermon on the Mount, which is almost universally recognized as an authentic piece of Jesus' teaching even by those who retain little else. To deny this section is to occupy the place of almost total skepticism; and total skepticism with regard to the basic documents of early Christianity is not a position that has commended itself to careful scholars. Furthermore, this saying of Christ has a parallel in Luke (as also the remark about His own words, Luke 21:33). The doubly-attested sayings of Christ have been regarded by modern scholarship as belonging to extremely early and genuine sources.[2] The fact that this verse has a parallel in Luke 16:16, 17 supports the conclusion that the doctrine of verbal inspiration is indeed basic to Jesus' teaching. Thirdly, we may add, though we shall not prove it at once, that this same thought recurs again and again in Jesus' teaching. We cannot suppose that with so many evidences it has no basis in the actual words of Christ.

But first we must deal with an objection that is raised to our interpretation of Matthew 5:17f. It is said that this reference cannot teach verbal inspiration because Jesus in the following verses denies the Old Testament. Many argue that He proceeds to quote the Old Testament and then to set His own authority on a higher plane.

Now, truly Jesus never hesitated to claim all authority possible for Himself and His own words. But that He contradicted the Old Testament is not considered as a possibility in Matthew 5:17f., nor is it so considered in any other part of the Gospel record. Must it be found in the later verses of Matthew 5? We think not. Fair and careful exegesis will, we believe, show that in this portion of the Sermon on the Mount Christ sustains the Old Testament also.

There are six verses in this chapter in which Jesus says, "Ye have heard that it hath been said by them of old time . . . but I say unto you," or some similar phraseology. Now, it will be noted that He does not say, "It is written, but . . ." Again, it should be emphasized that the matters said "by them of old time" (or "to them of old time") are not all direct quotations of Scripture.

LOVE THY NEIGHBOR

Verse 43 is the clearest example: "Thou shalt love thy neighbour, and hate thine enemy." The first part is truly a quotation from Leviticus 19:18, but the last part is not found in the entire Old Testament. Indeed, the Old Testament itself contradicts that last part; cf. only Leviticus 19: 17 and 34, "Thou shalt not hate thy brother in thine heart. . . . The stranger . . . thou shalt love him as thyself." And Jesus is not against the first part of the quotation, the part which is found in the Old Testament. What, then, is Jesus opposing? Quite obviously here, as often, He is opposing the Jewish traditions, the sayings of the Fathers with which they had overlaid the Word of God and made it of none effect. He is contradicting the scribal commentary, but not the Scripture.

OATHS

Another example of a similar situation is found in verses 33ff., the law of oaths, the fourth in this series of six. Now, fortunately, we know the scribal attitude toward oaths. Jesus refers to the subject again in Matthew 23:16-23. The scribes and Pharisees evidently distinguished degrees of obligation in oaths. Some oaths did not count. Some carried, as it were, the penalties of perjury. Their attitude was not the God-ordained attitude of regard for truth, but rather the lawyer's attitude of finding penalties for various infractions. Their "lawyers" were evidently eager to profit by loopholes in the traditional regulations of Phariseeism.

Now, the principle had been accepted that the seriousness of a man's oath could be measured by the object he swore by. If he swore by the gold of the Temple, he was obligated. If he swore by the lamb on the altar, he was obligated. But, curiously, they held that if a man swore by the Temple, he was not obligated — apparently because it was not for sale! Likewise, an oath by the altar could be broken with impunity. It would obviously be easy for a sharp lawyer operating by these principles to devour the estate of a poor widow who did not know the right things by which to swear! It was like putting exception clauses in fine print at the end of a contract! That this was the Pharisaic doctrine is further proved by reference to the Mishna, the Jewish codification of Jewish law of about 200 A.D. It says, "If a man said, 'I adjure you,' or 'I command you,' or 'I bind you,' they are liable. But if he said, 'By heaven and by earth,' they are exempt." Again "If a claim concerns these, no oath is imposed: bondmen, written documents, immovable property, and the property of the Temple. . . . Oaths may only be taken about what can be defined according to size, weight, or number." [3]

These are precisely the foolish distinctions which Jesus denounces.

Jesus upbraids the hypocrites for such wicked practices. An oath taken in God's sight is enforceable by the Righteous Judge whatever men may say.

The Old Testament has no easy provisions for breaking of oaths such as the scribes had added by their tradition. Numbers 30 gives provisions whereby vows of minors and women were not obligatory unless there was the consent of fathers and husbands. But the third commandment, Deuteronomy 23:22, Deuteronomy 6:13, and other passages emphasize that the obligation of oaths is religious and depends upon the fact that there is a God of truth. In contrast, Jesus is quoting the scribes, who would distinguish between oaths.

Christ's answer is surely to be taken as a negative of comparison. Some have insisted on giving the negative its full force and have resisted taking any oath. Most Christians, having regard to the examples of Paul and James (Acts 18:8; 21:23), the answer of Christ Himself to the high priest's adjuration (Matt. 26:63), and the promise on oath of God to Abraham (Heb. 6:16, 17), etc., do not come to this conclusion. They say that Christ intended to teach veracity rather than sharp legal practice. He condemned iniquitous oaths and double talk and insisted that the word of a child of God should be as good as his bond.

In this, Christ is in strict accord with the Old Testament. But the scribes and Pharisees were woefully out of line with its high moral teaching. They were breaking the commandments and teaching men to do so. And the result is that Christ, in powerful language, condemns not the Old Testament but the sophistry of the scribal and traditional commentaries thereon.

AN EYE FOR AN EYE

The fifth of the examples of poor scribal exegesis is the famous law of retaliation in Matthew 5:38-42. The old rule of an eye for an eye and a tooth for a tooth is here contradicted. In handling this comment of Jesus, we shall see that the scribes had committed the familiar error of taking a text out of its context.

The quotation is indeed found in the Old Testament — in three places: Exodus 21:24; Leviticus 24:20; and Deuteronomy 19:21. In each case the context shows clearly that this maxim was a divinely given guide for Israel's judges. In Exodus 21 we have a series of institutions for applying the Ten Commandments to the life of Israel. The judgments concern servants, manslaughter, capital punishment for first-degree murder, criminal negligence, etc. Among the prescriptions treated is the case of abortion caused by assault and battery. The law is that such abortion is punishable by fine, but that if the mother dies as a consequence, then it is punishable by death — life for life is the rule, eye for eye, tooth for tooth, hand for hand, etc.

Also in Deuteronomy 19:21 the verses are in a context of court procedure. The previous verses are instructions to judges on rules of evidence. Perjury is to be punished according to the magnitude of the offense. The false witness is to be given the penalty that his perjury would have brought upon the accused. If his false witness would have condemned an innocent man to death as a murderer, the false witness should be executed. If it would have caused an innocent man to pay a heavy fine as a thief, the false witness should pay such a fine. "And thine eye shall not pity; but life shall go for life, eye for eye, tooth for tooth, hand for hand, foot for foot." Again in Leviticus 24:20 the consideration of the judgment to be given for a blasphemer brings up this principle of judgment that the penalty must fit the crime.

There has been a question in the minds of many whether this is a proper principle even for court procedure. We may remark that it was far more proper than the court penalties meted out in early eighteenth-century England, where hanging was the penalty for 160 offenses ranging from murder to shoplifting of items worth more than a dollar! And in the case of Israel, where prisons were unknown, it was a practical expedient in line, evidently, with current practice. We can point out that there is no clear case in the Old Testament where it was applied. It is possible that the phrases "eye for an eye," etc., are more or less proverbial expressions in the common law expressing the very important legal principle that the severity of the punishment must match the gravity of the crime.

Now, the scribes of Jesus' day, literalists as they were, apparently were taking passages out of the context of court procedure and were using them for the justification of all kinds of personal vengeance. The Pharisees were not the kind that commonly turned the other cheek — at least the Pharisees and Sadducees engaged in a veritable scuffle when Paul in the council declared his belief in the Resurrection (Acts 23:6). And the Pharisees lived by their lawsuits; they are often mentioned as in a class with the lawyers. Surely none of them would have thought of giving an extra coat to settle a matter out of court! And there is a hint in Matthew 5:41 that the Pharisees' vengefulness toward Roman rule is singled out. The words reflect the Roman officers' practice of impressing someone into messenger service for the government. Imagine a Pharisee who thus impressed by the hated Romans would have no feeling of vengeance, but would go a second mile! The very wording is a burning exposé of the Pharisaic attitude of personal vengeance which they apparently excused by reference to these rules for Israel's judges — rules which in context are proper. But as to personal vengeance, when Paul warns against it in Romans 13:9, he appeals to the Books of Deuteronomy and Proverbs for substantiation of his warning. So we conclude that in this case also Jesus is not contradicting the Old Testament but is arguing against the Pharisaic misinterpretation which took the verses out of context and missed their true meaning.

ADULTERY

With these examples in mind, we are prepared to consider the second of the six matters that Jesus mentions: adultery. The quotation is directly from the seventh commandment. But Jesus says, "But I say unto you, That whosoever looketh on a woman to lust after her hath committed adultery with her already in his heart."

It is commonly supposed that Jesus here so applies the commandment that it may reach beyond the external act to the heart motive. It is thought that Jesus does not contradict the commandment but amplifies it. But the question is: Does Jesus actually amplify the meaning of the Old Testament text? Did the commandment merely forbid external acts?

An interpretation of this commandment is found in the legislation in Deuteronomy 22:22-27. There it is expressly stated that the external act without the consent and purpose is not accounted as a guilty act. The Levitical regulations were not merely external legalism but included motives and internal attitudes. Indeed, Proverbs 6:25 already gives this teaching of Jesus. The Old Testament forbids heart lust as well as the outward act. And Jesus was thus in full accord with the Old Testament.

But it seems clear that the Pharisaic doctrine, emphasizing externalism as it did, was here rebuked by Christ. The attitude of the Pharisees is clearly shown in several places in the Gospels. In Matthew 12:39, in answer to the question of the scribes and Pharisees, Jesus calls them "an evil and adulterous generation." Such language is also used in Matthew 16:4 and elsewhere. When Pharisees, according to the pericope in John 8:1-11, brought to Jesus the woman taken in adultery, they emphasized that she was taken in the act, but under Jesus' skillful accusation they tacitly confessed that they, too, had sinned, though not, evidently, thus overtly. In the parable of the Pharisee and the publican (Luke 18:9-14) the Pharisee thanked God that he was not an extortioner, unjust, or an adulterer, when the implication is that he was at heart all three. Paul, who

knew the censorious Pharisees well, accuses them directly
of adultery in Romans 2:22. It seems to fit the total picture
best to say here also that Jesus was contradicting the legalistic misinterpretation of Pharisaism; He surely was not contradicting the Old Testament or even greatly expanding
its teaching.

MURDER

This conclusion is re-enforced by study of the first of
Jesus' declarations, Matthew 5:21-26, where, be it noted, the
commanded righteousness is contrasted with that of the
scribes and Pharisees in verse 20.

Here the only part of the quotation coming from the
Old Testament is the sixth commandment itself, "Thou
shalt not kill." The remainder, "and whosoever shall kill
shall be in danger of the judgment [liable to the court],"
is from an unknown source, but is typical of the interest
in legality and the regulations of the time. Now, Jesus'
answer, "But I say unto you, That whosoever is angry with
his brother . . . shall be in danger of the judgment," by
no means contradicts the Old Testament. Indeed, it is
directly in line with the Old Testament, "Thou shalt not
hate thy brother in thine heart" (Lev. 19:17), and "The
stranger that dwelleth with you . . . thou shalt love him
as thyself" (Lev. 19:34). The Old Testament commands
proper heart attitudes and Jesus upholds it by opposing
Pharisaic externalism.

The next two phrases of Matthew 5:22 may be variously
interpreted. It is usually said that the argument proceeds
by way of climax; the lesser sin of saying "Raca" and the
least sin of saying "thou fool" are punishable by the Sanhedrin or even the Gehenna of fire. But it is not clear why
saying "thou fool" is a lesser sin than saying "Raca" or
why Jesus should threaten anyone with punishment by
the Sanhedrin.

Rather it seems to the writer that we have here a new
alternation between the quotation of a common error and
Jesus' answer thereto. "You say that to say 'Raca' will
make one liable to the Sanhedrin; I say that to say 'Mo-re,'

'thou fool,' makes one liable to hell." What is the difference between "Raca" and "Mo-re"? It seems that "Raca" is Aramaic for "empty head" and that "Mo-re," "thou fool," is a rather close Greek equivalent. The point of Jesus' words may well be that the Jews for some time had regarded "Raca," the Aramaic expression, with disfavor and had prescribed, as usual, penalties for the external curse word rather than recognizing the sinfulness of the attitude. The Greek equivalent, though just as bad in revealing an angry heart, had perhaps not yet attained a place on the Pharisaic index! They forbad vile language only when it was in Aramaic! Jesus, of course, has no use for such sophistry and says the slightest sin is sin in any language, and makes one liable not to a human court but to the judgment of God. A parallel instance of such alternation of quotation without the repetition of "You say . . . but I say" is found in Matthew 23:16-19.

DIVORCE

We come finally to Christ's teaching on divorce, Matthew 5:31, 32. Does He here contradict the Old Testament and give a higher New Testament revelation? It seems not. Rather, He is here contradicting a mistranslation of Deuteronomy 24:1-4. The King James translation of this passage implies that divorce for unspecified offenses received divine sanction. "Let him write her a bill of divorcement." This seems also to have been the interpretation of the Pharisees of Jesus' day, for, as is well known, they were divided on the question as to what constituted legitimate grounds for divorce. One group — the followers of Shammai — said that adultery was the only proper grounds; the other group — Hillel's disciples — said that almost anything justified divorce.

Examining the passage in the Hebrew, we see that actually the verse probably should not be taken as giving a divine approval of divorce at all. The clauses of the first part, the protasis, are so closely joined together by conjunctions that there seems to be no good place for the conclusion, the apodosis, until verse 4, where the negative *lo* gives the conclusion to the *ki* of verse 1, meaning "when" or "if." Also note that the protasis includes different possible situations to all of which the apodosis of verse 4 applies. It says that if a man marries and he divorces his wife and she marries another and the second husband divorces her or dies, she may not return to the first husband. According to this, the passage is not an allowance of divorce but a forbidding of "wife trading." The Septuagint translation of these verses supports this rendering of the Hebrew and it is followed in the Revised Standard Version. Actually, the propriety or impropriety of divorce is not taken up in Deuteronomy 24 according to this interpretation. Divorce is simply accepted as a regular social custom, but its grosser evils are regulated. There is here no blanket approval of divorce for indiscriminate causes.

But the Pharisees, in tempting Jesus, tried to get Him to side with either Hillel or Shammai and thus secure the hatred of the other group (Matt. 19:3-9). Christ answered them with reference to the institution of marriage at creation. The Pharisees asked, "Why, did Moses then command to give a writing of divorcement?" Jesus answered that Moses "suffered" divorce for unspecified causes, but this was not God's moral law and did not have divine approval. The civil legislation of Moses winked at various sins like polygamy, slavery, etc., without giving them divine approval. The civil legislation was based on moral law, yet it was a practical regulation for the people. It did not deal with all possible matters. Moses' lack of prohibition of these things does not make them right, as is clearly seen by other passages in the Old Testament (Mal. 2:16). Actually, the Pharisaic mistranslation of Deuteronomy 24:1-4 would have been avoided if sound principles of translation had been applied. Jesus' translation is accurate and in full accord with the Old Testament itself. That divorce does have one proper ground, fornication, Jesus makes clear in His additional statement (Matt. 5:32).

From the foregoing detailed treatment it can surely be seen that Christ in these verses by no means contradicted the basic law of Israel. The authorities accused Him of many things, but they did not accuse Him of that. Christ agreed fully with the Jews on the authority and full truthfulness of the Bible.[4]

We have said that the uniform attitude of Christ toward the Scriptures is one of complete trust. In this regard the record of the rich man and Lazarus is instructive. It may be debated whether or not this story in Luke 16 is a parable or an actual happening. It would seem to make little difference in its teaching, for Jesus' parables were not fairy tales but always true-to-life illustrations. The concluding verses, however, have a special emphasis, stating the point of the story. The poor rich man in hell begs that a testimony be given to his five living brothers. But the answer comes that they already have a testimony — Moses and the prophets. The rich man urges that a further appeal be made by a message from the dead. The answer is doubly emphatic: "If they hear not Moses and the prophets, neither will they be persuaded, though one rose from the dead." The emphasis here is tremendous. The witness of Scripture is the ultimate voice from the beyond, says Jesus. And we may note that the story is in close proximity with the saying in Luke that a tittle of the law cannot fail.

John's gospel gives many witnesses of Jesus' views on this point. One of the most striking is John 10:35, "The scripture cannot be broken." An effort is made by some to say that this is only an argument *ad hominem*, arguing on the basis of what the Pharisees admitted and declaring that on their principles He was guiltless. Meyer's commentary[5] takes a somewhat different view, arguing that the Greek particle *ei*, "since," "inasmuch as," governs both halves of the protasis: "Since it is written, and since the Scriptures cannot be broken, it follows that . . ." There is in the grammar no hint of doubt expressed by Jesus that He is merely assuming this for the sake of the argument. Rather, He rests His case upon the Scripture, and, we may add, upon a verse of the Psalms, which were in the third division of the Hebrew Bible, a division thought by some to have been held in lower regard by the Jews. It apparently was regarded highly by Christ.

Another section to the same effect is found in John 5: 39-47. For vindication of His own claims Christ appeals to Moses, in whom they claimed to trust. But He says that they did not really believe Moses: "For had ye believed Moses, ye would have believed me: for he wrote of me. But if ye believe not his writings, how shall ye believe my words?" Here is no *ad hominem* argument. He meets His Jewish persecutors with a head-on declaration that their Bible is true, though they have misconstrued it. He declares the Pentateuch to have been written by Moses and to be prophetic of Himself. Strangely, these two points are denied by the entire group of higher critics of our day. That the Old Testament was supernaturally written and made predictions about Jesus Christ is not accepted by modern scholarship. With a thoroughly naturalistic bias they rule out direct Messianic prediction.[6] It is a curious study to check the Revised Standard Version of the Bible, a monument of higher critical scholarship, and note how every important Old Testament passage purporting to predict directly the coming of Christ has been altered so as to remove this possibility. Sometimes the alteration is by translation, and sometimes by unfounded alteration of the Hebrew consonants. Cf. Psalm 2:12; 16:10; 45:6; 110:1 (the small *l*); Isaiah 7:14; Daniel 9:25f.; Micah 5:2, etc. Comparison of all of these verses with the New Testament and with the translations of the pre-Christian Greek Septuagint is most instructive. It is almost impossible to escape the conclusion that the admittedly higher critical bias of the translators has operated in all of these places. The translations given are by no means necessary from the Hebrew and in some cases, like Psalm 45:6, are in clear violation of the Hebrew. But the man who does not believe in the supernatural Christ cannot believe in the Old Testament, for, as Jesus said, the two stand or fall together.

Turning to Mark 12:36, we find a detail, not found in the parallel gospel accounts, which re-emphasizes our point. The quotation from Psalm 110 is said to predict Christ. The Psalm is said to have been written by David, which modern critical scholarship would deny. But Mark makes it clear that Jesus held that David spoke this word "by the Holy Ghost." In Mark 12:36 as in John 10:34 the argument turns on a single word.

The narrative in Luke telling of the walk to Emmaus also gives prominence to this element in Jesus' teaching. He rebuked them because they did not "believe all that the prophets have spoken" (Luke 24:25). He assured the assembled disciples that "all things must be fulfilled, which were written in the law of Moses, and in the prophets, and in the psalms, concerning me" (v. 44). He had "opened to [them] the scriptures" (v. 32).

Other passages can be treated more briefly by classifying them together. Not only the New Testament authors but Christ Himself refers repeatedly to the divine necessity of the fulfillment of the Scripture. This was the note on which He began His ministry at the synagogue in Capernaum (Luke 4:21). He recognized during His ministry that the Passion was appointed to Him by the prediction of Scripture (Mark 9:12). He could have called upon twelve legions of angels to avert His arrest, "But how then shall the scriptures be fulfilled, that thus it must be?" (Matt. 26:54). Even in the detail of Judas' enmity, Christ recognized a fulfillment of Scripture (John 13:18). His very words from the Cross apply the Messianic Psalm 22 to Himself. It is not too much to say that although Jesus declared that He came from heaven as the incarnate God, yet He was at the same time governed by Scripture and recognized that it also had come from heaven.

Not only the predictions but also the didactic and historic portions of Scripture are received and used by Christ. The very propositions which higher criticism insists upon are pointedly denied by Christ. We have cited one occasion where He affirms the Mosaic authorship of the Pentateuch.

There are others. He quotes from the Book of Daniel and ascribes it to Daniel the prophet (Mark 13:14). Jonah, He declares, was in the whale's belly (Matt. 12:40).[7] He affirms the divine creation of Adam and Eve (Matt. 19:4). The days of Noah are cited as historical fact useful to warn us to be ready against His coming on the clouds (Luke 17:26). Remember Lot's wife (Luke 17:32), Christ warns us, though critics would argue that her being turned into a pillar of salt is merely an aetiological tale suggested by the peculiar salt formations in the region south of the Dead Sea. Quite clearly, Jesus Christ was not a higher critic. Nor was the Devil, it seems, for he had no answer when Christ quoted Scripture to him. Jesus Christ lived in the Scripture. As a boy of twelve He confounded the doctors of the law because He knew their law and distinguished it from foolish human traditions. He declared that the Sadducees erred in the matter of the Resurrection because they did not know the Scripture. As we have said, He explained the Scriptures to His disciples in His post-resurrection appearances. You cannot separate Christ from the Scriptures.

A grasp of the evidence will show why this doctrine of verbal inspiration has had a powerful hold upon the Christian Church. It will not do to explain it away by saying it is Jewish, or that it smacks of Mohammedanism, or that it was the creation of the post-Reformation period, or that it was the invention of old Princeton Seminary. It was indeed held by the Jews, by the Early Church, and through the centuries of Church history. A similar, though not the same, view is found in Mohammedan circles, a fact which is best explained, probably, by Mohammed's Judaeo-Christian contacts. The view is held today by a large group of Christians often called Fundamentalists. But the reason all these Christians and many more have held to this view is simply that they are Christians and hold supreme the authority of Christ. They therefore believe what He told them to believe. They cannot do otherwise without betraying their Saviour afresh.

If there are problems which may beset full belief in

the Bible, those problems should be recognized and an answer sought, or faith encouraged where full evidence is lacking. But to deny the Bible, with its consequent denial of Christ, brings other problems which have in our day well-nigh brought the Western world to the brink of despair. We cannot feel that the retreat from the Bible in the twentieth century has been productive of spiritual power, growth in grace, assurance of salvation, peace of mind, sanctity of the home, or any other of the fruits normally associated with Christianity. Something is rotten in the household of faith. Perhaps it is because the prophets of modern theology have lost their faith in the Christ of the Book.

It is, of course, true that Jesus' doctrine of inspiration was not peculiar to Himself. In this point He shared the teaching of the Old Testament and the Jews of His time. Yet no one need hold that He was a mere child of His time not responsible for His teachings. It must be remembered that He never hesitated to contradict His contemporaries on other matters. No, Christ held this doctrine because it was the truth of God.

CLAIMS OF INSPIRATION IN OTHER BIBLICAL PASSAGES

A little reflection will show that the doctrine of verbal inspiration was held by the authors of the Old Testament. Joshua 1:8 insists that all the things written in the book of the law must be obeyed. Joshua 22:5 also enjoins similar respect for the law of Moses. David, in II Samuel 23:1, claims an inspiration similar to that assigned to him in Mark 12:36. The prophets throughout claim to speak the word of the Lord in truth and in detail. Daniel 9:2 contains an interesting reference to Daniel's study of "the books" (the Hebrew has the article), which included the prophecy of Jeremiah. He believed its prediction and prayed accordingly. Nehemiah, one of the last books of the Old Testament, shows a full knowledge of and high regard for the law of Moses and the prophets, who spoke by God's Spirit (cf. Neh. 9:3, 30; 10:29, etc.). Our present point is not affected by the fact that higher criticism may declare that these passages are not genuine. At the very least they were written long before Christ. Reverence for the Scriptures was well established in the Jewish community. The remarkable discoveries of the Dead Sea Scrolls, including a complete scroll of Isaiah from a century before Christ, another long section of the Book of Samuel, and fragments of all the Old Testament books, are illustrating afresh the care with which the Jews guarded their sacred Scriptures in an early time. Christianity, based as it was upon Old Testament teachings, was from the start a "book religion."

The Judaism of Christ's day revered the book. Probably the best firsthand witness is Flavius Josephus. This famous Jewish historian, who wrote toward the end of the first century A.D., tells us that the pious Jew held his Scriptures dearer than life itself. In his epistle *Against Apion* he writes: "How firmly we have given credit to these books of our own nation is evident by what we do; for during so many ages as have already passed no one hath been so bold as either to add anything to them, to take anything from them, or to make any change; but it is become natural to all Jews, immediately and from their very birth, to esteem these books to contain divine doctrines, and to persist in them, and if occasion be, willingly to die for them."[8] In this valuable quotation he also gives us a listing of the books of the Jewish Scriptures, which, as we shall see in Part II, are the exact equivalent of the thirty-nine books found in the Protestant Old Testament and in the Jewish Bible. The Apocrypha are not included.

But not only did Christ's Jewish forbears believe the Old Testament to be true in its entirety; the apostles and the later Church also held the same view. There is no hint of a difference between Christ and the apostles on this point. The New Testament writers quote the Old Testament as freely as do the recorded speeches of Jesus. If Jesus insisted that the Scriptures must be fulfilled, the gospel authors do also (cf. only Matt. 26:56; Mark 15:28; Luke 3:4; John 12:38). The Book of Acts from 1:16 to 28:25 also is filled with this doctrine. Paul's constant appeal in his Epistles is to the Old Testament. His proof of the sin of the Jews as well as the Gentiles is a catena of quotations from the Old Testament (Rom. 3:10-18). His constant opposition to the idea of justification by the works of the law is not against the law itself, much less the Scripture. He recognizes that the "law is holy" (Rom. 7:12), declares that the Scripture foresaw the Gospel Age (Gal. 3:8), and finds the Scripture sufficient for hope as well as learning (Rom. 15:4). It is here doubtless that the famous verse II Timothy 3:16 should be mentioned. It has been treated so thoroughly by many commentators that little needs to be said. It surely does not mean, as is sometimes deduced from the old Revised Version, that every Scripture which is inspired is also profitable. The Revised translation was a mistake acknowledged by almost all and has been corrected in the Revised Standard Version. The verse says that all Scripture is inspired of God. And the word "inspired" is not used in the loose sense of exhilaration so common in our day. It indicates that Scripture is literally God-breathed, spoken out by God. More significant than the details of the exegesis, however, may be the context. What was this Scripture that Paul eulogizes? It was the book which Timothy had known as a child (3:15). His godly mother and grandmother had instructed him well. And the basis of their instruction had been the law of God. This could have been only the Old Testament. Paul's conclusion (4:2) comes with force to one who would serve God today: "Therefore . . . preach the word," because in truth it is the Word of God.

The same remarks can be applied to II Peter. If it is by Peter (as the present author believes), it supports the fact that he believed in verbal inspiration, just as Acts 1:16, etc., says he did. If it is by a later hand, it proves that the Church of a succeeding period held the doctrine, for the Epistle clearly teaches such a view of the Scriptures.

In 1:21 the human origination of Scripture is denied in favor of the divine superintendence. The prophetic Scriptures, i.e., the Scriptures of the prophets, are said, in comparison with the solemn report of the glory of the Transfiguration scene, to be "more sure." In view of the occasional use of a Greek comparative as a superlative,[9] and since the Scriptures are not easily seen to be more sure than the eyewitness account which is given such emphasis, it seems best to translate, "We have also a most certain prophetic word . . ."

A further detail may be allowed on this interesting passage. Verse 20 seems in the Authorized Version to be concerned with principles of interpretation. The Revised Standard Version goes even further in claiming that the Scripture is not of one's own interpretation. But interpretation is not in view in the context. The trouble concerns one word, *epiluseos*, used only here in the New Testament. Its meaning is not clear. It is used in connection with the account of Joseph's dream recorded in the Septuagint, where it means "interpretation." But the context of the passage in Peter indicates that the etymological significance "unloosing" would seem to be preferable. The question at issue is the origin of Scripture, not hermeneutics. The thought is that the Scripture did not spring up, it was not let loose, of itself, nor did it come by the will of the prophets: it was written by God. This was Peter's doctrine and it was the doctrine of all the early Christians.[10]

Now, the remarkable fact is that not only do the Epistles claim this high view of inspiration for the Old Testament but the writings, indeed, the oral teachings, of the apostles are put on an equally high plane.

It is occasionally assumed that the apostles were not conscious of writing authoritative books. From time to time a fable appears in current religious periodicals. It pictures the Apostle Paul returning to one of our metropolitan churches for prayer meeting and finding, to his surprise, that the study concerned the Book of Romans. "How interesting," he is made to say. "I hardly thought that my casual correspondence would be treasured so long, but I shall be glad if you find it helpful." This easy assumption of modern religious journalists, of course, in fact contradicts Paul's express testimony in his undoubted Epistles. Several of these passages should be noted.

In I Corinthians 14 Paul is giving the Christians directions for the exercise of spiritual gifts. He had said in 12:28 that God had set the apostles in the Church first. Now he concludes his instructions in 14:37 by declaring that the mark of a spiritual man is to receive his, Paul's, writings as "the commandments of the Lord." To the same effect he maintains in I Corinthians 2:10-13 that he speaks what God has revealed to him, not in words of human wisdom, but in words taught by the Holy Spirit. About the only way to avoid the plain conclusion that this passage is, as Hodge calls it, the most clear didactic passage on verbal inspiration in the New Testament is to interpret the use of "we" in verse 13, etc., as referring to all spiritual Christians. This is done, for instance, in the *New Commentary* by Gore, Goudge, and Guillaume.[11] This interpretation is certainly not necessary, for in II Corinthians 10 there is an alternation of the pronouns "I" and "we" in just the same manner as in I Corinthians 2, and the reference there is clearly to the Apostle Paul all the way through. It is an editorial "we." Further, the allegations in I Corinthians 2:10-13 are not true of spiritual Christians in general, nor are they alleged of them elsewhere. And, finally, the claim of verse 13 is made by Paul in the first person singular in verse 4. Paul and the apostles claimed a special gift for their written and oral teaching, and it was specifically in this gift that the apostles' pre-eminence as teachers lay. Paul makes the claim again in I Thessalonians 2:13. Here again the word that Paul preached — orally this time — is called not the word of men but truly the word of God. That the first person plural should be used again is no problem. The situation is precisely the same in the Second Epistle to the Thessalonians, where they are commanded to receive and hold the traditions given them "by word, or our epistle" (2:15); yet the Epistle is very carefully signed by Paul himself, a signature and characteristic closing which was to be a token in every epistle he was to write. Paul clearly wrote and preached expecting to be believed because he brought a revelation that was divine — even in detail. Peter (II Pet. 3:2, 15) and John (Rev. 22:18, 19) present the same teaching, as will be shown in detail later.[12]

There are two exceptions to this conclusion which are sometimes cited. They are, however, only apparent exceptions. In I Corinthians 7:6, 10, 12, 25, much is sometimes made of Paul's distinguishing between his own word and the Lord's commands. The unusual character of these expressions makes us wonder if there is not another and better explanation. It is found in the fact that a frequent name used by Paul for the second person of the Trinity is "the Lord."[13] If we understand the word "Lord" in this section to be Christ speaking during His earthly ministry, all becomes clear. True, Paul had not heard Christ first hand, but with his associates he had a source of such quotations (cf. Acts 20:35). Against divorce Paul could quote the Lord (v. 10). With regard to the leaving of an unsaved partner in a mixed marriage he could not quote Christ's instruction, for He had left us none. Nor had He left us a commandment about virgins (v. 25) nor about continency (v. 6). But Paul feels fully competent to add his own apostolic directions regarding these matters. Indeed, with a fine touch of irony, Paul, at the conclusion of this very chapter, reasserts his apostolic authority, insisting that surely he had a right to claim the Spirit of God as truly as did the puffed-up prophets of Corinth (I Cor. 7:40).

The other apparent exception is given in the contrast Paul draws between the letter and the spirit in II Corinthians 3:6. Attention to the context will save us from an interpretation that might make Paul appear to contradict his teaching elsewhere. He is not making here a contrast between a belief in verbal inspiration and a general spiritualizing of Scripture that denies its full truthfulness. Paul is contrasting the legalism of the scribes and Pharisees — which had entered the Christian Church as the teaching of the Judaizers — with the true doctrine revealed to us by the Holy Spirit. The word for scribe is *grammateus*. The word for letter is *gramma*. The scribal legalistic doctrine is denounced as "of the letter." The Christian doctrine is praised as "of the spirit."

The same contrast is given in Romans 2:27-29. There the Judaizing teaching of righteousness through letter and circumcision does not avail but is an actual transgression of the law and is condemned. The true teaching is justification by faith which touches the heart and spirit. Circumcision was not wrong. But what the Jews made of it was wrong. Likewise, the Old Testament was not wrong, but what the Judaizers read into it was wrong. Their very error Paul says was in *not* believing the Old Testament, in fact misinterpreting it (II Cor. 3:14-16). Christ had said the same (Mark 7:9). This explanation is reinforced by a third passage, Romans 7:6, where again the contrast cannot be drawn between some Fundamentalists' belief in the Bible and Modernists who accept it in a general, vague way. Rather, Paul says, the bondage of the letter was the legalism of justification by circumcision, feasts and fasts, and such works of the law, while the newness of the Spirit is his preaching of freedom from the law in order to find salvation by grace. The evidence is clear and overwhelming that Paul and the other New Testament authors both believed the Old Testament verbatim and expected their writing to be believed the same way.

One further objection may be raised: since the New Testament most frequently quotes the Old Testament in the Septuagint version, and as this is erroneous in spots, does this not indicate that the New Testament authors were not careful in their handling of the Scripture? That the New Testament authors usually quoted from the Septuagint is true enough. In fact, all seem to do so except Matthew in those quotations peculiar to his gospel. But it does not follow that the New Testament authors had no regard for their Old Testament text. In the foregoing pages the author has quoted many times from the King James Version of the English Bible merely for convenience and without in the least departing from the view that the original only is inspired. In the same way the Septuagint is used by the New Testament. Notice the obvious fact that the New Testament authors, writing in Greek, had to quote the Old Testament in translation. The only question was: should they use the commonly known translation or should they translate *de novo* for each quotation? It should occasion no surprise that they have usually used the standard translation for the convenience both of themselves and of their audience.

Moreover, we cannot be so sure as scholars once were that the Septuagint is a poor version. There has been a tendency in the past to consider the Massoretic text of the Hebrew Bible well nigh the ideal and to treat all divergences from it as errors. On this assumption naturally the Septuagint is guilty of many mistakes. But the methodology is bad. Preliminary reports of a scroll of Samuel in Hebrew found in the region of the Dead Sea indicate that it also shows several striking divergences from the Massoretic text which are in the direction indicated by the Septuagint.[14] The Septuagint may be right more frequently than has been supposed. Of course, we must make allowances for errors made in copying the Septuagint during the period before the fourth century A. D. when our major Septuagint manuscripts were made. The New Testament naturally did not quote from the Codex Vaticanus copy which was made about 325 A.D. It quoted from a copy of the Septuagint which seems to agree more closely with the Codex Alexandrinus, which was made in the fifth century A.D. But, of course, Alexandrinus has errors in it which were not in the first-century text used by the apostles.

In several instances it seems clear that the New Testament prefers the Septuagint against the Massoretic text

WHY WE BELIEVE THE BIBLE

when the latter is clearly wrong. A typical example is Romans 10:18, quoting from Psalm 19:4. The verse in Romans says "their sound" went into all the earth. The Psalm says "their line" went into all the earth. The New Testament here follows the Septuagint. But is the Septuagint possibly not correct? The difference in Hebrew between "their line," *qwm*, and "their sound," *qwlm* or *qlm*, is very small and easily mistaken by a copyist. The evidence of the minor Greek versions made about 200 A.D. is somewhat divided. Some translate it "sound"; one translates it "line." These translations, basing themselves generally on the Hebrew of that day, would seem to indicate that the Hebrew manuscripts differed among themselves on this point in post-Christian times. Turning to internal evidence, we find that the poetic parallelism of the verse in the Psalms seems clearly to prefer the reading "their voice." If it be held that the original reading was *qlm*, "their voice," the Greek translations are explained, the context is satisfied, and the existing Hebrew copies are accounted for as a slight mistake by later copyists. In this case, the New Testament indeed follows the Septuagint, but in doing so avoids an error which has apparently crept into the Hebrew text. In this case the New Testament is fully justified in its method of quotation. Other examples will be given later[15] under the subject of textual criticism. It may be added that others have explained the reading "voice" in this passage as a free and justifiable interpretation of the Hebrew reading "line." That is a possibility that should be kept in view. But evidence for such an idiomatic use of "line" seems to be lacking. It seems rather that the Septuagint has preserved the true text. Several of the discrepancies between the Old Testament and the New can be handled in this manner. The New Testament usually followed the Septuagint where its translation was acceptable. In some few cases where the Septuagint differs from the Massoretic text and the New Testament follows the Septuagint, it can usually be clearly shown that the Hebrew text is suspicious and probably wrong. One interesting case of a slightly different character can be mentioned. In Romans 11:26, where the New Testament says, "There shall come out of Sion the Deliverer," the Septuagint of Isaiah 59:20 reads, "The Redeemer shall come to Zion." The curious thing is that new evidence from the Canaanite literature of Ugarit indicates that the Hebrew preposition *Lamedh* can be translated not only in the usual way "to," as in the Septuagint and the King James Version, but also "from," as the New Testament does in this quotation.[16] In this case Paul departs from the Septuagint, where a different translation is allowable and desirable. The entire principle of quotations from the Old Testament in the New is fully defensible.

We are left with a solid basis for the doctrine of verbal inspiration. It was clearly the teaching of Jesus Christ, and for Christians this should be sufficient. Christ's own doctrine was in full accord with that of the ancient Jews and with His Jewish contemporaries. The Old Testament itself alleges such a view. When we add to this that the apostles who were taught by Christ advanced this same view, we see that the doctrine is so basic, so pervasive in the origins of the Church, and so necessary to our faith that we cannot relinquish it without the direst peril. It is not an elective in the Christian curriculum. It is required. The Bible is the Christian's infallible guide in a dark world. We gladly believe it as true and turn to it as profitable for doctrine, for reproof, for correction, for instruction in righteousness.

In Bunyan's *Pilgrim's Progress* we read that at one point in his journey Pilgrim slept awhile and lost his scroll. Bunyan grippingly pictures the anxiety and trouble that ensued until Pilgrim retraced his steps and found his book. America has lost its belief in and emphasis upon the Bible. There was a time when it was read and taught in our schools. Now more than the most perfunctory reading of it is said to be illegal. It used to be preached, memorized, quoted, studied, and believed. Now this is true only in restricted circles. America must return to the Bible. But we shall not return to the Bible as long as it is regarded merely as great literature. It is only when we receive it as God's holy and infallible Word that it will bring the promised blessing. "Blessed is he that readeth, and they that hear the words of this prophecy, and keep those things which are written therein: for the time is at hand" (Rev. 1:3).

CHAPTER 3

VERBAL INSPIRATION IN CHURCH HISTORY

In this section only a survey of the doctrine through the great periods of Church history will be attempted. The situation is clear and is freely admitted by many — even of those unfriendly to the doctrine. We shall consider only the post-Reformation era, the Reformers themselves, and the times of the Early Church.

It is safe to say that there is no doctrine, except those of the Trinity and the deity of Christ, which has been so widely held through the ages of Church history as that of verbal inspiration. This, however, is by no means the common conception of the situation. Occasionally an effort is made to picture this doctrine as a recent growth, the product of the Hodge-Warfield-Machen School of Princeton Seminary. This was the contention of men in the Presbyterian Church in the U.S.A. who defended the Auburn Affirmation of 1924. They asserted that in 1923 the General Assembly of that Church had erred when it re-adopted five basic points, including the doctrine of verbal inerrancy, as essential to Presbyterian standards. They maintained that the Westminster Standards teach that the Bible is "our only infallible rule of faith and practice," that is to say, an infallible guide in spiritual matters. But the Auburn Affirmation argued that "the doctrine of inerrancy of Scripture, intended to enhance the authority of the Scriptures, in fact impairs their supreme authority for faith and life."[1] It was argued that inerrancy is not found in the Westminster Standards, but was a new development adopted by the General Assembly under pressure from the Fundamentalist groups.

This argument had already been considered by Warfield and dealt with at length.[2] Philip Schaff had written in 1893, at about the time of the heresy trial of his colleague, C. A. Briggs, that "the theory of a literal inspiration and inerrancy was not held by the Reformers."[3] Warfield goes on to consider the argument by Briggs that the Westminster Confession does not teach this doctrine. The Confession, of course, devotes its first chapter to the Scriptures, and declares that the canonical books and these alone are of authority. The Apocrypha are not, but are mere "human writings." The authority of Scripture depends "upon God (who is truth itself), the author thereof; and therefore it is to be received, because it is the Word of God." "Nothing at any time is to be added" to Scripture. There is a wonderful "consent of all the parts" among its "many other incomparable excellencies." "The Old Testament in Hebrew . . . and the New Testament in Greek . . . being immediately inspired by God . . . are therefore authentical . . . the Church is finally to appeal unto them."

It would seem that the Confession speaks positively enough, although the word "inerrant" is not used. Why the word "inerrant" is not used is easy to see. Three hundred years ago the modern critical problems and the conflict of science and the Bible or serious questions of historical accuracy had not yet arisen. The Confession does speak of "the infallible truth" of the Word of God and this should be sufficient. "Inerrant" means "without mistake"; "infallible" means "incapable of error." It is actually a stronger word. In 1646 there had not yet arisen the distinction Modernist theologians now attempt to draw between spiritual truth and historical error. The old creed therefore does not specifically say that the Bible is true also in matters of history and science as well as in the spiritual sphere. It simply emphasizes that the Bible is all true. As Chapter XIV of the Westminster Confession puts it, "By this faith [saving faith], a Christian believeth to be true whatsoever is revealed in the Word, for the authority of God Himself speaketh therein." It is also to be noted that the matter of self-contradiction in the Bible had repeatedly arisen,[4] but that here the Confession took its stand with the other Reformation creeds to insist that there are no contradictions in Scripture. It mentions "the consent of all the parts." So the Westminster standards actually teach Biblical inerrancy, even though they do not use the modern terminology which has been developed to meet a new attack.

Warfield carefully considers this in the above mentioned article, but, with his characteristic thoroughness, he does even more. He treats in detail the writings of eminent Westminster divines that have been preserved for us and shows that they clearly deny the possibility of mistakes in Scripture. He quotes John Ball's catechism, which declared that "the Holy Scriptures in the Originals were inspired both for matter and for words."[5] Richard Capel is quoted also as saying that the original writers of Scripture were "indued with the infallible Spirit" and "might not err."[6] The great Richard Baxter is briefly quoted to the same effect. "No error or contradiction is in it, but what is in some copies, by the failing of preserver, transcribers, printers, or translators."[7]

Warfield quotes many of the other authors of the Westminster Confession to the same effect, much to the detriment of the contrary view which C. A. Briggs had set forth in his still-sold book *Whither?* Warfield showed how Briggs had, in a serious manner, taken quotations of these men out of context. They believed precisely what we believe when we affirm the doctrine of verbal inspiration today.[8]

Happily in this point, Warfield's argument is admitted today. The tendency now is to say that the awful doctrine of verbal inspiration was not held by the Reformers but was the product of an atrophied orthodoxy of the century after the Reformation, when the high character of the Reformers had been superseded by the sterile intellectualism and cold orthodoxy of the creed-making age.

Barth speaks almost as if this doctrine were the invention of the post-Reformation era: "The historistic conception of

the Bible with its cult of heroes and the mechanical doctrine of verbal inspiration are products of the same age
and the same spirit. They have this in common, that they
stood for the means by which men of the Renaissance
claimed to control the Bible."[9] He speaks of the "period
of orthodoxy (subsequent to Calvin) which was the counterpart of the fatal doctrine of inspiration."[10]

Brunner speaks a bit more accurately and at length. His
view is that Luther had come to the grand conclusion that
it is not the Bible that counts but Christ therein contained.
We should note that this position invents a false antithesis.
It is our view that the Bible counts because it is the true
revelation of Christ. And as to Luther's view, which has
been much discussed, Marcus Reu has admirably drawn
together the evidence from the great Reformer's writings
to show that he fully believed in verbal inspiration.[11] But,
Brunner declares, "Calvin is already moving away from
Luther toward the doctrine of verbal inspiration. His *doctrine* of the Bible is entirely the traditional, formally authoritative, view. From the end of the sixteenth century
onwards there was no other 'principle of Scripture' than this
formally authoritarian one."[12] Brunner here at least agrees
with Warfield and disagrees with Briggs and older Modernists when he declares that verbal inspiration has been the
teaching of the Protestant Church and its creeds. Most
students of the Reformation will be astonished at the suggestion that Calvin believed anything else. Luther has been
quoted as questioning the doctrine because of his oft-
mentioned remark that James is a "right strawy Epistle."
It should be noted, however, that Luther's problem was
not one of inspiration but of canonicity. Luther had denied
the Apocryphal books of the Old Testament, a denial in
which he was on solid ground and had much support from
previous as well as contemporary scholars. But it need not
be wondered at too much if, in facing the problem of the
reconciliation of the Epistle of James with Luther's essential doctrine of justification by faith, Luther was perhaps
led to solve it too easily simply by questioning the canonicity

of James. After all, the Epistle had actually been questioned in certain circles of the Early Church and its apostolic origin was not thoroughly demonstrated. Luther, a pioneer, might well have questioned it. However, in Luther's defense it should further be said that he kept the Book of James in every edition of his Bible. Actually, the context of his reference to James shows that he only argues that James is an "epistle of straw" in comparison with the greater and more basic books of the gospels, major Pauline Epistles, etc. In this we admit that he was right. Verbal inspiration as a doctrine by no means teaches that Obadiah is as important as Genesis. It merely insists that the entire Bible is true. Luther plainly accepted the doctrine of verbal inspiration.

Brunner makes the further admission that the doctrine is an ancient one: "The doctrine of verbal inspiration was already known to pre-Christian Judaism . . . and was probably also taken over by Paul and the rest of the apostles."[18] He proceeds to argue that the doctrine was of no great consequence through the medieval period because the principle of allegorical interpretation allowed the scholastics to make what they would out of the Bible. The doctrine was revived in the Reformation. Probably Brunner does not realize the import of what he is here saying. He says that this doctrine — which he cordially castigates — was the legacy of Judaism, accepted by the apostles, and held by the Early Church through the years of her strength down to the times of Origen and Augustine, who set the pattern of allegorical interpretation for a thousand years. The loss of this doctrine as a practical element in theology (though it was by no means lost in theory) corresponded with the Dark Ages. After the Reformation, the doctrine lasted through three centuries of the Church's strength till the rise of higher criticism. It was held by the Church which spread abroad in the great missionary movement of the nineteenth century. It has been denied by the scholars of the late nineteenth century and by the laity and churchmen of the twentieth. This terrible doctrine seems to be absent in the times of the Church's apostasy and present in the times of her power.

At least Brunner is historically rather accurate. One might well here urge Brunner to reconsider and embrace a doctrine evidently so productive of spiritual power and blessing![14]

With these admissions it perhaps is a work of supererogation to search the old Christian writings to prove that the Early Church was faithful in following its Lord in this doctrine. The evidence has been set forth in some detail by Sanday in his Bampton Lectures on "Inspiration," especially in his first chapter, where he gives a great number of brief references to the writers of the early centuries, especially after 200 A.D.[15]

It might be of interest to quote Warfield's estimate of Sanday's work: "Dr. Sanday, in his recent Bampton Lectures on 'Inspiration' — in which, unfortunately, he does not teach the Church doctrine — is driven to admit that not only may 'testimonies to the general doctrine of inspiration' from the earliest Fathers 'be multiplied to almost any extent'; but (that) there are some which go further and point to an inspiration which might be described as 'verbal'; 'nor does this idea,' he adds, 'come in tentatively and by degrees, but almost from the very first.' He might have spared the adverb 'almost.' The earliest writers know no other doctrine."[16] With this we heartily agree. Sanday does not hold to verbal inspiration. But, like Brunner, quoted above, he is constrained to admit that this has been the teaching cherished by Christians through the ages. He is an unwilling witness to the fact that the early Fathers believed in a verbally inspired Scripture. Much of the evidence is referred to also by Gaussen in his well-known book *Theopneustia*,[17] but the quotations are not printed nor classified as conveniently as in Sanday.

A very few of these early statements should be given. The First Epistle of Clement, written near the end of the first century A.D., speaks of the Old Testament with the greatest reverence and tells also of the inspiration of the apostles and their high authority. Several times[18] Clement quotes from the Old Testament and ascribes the words of the human author to God, Christ, or the Holy Ghost. It is

called the "Scripture," "Sacred Scriptures," the "Holy Word,"
etc. Specifically he says, "Look carefully into the Scriptures,
which are the true utterances of the Holy Spirit. Observe
that nothing of an unjust or counterfeit character is written
in them."[19]

Ignatius, the bishop of Antioch, who was martyred about
117 A.D., has left us a similar witness. By this time references to the New Testament abound and an exceedingly
high view of the apostles is held. He speaks rather depre-
catingly of the Jewish law, but it is plainly the Judaizing
doctrine that is meant, for he commends the prophets. However, he emphasizes that the word of the new dispensation is far superior. He remarks concerning those who
ignorantly deny Jesus that "these persons neither have the
prophets persuaded nor the law of Moses nor the Gospel
even to this day."[20] The way in which he here places the
Gospel on a par with the Old Testament is very instructive. Of these prophets he says, "The divinest prophets
lived according to Christ Jesus. On this account also they
were persecuted, being inspired by His grace to fully convince the unbelieving that there is one God, who has
manifested Himself by Jesus Christ His Son."[21] He says
also that we who have received the things of the new dispensation should follow Christ when the "prophets themselves in the Spirit did wait for Him as their teacher."
Again he uses such terms when he urges us to flee to "the
Gospel as to the flesh of Jesus, and to the apostles as to
the presbytery of the Church. And let us also love the
prophets because they, too, have proclaimed the Gospel,
and placed their hope in Him, and waited for Him; in
whom also, believing, they were saved, through union to
Jesus Christ, being holy men, worthy of love and admira-
tion, having had witness borne to them by Jesus Christ."[22]
Ignatius is full of the thought that the new is better than
the old. But he does not hint that the new is truer than
the old. For him, as he says, "It is written" refers not only
to the old dispensation but applies equally well to the
gospel.[23]

Polycarp, the great martyr and disciple of John, writes near the beginning of the second century, just after Ignatius' martyrdom, "Whosoever perverts the oracles of the Lord to his own lusts, and says that there is neither a resurrection nor a judgment, he is the first-born of Satan."[24] Polycarp here is probably speaking of the New Testament. His opinion of the apostles is most high: "For neither I nor any other such one can come up to the wisdom of the blessed and glorified Paul. He, when among you, accurately and steadfastly taught the word of truth."[25] The prophets — surely the Old Testament authors — are said to have "proclaimed beforehand the coming of the Lord,"[26] thus evidencing a belief in prophecy. The quotation from Psalm 4:4, "Be ye angry, and sin not" (in the Psalm, "Stand in awe, and sin not," A.V.), and from Ephesians 4:26, "Let not the sun go down upon your wrath," are linked together and called Sacred Scriptures.[27] (Ephesians 4:26 quotes Psalm 4:4, and possibly Polycarp is taking the whole quotation from Ephesians.) In this short epistle Polycarp has comparatively few references to the Old Testament, but his doctrine of Scripture is clearly the standard one of complete belief therein.

There are a few other fragments and short writings from authors of this early time which do not speak so positively as these, but it must be remembered that neither they nor any of the rest of the authors quoted give any hint that the Scriptures, either Old Testament or New, are not to be trusted. Rather, the spirit of their extant remains is in full agreement with the doctrine so widely witnessed in the apostolic writings that the Holy Scriptures are true and without the slightest mistake.

When we come to the great authors of the late second century where the witness abounds, we also find full testimony to belief in a doctrine of inspiration that must be described as verbal. Irenaeus, the disciple of the aged Polycarp and therefore closely linked to the Apostle John, complains that these men, "when . . . they are confuted from the Scriptures, they turn round and accuse these same

Scriptures, as if they were not correct."[28] But Irenaeus declares that they are correct in whole and in part. He objects to the fact that Marcion and Valentinus use only a part of Luke: "It follows then, as a matter of course, that these men must either receive the rest of his narrative or else reject these parts also. For no person of common sense can permit them to receive some things recounted by Luke as being true and to set others aside, as if he had not known the truth."[29] He maintains that the author of Matthew was so endowed with the Holy Ghost that he, "foreseeing the corruptors," wrote certain words and not others so as to preclude the Gnostic heresy.[30] He declares that the apostles after the Resurrection "were invested with power from on high when the Holy Spirit came down (upon them), were filled from all (His gifts), and had perfect knowledge."[31] A final quotation may be given from the many more which could be cited. He says with the humility of true faith, "If, however, we cannot discover explanations of all those things in Scripture which are made the subject of investigation, yet let us not on this account seek after any other God besides Him who really exists. For this is the greatest impiety. We should leave things of that nature to God who created us, being most properly assured that the Scriptures are indeed perfect, since they were spoken by the Word of God and His Spirit."[32] What good advice from the second century to the twentieth!

We close this section of our study with a few quotations from Justin Martyr, who wrote just after the middle of the second century and is thus an earlier contemporary of Irenaeus.

Commonly quoted is Justin's description of the inspiration of "the holy men" who would "present themselves pure to the energy of the Divine Spirit, in order that the divine plectrum itself, descending from heaven, and using righteous men as an instrument like a harp or lyre, might reveal to us the knowledge of things divine and heavenly. Wherefore, as if with one mouth and one tongue, they have in succession, and in harmony with one another, taught us both concerning God, and the creation of the world, and the formation of man," etc.[33] Note that this quotation not only gives an illustration which is by no means a part of our doctrine but also points out that the product is divine and true, without contradictions. This last point is made more explicit in another passage: "I am entirely convinced that no Scripture contradicts another; I shall admit rather that I do not understand what is recorded, and shall strive to persuade those who imagine that the Scriptures are contradictory to be rather of the same opinion as myself."[34] To this end he was arguing with the unbeliever Trypho.

A final quotation from Justin's first *Apology* tells of the rise of the Old Testament: "There were, then, among the Jews certain men who were prophets of God, through whom the prophetic Spirit published beforehand things that were to come to pass, ere ever they happened." These prophecies, he says, were "carefully preserved when they had been arranged in books by the prophets themselves in their own Hebrew language."[35] Justin then presents two or three pages of Old Testament citations predicting Christ's coming and work. A great deal of this material is equal to much that is written on the subject today, and it is all from the point of view of one who accepts without question the supernatural inspiration of the authors of Scripture so that it can be trusted entirely even in small details.

During the immediately following period of the third century our witnesses are abundant. Sanday says, "Indeed on both sides, the side of doctrine and the side of practice, the authoritative use of Scripture — the New Testament equally with the Old — underlies the whole of the Christian literature of this period. Not only might we quote it for page after page of Irenaeus, Clement of Alexandria, Tertullian, Hippolytus, Origen . . . but — what is of even more importance — the method is shared alike by orthodox writers and heretical."[36] We may summarize the matter by citing a quotation from Augustine a bit later, who says of the canonical Scriptures that he "firmly believes that no one of their authors has erred in anything, in writing."[37]

Sanday strangely tries to add a caveat that side by side with this high view was a lower opinion which he imagines to be "in closer contact with the facts."[38] This lower view of Scripture he finds in the fragments of Papias, the preface to Luke's Gospel, and the Muratorian Canon. His main substantiation for this idea is apparently a willful misunderstanding of what is involved in verbal inspiration. He assumes that verbal inspiration involves that the authors did not study or use sources for their work.

No one who reads his Bible at all would wish to claim that the human authors were entirely passive in the process of inspiration. God did not lay hold of a Persian to write Hebrew nor of a mystical John to write the logical Epistles of Paul. God chose John to write according to his nature, but superintended his writing. Paul, trained in the schools of Jerusalem, reflects his background, but writes only God's truth. If human industry in preparation of material precludes inspiration, then no one from Moses to the Apostle John was inspired. Of course Moses counted the Israelites before he wrote the Book of Numbers. The census was not a matter of revelation to Moses, but it is none the less true and a part of God's Word. Of course Mark took care to gather his material carefully from Peter just as Papias says, and Luke worked industriously, as he outlines in Luke 1:1-4. But hard labor is not antithetic to usefulness for God! God would probably not have chosen Paul as a vessel of inspiration and an author of Scripture if he had not been one who would labor more abundantly than all. Very few have been the theologians who have held that verbal inspiration involved a trancelike receptivity and mechanical dictation of the Word without human activity. None of the great creeds so define it. To liken the Fundamentalist view to a mechanical thing such as Mohammed claimed is only to evidence a lack of knowledge of what one's opponents believe and what the Church has so widely held. These misconceptions are so unnecessary and yet frequent that they can only be called willful. They have been considered above.[39]

Others have objected that such incidental details as the apostle's asking for his cloak left at Troas (II Tim. 4:13) or requesting lodging (Philem. 22) surely cannot be considered as inspired because they are too mundane. Of course this is not a positive argument, but merely an appeal to propriety in what one thinks to be a fit object of divine superintendence. And presumably the answer is that we are not the measures of the divine interest in our mundane existence. In the Old Testament the interest of God descended to ailments of the body and the handling of unclean vermin and animals in the Hebrew home. The view perhaps forgets that the God who cares for sparrows is much more concerned about warm clothing and lodging for His aged apostle. If God could superintend the arrow drawn "at a venture" which smote King Ahab "between the joints of the harness" in fulfillment of Micaiah's prophecy (II Chron. 18:33), surely He is interested in our little problems, too, for in the life of a prophet or apostle, just as in our own, it is very difficult to separate the little from the big. It was a little thing that Paul happened to be in Jerusalem the day that Stephen was stoned and held the coats of his attackers, but it left an indelible impression which God doubtless used in the apostle's conversion. As a matter of fact, the little detail about the coat left at Troas, if it be accepted as genuine and believed, furnishes the clue to the later history of Paul. It proves correct the view that he was delivered from the first Roman imprisonment, then traveled about — at least to Troas —before being captured a second time for his execution a short time after Second Timothy was written. Let us not despise the small things in the Bible or in any of God's work. Even the jots and tittles have their place. By verbal inspiration we merely mean that God superintended the process of writing so that the whole is true — the historical, the doctrinal, the mundane, the minor, and the major. The genealogies are not so ennobling as the Passion narratives, for instance, but they truly give the antecedents of Him who was the Seed of David according to the flesh, but the Son of God with power according to the Spirit of holiness, Jesus Christ, the central subject of the whole sacred volume.

This, under various names, has been the doctrine of the Christian Church from the earliest times, such unwilling witnesses as Sanday, Brunner, and Alan Richardson being proofs. Christ and the apostles believed it. So has the Church, with the rarest of exceptions, until the rise of Modernist theology in the nineteenth and twentieth centuries. This doctrine is by no means the hard and mechanical view it has been said to be. It has held before the Church a Book with the message of God. In a dark and sinful world the Book has rebuked kings, comforted the poor, encouraged learning, freed the downtrodden, brought peace of heart, and ennobled men for missions of service and evangelism. Its rediscovery has brought new life and power. Its neglect has resulted in darkness, war, and sin. Of course we do not worship the Bible. The caricature of "Bibliolatry" is manifestly unfair. We worship not the Book but the Christ of the Book. But the Book is the gracious instrument God has given us for the spread of His Gospel. And to that Book we do well to return for new supplies of grace and power.

> Holy Bible, book divine,
> Precious treasure, thou art mine;
> Mine to tell me whence I came,
> Mine to teach me what I am.

Christianity has always been a book religion!

CHAPTER 4

TEXTUAL CRITICISM AND INSPIRATION

THE NEW TESTAMENT

It is not our purpose in these pages to discuss the principles of the study of textual criticism. That has often been done.[1] Our purpose is rather to discuss the bearing of the science of textual criticism on questions of inspiration. For it is supposed by some that one cannot practice textual criticism and at the same time believe in verbal inspiration. The modern science of textual criticism has for these men made the old belief untenable.[2]

There is in the opinion a double error. Not only do these men misunderstand the historic Christian doctrine, but they also underestimate the textual critical efforts of the ancients. For the study of the textual criticism is not new. One of the most elaborate attempts at textual criticism was made by Origen in the *Hexapla,* his work on the Old Testament text, written about 250 A.D. It is only in modern times that textual criticism has been put on a solid and logical basis by the work of Tischendorf, Westcott and Hort, and many others. But the practice of textual criticism is not new.

The results of the modern science of textual criticism are no more surprising than those of the textual criticism of the Middle Ages and before. The picture is not that the early scholars thought the text had one minor error in every ten pages and that the modern scholars have found ten major errors in every page. This is not the case at all. Rather, the ancients, like the moderns, were cognizant of some errors in the various copies and some uncertainties,

85

but both agree that errors of any consequence are few and far between.

We should also note that new discoveries of manuscripts and textual critical materials have not altered the picture as far as the doctrine of inspiration is concerned. Tischendorf, while on a memorable expedition looking for new materials, brought to light the famous Codex Sinaiticus of the fourth century A.D. In modern times also the Codex Vaticanus, which long lay unnoticed in the library at Rome, has come to light. These two manuscripts form the basis of the preferred neutral text in modern New Testament textual study. But have these manuscripts unsettled our faith in the New Testament? Far from it. They have corrected our copies in many details. And they were rightly used with other material in the making of the Revised Version of a generation ago. But, as we shall show, they are so close to the rather poor type of text upon which the King James Version was based that still the differences in reading between the Authorized Version and the Revised Version are of no great moment. Most people, regardless of the excellency of text of the Revised Version, still prefer the Authorized Version, because of its other values. And it should be emphasized that the recent Revised Standard Version of the New Testament has used no manuscripts of any consequence that were not available to the translators of the Revised Version.[3] It is not *new* textual critical study that is a problem for verbal inspiration, but *any* textual criticism.

The second error involved in the view given above is the contention that verbal inspiration cannot be held — or, at least, that it is a useless doctrine — if we do not have the original autographs as they left the hand of the apostles. Now, it is quite true that we do not believe in the verbal inspiration of the King James Version of the Bible, which was translated in England in 1611 A.D. It is doubtless true that some young or unschooled Christians who know only the King James Version have considered it inspired. Such errors of sincere, but simple, Christians need not be charged against a doctrine which has been ably defended by the best minds of the Church and has been held throughout its history. The Mohammedans think their Koran is so sacred in its official form that it must not even be translated. In Christendom only in Roman Catholic circles has this view been approached. According to Roman Catholic opinion, the Latin Vulgate, translated out of the Greek and Hebrew by Jerome about 400 A.D., is to be held authentical. In 1590 Pope Sixtus V, in his bull *Aeternus ille,* even declared that the "Vulgate edition of the sacred page of the Old and New Testaments, which was received as authentic by the Council of Trent, is without doubt or controversy to be reckoned that very one which we now publish." He called it "true, legitimate, and authentic,"[4] and prohibited any new edition to be published unless it was exactly like this one. It would seem that he regarded his Vulgate edition as inspired.

In a short time, however, Sixtus V died. His Vulgate had manifest imperfections. In two years his successor, Clement VIII, brought out a new edition which is the one now in general use! Roman Catholics today apparently do not hold that the Vulgate is inspired, although the words of Sixtus V come very close to teaching that his edition of it was to be so considered.

The Westminster divines of 1646 may be considered representative of orthodox Protestant scholars whose work has been widely received and who represent the usual Reformed theology of the seventeenth century. Warfield gives ample evidence from their writings that even their copies of the Greek and Hebrew Testaments they did not consider to be inspired. They recognized errors in transcription but insisted that they were negligible — just as we do.[5]

The fact is, as the writings of the Westminster divines and others clearly show, that the doctrine of verbal inspiration is complemented by its twin, providential preservation of the text from serious error. We believe it was perfect as it came from God and that our copies thereof are reasonably accurate and a completely suitable basis for our faith and instruction.

But, if this be the case, is verbal inspiration a worth-while doctrine, and can the providential transmission be proved? We believe the answer to both questions is in the affirmative.

Verbal inspiration, as explained in chapter 2, is not to be accepted because it is necessary, or desirable, or can be shown in every verse to be according to fact; it is to be believed on the authority of Christ. Many confirmations of the Scripture have appeared in recent years, especially in the field of archaeology. We are thankful for all of these. And yet it is obvious that $99^{44}/_{100}$ per cent of the Old Testament cannot be proved to be true by archaeology. So much of the material concerns spiritual things or incidental items in daily life that archaeological confirmation is impossible. We believe it on the basis of the authority of Christ. It may be confirmed in several ways — by newly discovered facts, by experience, etc. But the doctrine is to be held regardless of whether or not it is a useful dogmatic teaching.

Reflection will show that the doctrine of verbal inspiration is worth while even though the originals have perished. An illustration may be helpful. Suppose we wish to measure the length of a certain pencil. With a tape measure we measure it at $6\frac{1}{2}$ inches. A more carefully made office ruler indicates $6^{9}/_{16}$ inches. Checking it with an engineer's scale, we find it to be slightly more than 6.58 inches. Careful measurement with a steel scale under laboratory conditions reveals it to be 6.577 inches. Not satisfied still, we send the pencil to Washington, where master gauges indicate a length of 6.5774 inches. The master gauges themselves are checked against the standard United States yard marked on a platinum bar preserved in Washington. Now, suppose that we should read in the newspapers that a clever criminal had run off with the platinum bar and melted it down for the precious metal. As a matter of fact, this once happened to Britain's standard yard! What difference would this make to us? Very little. None of us has ever seen the platinum bar.

Many of us perhaps never realized it existed. Yet we blithely use tape measures, rulers, scales, and similar measuring devices. These approximate measures derive their value from their being dependent on more accurate gauges. But even the approximate has tremendous value — if it has had a true standard behind it.

One may object that we have never seen the originals. No, but other people have. Tertullian, in 200 A.D., said that the originals of the New Testament books could still be inspected in the churches founded by the apostles. We have some portions of the New Testament from near Tertullian's day and one fragment from even seventy years earlier. During all these early years the copies of the New Testament in daily use were made from and checked with the originals. Some of our manuscripts, it appears, are in close dependence upon the originals. They are like the engineer's scale which is for accurate work. Other copies are close enough for all practical purposes. They are like the office ruler. Some of our translations are more or less close to the original. They are like a tape measure which is useful but will give only an approximately correct measure if it is stretched. But all these measures have their place and value. So do our copies and translations. If our copies were good copies of a text of no particular value, we would have a book containing much human wisdom but nothing that we could consider as coming from God. If, however, our copies are good copies of a book indited by the Spirit of God, we have a message from heaven upon which our souls can rest.

We must emphasize that we have good and reliable copies. The New Testament is the best-attested book in antiquity in regard to its text. The words of Plato, Josephus, the Greek tragedians, etc., exist in only a few copies, and these of a date long after the originals. The New Testament text is established from about three thousand manuscripts, several early translations, and innumerable quotations from the early Church Fathers. Some of this material dates back to very early days. Its cumulative value is exceedingly great.

Most students view the science of textual criticism as primarily the study of these early remains for the purpose of establishing the original text of the Bible to the extent that this is possible. Textual criticism of the New Testament has been highly successful in that endeavor. But Warfield, in a discerning passage,[6] adds that another function of textual criticism is to indicate to us how close we can come to the readings of the original manuscript. Are our copies poor and uncertain, or are they excellent or intermediate in value? To illustrate the answers to this question made by New Testament textual criticism, we shall outline briefly the manuscripts available and the conclusions that may be drawn therefrom.

It is clear from detailed study that the majority of New Testament manuscripts and other witnesses can be classified into major types of text. Simple inspection of the large number of medieval manuscripts written in small letters joined like those in our English handwriting (the cursives) shows that the majority of them agree fairly well in the text they present. Each manuscript has a few mistakes of its own, a letter dropped here or a couple of words reversed there, or a line omitted, etc., but by and large these cursives form a rather homogeneous family. If one of them in a particular passage omits a pronoun or uses the name Jesus instead of Jesus Christ, the great majority of the other cursives do likewise. They form a homogeneous family and evidently were copied from copies of copies of one great edition. From various angles of study it seems probable that this great edition was used in Constantinople in about the fourth century. It is often called the Byzantine text or the commonly received text. It was from a representative of this family that Erasmus printed his Greek Testament, and since this was widely received, it is called the *textus receptus*. Luther translated his German New Testament from this, and our King James Version was made from this type of text.

There are, however, other families. Some of the older manuscripts written in capital letters (uncials) belong to this same type of text. Upon inspection other uncial manuscripts are found to disagree with the Byzantine text in these details, but they agree with one another. If the Byzantine text omits a pronoun or uses the name Jesus, this other group may agree in having the pronoun or using the name Jesus Christ. This occurs with sufficient frequency to indicate that they are copies of copies of a different great edition. Now, the chief manuscripts of this family are the Codex Sinaiticus and Codex Vaticanus, both dating from the fourth century. This is called the Neutral text, or the Hesychian text, after the Church Father who may have had something to do with this great edition in the first place. By similar methods a third important family, the Western text, is observed to appear by the comparison of important manuscripts. This type of text is represented by the fifth-century Codex Bezae, among others, and usually by the text evidenced in the Latin and Syriac translations, some of which were made as early as the second century, and some a bit later. There are still other less important and less familiar subgroups which have been recognized and studied.

It thus develops that we do not have an embarrassing welter of three thousand manuscripts disagreeing in confusing ways, but that these manuscripts have been copied with considerable care from a few old and standard editions. We should notice that these old standard editions were made some time before our oldest manuscripts, since the latter show slight divergences from their standard. Our manuscripts are related as cousins. The grandfathers are not directly known.

Two questions then arise. First, which of these three or more families preserves for us the best text? Second, how much better is one than the other? If these three families agree in essentials, and therefore we assume that the three great editions were not far apart, our conclusion is that we are very close to the original text. If one of these families proves to be especially excellent, we may feel confident that this family is very, very close to the original. That is precisely the situation.

If three stenographers are applying for a position and each does ten pages of copying, it is not difficult to judge each applicant's accuracy. If the first girl's work is marred by many mistakes, such as "aftex," "moreever," and "appareently," one can conclude at once that she is not painstaking, and that worse mistakes can be expected. If the second girl makes only two mistakes and the third makes none, one can conclude that the latter's work, though not infallible, is to be trusted, and she will receive the position.

Scrutiny of the Byzantine family reveals a multitude of small mistakes and numerous unexpected readings which seem unreasonable. Numbers of them can be corrected at first glance. The Neutral text, however, is a text that commends itself to the careful student. It has mistakes, but, on the whole, it gives the impression of being a trustworthy and careful piece of work. The Western text is also good, but is generally less highly regarded. Advanced study and new materials may change, occasionally, the decisions on individual readings, but it seems that in general the basis for these conclusions is well established. We can hold that the Neutral text is much better than the Byzantine, and apparently it has been made from a great trustworthy edition of the New Testament. We must emphasize that the superiority of the Neutral text does not rest alone on the early date of its manuscripts but upon its inherent worth recognized after careful scrutiny of its character. True, our oldest nearly complete manuscripts show the Neutral text, but the translations which exhibit the Western text are very, very early, dating from the second century A.D. The Western text is probably as old a type of text as is the Neutral, possibly even a bit older. But still the Neutral is the more carefully made and better copy of the original. Warfield[7] pictures the Western text as a popular text of the early days. Through much use, marginal notes and explanatory simplifications were made.

Some of these were then taken into the text by undiscerning copyists and the result is a less perfect text.

But how great is the difference between these two older and more worthy families? The answer, as already indicated, is that the difference is not great. Anyone who desires can compare the two texts by using the King James Version, which was based upon the Byzantine type of text, and the Revised Version of 1901, which favored the Neutral family. The differences are minor.

We may, for instance, compare John 18:31-33 and 37, 38. These verses are found on our earliest fragment of the New Testament. The differences are exceedingly minute. The Revised Version uses "therefore" several times where the Authorized Version uses "then," and uses "praetorium" where the Authorized Version uses "judgment hall," and says "I find no crime in him" where the Authorized Version says "I find in him no fault at all," but these are merely matters of translation. The Greek words are the same. No difference at all appears, and this is typical of the entire work of the Revisers. Differences of translation are probably of more moment in comparing the two versions than are matters of text.

A further experiment may be instructive. The Greek text of Alexander Souter is substantially the text used by the English Revisers of 1881, which is reflected also in the American Revised Version of 1901. It represents the best conclusions of textual critical scholars up to 1881 and it heavily emphasizes the Neutral text. Now, in about 1900 a group of papyri were found in Egypt and brought to England, some of which found their way into the John Rylands Library. In the 1930's, after careful evaluation of this material, C. H. Roberts discovered a little fragment which proved to contain the verses from John 18 which have been noted above.[8] Comparison of the style of the handwriting has convinced experts that it was written in "the first half of the second century."[9] Let us compare this fragment — which would have been copied within fifty years[10] of the death of the apostle — with the standard text of Souter. We find that in the preserved fragment there is a difference in three letters, in every case a merely alternative spelling as in our words "honor" and "honour." In this Rylands fragment the pronoun "to us" is spelled *hemein* instead of *hemin*, the word "he said" is spelled without the final meaningless "movable *Nu*," which, Greek students will realize, is a free variant, and the word "he entered" is begun with the spelling "is" instead of "eis." All are purely stylistic variations. Apparently during those crucial two centuries from about 150 to 350 A.D., where we formerly had little direct evidence, the New Testament was changed only in the most trifling manner, and these changes concerned matters of style or spelling. All the evidence of early fragments and translations is in this direction. Is it not clear that in the New Testament field we are probably so close to our originals that we have no room for skepticism as to the autographs? To all intents and purposes we have the autographs, and thus when we say we believe in verbal inspiration of the autographs, we are not talking of something imaginary and far off but of the texts written by those inspired men and preserved for us so carefully by faithful believers of a long past age.

No mention has been made so far of other remarkable papyrus finds — several shorter pieces and especially the Chester Beatty papyri. These papyri cover portions of the Gospels, Acts, most of the Pauline Epistles, and about half of Revelation. They come from the third century and therefore are intermediate between our major codices and the Rylands fragment. They include a considerable portion of the Old Testament in Greek also, and are very interesting. But their value is largely confirmatory. They became available between the fifteenth and sixteenth editions of Nestle's Greek Testament, but it cannot be said that they necessitated any revision of importance in that work. We may expect further papyrus discoveries in all probability, but we need expect none which will upset our conclusions. Scholars may still argue as to how the New Testament books came to be written (though we believe that II Peter 1:21 treats this subject very well with respect to the New Testament as well as the Old). But the witness of the Fathers and the united voice of these old manuscripts and the early translations into Latin, Syriac, Coptic, etc., assure us that we are close enough to the original to have great confidence in our copies; and of all the copies that we have, the very poor are actually so close to the very good that for practical purposes one is as good as another. Westcott and Hort's oft-quoted dictum still holds: "If comparative trivialities, such as changes of order, the insertion or omission of the article with proper names, and the like, are set aside, the words in our opinion still subject to doubt can hardly amount to more than a thousandth part of the whole New Testament."[11]

The Old Testament

All of the foregoing comments on textual criticism apply, of course, to the New Testament. What about the Old? Again, we are not concerned with the details of Old Testament textual criticism, but only with the way it affects our doctrine of verbal inspiration. Do we have good copies of the Old Testament books?

Here it must be confessed that much less solid work has been done in this area than in the New Testament field. The principles of textual criticism are virtually the same for any manuscript. But the practice of these principles may differ widely with the availability of differing materials. The original Old Testament writings are much older, and until quite recently our copies were much younger. We might therefore jump to the conclusion that our Hebrew manuscripts are consequently much more faulty than the New Testament ones. But, interestingly enough, that is not the case. In the Old Testament field, moreover, there are available two or three translations earlier than the New Testament age, and therefore one might think that these would be of considerable help. Here, too, our first thought needs qualification.

The major Hebrew manuscripts of the Old Testament

date from the vicinity of 900 A.D. and somewhat later. Those of an earlier date have apparently perished. Some have thought that the synagogues made it a practice to destroy the worn-out rolls of Scripture to prevent their possible desecration. In some cases they have put old documents in a Genizah — the equivalent of an attic closet. But few of these remain to yield us their old treasures. Upon inspection, these manuscripts show exceedingly few variations from each other; that is to say, they are all of one family and have been meticulously copied from extremely careful copies of one standard type of text. Evidences of this careful copying are found not only in Jewish tradition but in the Massoretic notes appended to our Hebrew Bibles. The middle verse of a book is marked, the total number of verses is mentioned, the middle letter is indicated, etc. The scribes went to extreme lengths to avoid mistakes. We might note that this care is not entirely an evidence that the Jewish scribes held their Scriptures in higher regard than did the Christians. Rather, it appears that the Christians regarded their Bible as so truly the Word of God that it had to be disseminated widely and published in the language of the people. The Jews with their erroneous doctrine of cabbala invested the Scripture with magical meaning in their very writing and format. They had regard to the numerical value of the letters in a word, and in their expositions they could even replace a word with another word of equal numerical value. Apparently the scribes were not interested so much in truth as in externals — but they were exceedingly careful in the externals, and we may be thankful for that.

But how far back did this accuracy of copying extend? Clearly as far back as 400 A.D., for the Latin Vulgate translated by Jerome at about that time evidences a text almost exactly like that of our later Hebrew copies. There are also earlier evidences in the same direction. About 200 A.D. there were three Greek translations made from the Hebrew: the translations of Aquila, Symmachus, and Theodotian. We have only fragments of these, but they indicate that the text of the Hebrew of that time was already standardized.

Concerning the time before 200 A.D. there had been very little information, but in the last five years the situation has changed greatly. The totally unexpected has happened. Geden, in his *Introduction to the Hebrew Bible*,[12] had deplored the fact that we had no early Hebrew manuscripts and had predicted that we never would have. Now we have portions of all of the Old Testament books represented in pre-Christian manuscripts found in the caves in Palestine near the Dead Sea. Since the story of the Dead Sea Scrolls has already been told,[13] only a sketch need be given. In 1947 some Arabs sold five scrolls to the Archbishop of the Syrian Church in Jerusalem, Mar Athanasius Y. Samuel. Questioning their value, he brought them to the American Schools of Oriental Research, where Dr. John C. Trever recognized their antiquity and persuaded the Archbishop to allow them to be photographed and published. They were thus promptly given to the scholars of the world. For a time discussion raged as to whether they were genuine or a forgery. Other such scrolls were purchased from Arabs by the late E. L. Sukenik, of the Hebrew University in Jerusalem, at the same time. Albright from the beginning championed a second century B.C. date for the one beautiful scroll which was a complete manuscript of Isaiah and a slightly later date for the related material. Albright's contention has been entirely confirmed by radiocarbon dating of the linen wrapper around the scroll and by further manuscript discoveries.

Soon occurred the discovery of the cave where the precious manuscripts had been preserved in large pottery jars during all these centuries. Immediately numerous cave explorations were conducted in an effort to discover, if possible, other such treasures. Unauthorized archaeological investigation is, of course, prohibited in the Near East, but the Arab Bedouins, who know well the desolate hills to the west of the Dead Sea, had the advantage of numbers and discovered additional scrolls, some of which have been purchased for study. Organized exploration conducted by the American Schools of Oriental Research and others has also resulted in the discovery of more caves and has yielded an embarrassing richness of manuscripts dating from these pre-Christian centuries to the revolt of Bar Cocheba in the second century A.D.[14] Some of the finds are papyrus and in poor condition. The long, tedious process of piecing together the scraps is going on apace, however, and several important discoveries are being made. A fragment of First Samuel has been published[15] which confirms a reading of the Septuagint in opposition to a Massoretic reading which was suspicious on internal grounds. On all counts the next ten years promise to be an exceedingly interesting decade in the field of Old Testament textual criticism.

The main piece of this literature so far published is the great Isaiah Scroll.[16] It is of special interest to compare this with the Hebrew text as we had previously known it. In this comparison it must be remembered that the writing of Hebrew manuscripts passed through three stages. First, in ancient Israel, when the prophets wrote, only the consonantal letters were written. The Hebrew alphabet did not have vowels. At a later stage — probably after it had ceased to be a living language — certain of the weaker consonants were employed as vowel letters to mark long or especially significant vowels. Finally, during the early Middle Ages, an intricate system of vowel points, which involved marking all the vowels very carefully, was invented.

The Isaiah Scroll, being early, of course has no vowel points. It does, however, show a more extensive use of the vowel letters to mark long vowels than Hebrew grammarians had expected to find in literature dating from the second century B.C. A proper comparison of the text of the Isaiah Scroll with our Massoretic text can be made only by comparing the consonants, for the method of employing the vowel letters changed from age to age. Comparison of the first chapter of Isaiah in the scroll with the Massoretic text as given in Kittel's Hebrew Bible illustrates that the differences are small. Where it says, in verse 15, "Your hands are red with blood," the scroll adds freely (from Isaiah 59:3), "and your fingers with iniquity." Only in this one case do the two texts differ, to speak of, in wording. There are six places where freedom is shown in the use or absence of the Hebrew letter *Waw,* meaning "and." Once the letter *He,* meaning "the," is omitted from the scroll, and variant forms of a pronoun are used twice. There are in this chapter approximately twenty cases in all of variation between the two scrolls, and all but the first mentioned above are very inconsequential. Evidently the difference between the standard text of 900 A.D. and the text used in 100 B.C. is not nearly so great as that between the Neutral text and the Western text in New Testament study. Our text as used in the King James Version of the Old Testament is extremely close to what it was two thousand years ago.

To consult sources preceding the Isaiah scroll, except in the case of a few earlier Dead Sea fragments, is so far not directly possible in our textual study of the Old Testament. The Septuagint, the great Greek version, was translated a bit earlier, but only slightly. Tradition says that the Law, that is, the Pentateuch, was translated into Greek during the reign of Ptolemy Philadelphus, king of Egypt about 250 B.C.[17] Some elements in this tradition are clearly fanciful, but it is generally admitted that there is some truth in it. The next datum point is the year 132 B.C., when, in the prologue to Ecclesiasticus in the Apocrypha, Jesus ben Sirach refers to the Law, Prophets, and other books (clearly the Old Testament) in Greek dress. Especially with the discoveries of the Dead Sea Scrolls before us it is acknowledged increasingly that the Septuagint dates from the vicinity of 200 B.C.[18] This pushes our knowledge a bit further into the past.

Our earliest copies of the Septuagint, unfortunately, date from the second, third, and fourth centuries A.D., and it has always been a question whether these are reliable copies. It seems that the Hebrew from which the Septuagint was made differed in numerous particulars from the standard text represented by our present Hebrew copies.

The difference need not be overemphasized. The major features of the two text traditions are identical. But pronouns, articles, conjunctions, and the like may be dropped or added, words may be misunderstood, especially by the Greek translators, or letters overlooked, etc. It is always a question how many of these differences were the result of poor translation and how many were actually due to a variant Hebrew original. Careful use of the Septuagint in textual criticism must first of all make allowances for the mistakes made by translators and copyists of the Septuagint. When such allowances are made, the Hebrew inferred as lying back of the Septuagint is not extremely different from our Massoretic text. Actually, if the Hebrew were destroyed and only the Septuagint remained, the Christian Church would not suffer unduly. Indeed, for the first three centuries the Greek-speaking Christian Church used the Septuagint almost exclusively and with excellent results. The differences between the two texts are of interest and are definitely of importance to close students of the Word, but they are differences which do not alter the main facts and doctrines of the Old Testament.

When we consider writings dating from 200 B.C., we are as close to the time of the last of Israel's prophets as our New Testament manuscripts are to the time of the apostles. We can dimly discern two types of text in existence at that time — one the parent of our Massoretic text and the other the parent of the Septuagint.[19] But, as previously remarked, the two types agree closely enough to assure us that the text we have is a very good copy of that Bible or portion of that Bible used at the close of the Old Testament period, approximately 400 B.C. The manuscripts thus far are scarcely early enough to answer the questions of higher criticism — though the discovery of a copy of Daniel or Chronicles from the third century would be exceedingly embarrassing to higher criticism and is entirely possible. But it seems clear that we have in substantially correct form whatever sacred Scriptures were used in the post-Captivity days. Concerning the previous thousand years from Moses to Ezra, there is no manuscript information. But if we are to believe at all in the testimony of Christ and the apostles, if we are to give credence to the frequent assertions of the Old Testament itself as well as the Apocrypha, we must realize that during that entire period the prophets of Israel were active as organs of the revelation of God.[20] If, with naturalistic criticism, we deny that holy men spoke from God, then the prophets who wrote in the Old Testament will have little significance. But if we believe that the writers of our great prophetic books were not total impostors, then we may indeed hold that it was natural for the writing prophets, as well as the established priests and kings of Judah, to treasure God's revelation and commit the Word to faithful men who should teach others also.

One other indication of careful copying through the years is supplied by scattered archaeological material. In the long years of Israel's history many a king, city, nation, etc., has risen only to fall again into obscurity. The names of many of these kings, etc., have been preserved in the sacred history. Now the kings and their deeds are being resurrected anew from the dust of centuries; their names are given in their own annals, and contemporary references can be checked against the Biblical text. This argument has been followed by Robert Dick Wilson,[21] who shows that every one of the forty names known from the Biblical text and archaeological records has been preserved for us with great accuracy. Of the 184 letters of these names, scarcely one has been incorrectly treated. When we consider that these are names of kings and persons many of whom were different in race from Israel and whose languages contained sounds which the Jews found difficult to reproduce, the extreme fidelity of both the Hebrew author and later copyists is seen to be remarkable indeed. Since Wilson's day another dozen or more new names have given further support to his conclusions.

One example may be cited as noteworthy. In Jeremiah 39:3 certain officers of Nebuchadnezzar's army are mentioned.

Six names, two identical, are apparently given, and they are printed thus in the Authorized Version, the Septuagint, and the Massoretic text. These Babylonian names could not have had great significance for copyists through the centuries of captivity, Persian domination, and Greek influence. But true to their calling, the scribes copied the letters accurately. That the copyists were completely in the dark in their transcription of this section is shown by the newly discovered fact that there are not six names but three, with a title for each person. They should read "Nergal-Sharezer of Samgar (Sin-magir), Nebo-Sarsechim the Rab-Saris, Nergal-Sharezer the Rab mag." A list of the names of Nebuchadnezzar's officers has been found, and we learn that his chief lieutenant, Nergal-Sharezer of Sin-magir, succeeded him in the kingdom. The Babylonian name Sin-magir would by normal Hebrew sound-change assimilate to become *simmagir*, the double *m* not being represented in the ancient documents. The letters of these long-misunderstood names have been transmitted to us with perfect accuracy — a firm witness to the carefulness of the Hebrew copyists even in the early days.[22]

It is not our contention that the copyists made no mistakes. They did. Indeed, in the Massoretic text there are footnotes showing where the text contains a letter which should be another. These Qere variations (from the Aramaic word meaning "read"!) usually concern merely a vowel, but occasionally they point out errors in more or less dissimilar letters (like *Aleph* and *Heth*) or indicate that an entire word has been dropped (as in II Sam. 8:3). Recognition of these copyists' errors occasionally helps greatly in solving a difficulty in Scripture. Textual criticism is thus a help to the doctrine of verbal inspiration rather than a hindrance. It explains some difficulties in detail; yet it shows the reliability in abundant measure of the text which we have. We believe the authority of Christ provides adequate grounds for the doctrine of verbal inspiration. There are, furthermore, abundant and clear evidences for believing that God in His providence saw to it that the sacred text was preserved free from any errors of consequence so that we may with confidence declare that we have the text in substantially the form in which it left the hand of the author. The Old Testament and the New Testament as we have them are faithful copies of the original manuscripts. God in His providence not only sent prophets and apostles to communicate His word to men. He also gathered His people into the Jewish congregation and the Christian Church, where His Word would be treasured and preserved. Treasured it was, and hidden away in caves of the hills of Judea and multiplied in monasteries and churches of many languages and groups. We may truly say that by God's peculiar providence it has been preserved free from serious error. We may say that to all intents and purposes we have the words that prophets and apostles wrote — and this was nothing less than the verbally inspired Word of the living God.

CHAPTER 5

OBJECTIONS TO THE DOCTRINE OF VERBAL INSPIRATION

A number of objections to this doctrine have been anticipated in the foregoing pages. There are general and particular objections. The general objections base themselves on the larger questions of unbelief, such as the reality of revelation, the conflict of evolution and the Bible, and the theories of higher criticism. Some mention has been made of these. Further study demands that the voluminous literature on these subjects be consulted.[1] Some attention may be given, however, to small points which, in some circles, are used to bring the entire doctrine into question. These "difficulties and alleged contradictions"[2] in the Bible may be classified and representative problems treated briefly. Again, there is an abundance of literature treating these problems, most of which have been treated by men of ages past.

One of the most palpable problems we must face is that of apparent contradictions in the Bible. Many of these are cited, and some yield readily to study when all the facts are assembled. In some instances, however, one must freely grant, at this distance from the events concerned all the facts cannot be assembled. In these cases the skeptic can, of course, point to the apparent contradiction which is unresolved. The believer, with equal justification, can say that two or three resolutions of the difficulty can be suggested. Which of them is the correct one we cannot say in the light of our present imperfect information. It is not necessary for a believer to have all the facts bearing on a problem, but only to see how a solution is possible. Complete contradictions in the Bible are few indeed and yield rather readily to textual analysis.

An example of the latter case is the problem concerning the age of Jehoiachin. Second Kings 24:8 states that he was eighteen years old and had reigned three months when he was taken captive; II Chronicles 36:9 declares that at that time he was eight years old and had reigned three months and ten days. There is plainly a contradiction, but it is quite clearly the result of incorrect copying. The numeral ten of the expression "eighteen years" in Kings was dropped or misplaced in Chronicles and reappears in the mention of the ten days. The Hebrew writes "eighteen" as "eight and ten." The word "ten" was probably misplaced. Some manuscripts of the Septuagint and the Syriac translation state in Chronicles that Jehoiachin was eighteen years old, as the original surely had it. Second Kings 24:15 even mentions that Jehoiachin's wives were taken captive with him.

Another example concerns the mother of Abijah, the king of Judah after Rehoboam. In I Kings 15:2 she is called Maachah, the daughter of Abishalom, but in II Chronicles 13:2 she is called Michaiah, the daughter of Uriel. The Book of Kings is clearly correct in this case, because II Chronicles 11:20ff. records that Rehoboam married Maachah and determined to make her son, Abijah, king. The names Michaiah and Maachah are somewhat similar, and confusion easily arose. Where the name of Michaiah, daughter of Uriel, originated, we cannot tell. Possibly this was the traditional name of the unnamed mother of another Abijah, son of Jeroboam of the Northern Kingdom at this time. At all events, the confusing of the similar-sounding names seems to have been a merely textual matter. Indeed, the Septuagint and the Syriac version of II Chronicles 13:2 give the name as Maachah, daughter of Abishalom, just as the Hebrew of Kings does.

Another class of alleged contradictions is more closely

related to theology. For example, I Chronicles 21:1 states that Satan moved David to number Israel, whereas II Samuel 24:1 declares that the Lord moved David to do this. This is really not a contradiction. The Biblical authors understood that Satan operates under God's permission and control. This view is amply illustrated in Job. The same problem, ultimately the problem of God's sovereignty being consonant with the free will of His creatures, is stated by Christ in Matthew 26:24 concerning Judas.

Other examples of such alleged contradictions can be cited. The Bible says that God cannot lie or repent (I Sam. 15:29) and also states that God repented that He had made man (Gen. 6:6). Again, Scripture tells us that Moses saw God (Ex. 24:10), and yet no man can see God at any time (John 1:18). These, of course, are mere verbal contradictions which are not actual contradictions. In one sense God will not change His eternal purpose; in another sense He changes His dealings with men as men's actions change. In one sense God cannot be seen. Moses was told that he might not see God's "face" or "presence." But in another sense God can be seen. Moses was allowed to see God's "back" (Ex. 33:23). This, by the way, is not the word meaning the "back" as a part of the body, but refers rather to the after-effects as God passed by Moses on the mount. There is no contradiction in these various statements; they simply approach the subject from various viewpoints.

Another large class of alleged contradictions consists of the various accounts of the same or similar events in the New Testament, especially those in the Synoptic Gospels. If these accounts are approached from the viewpoint of skepticism, a contradiction can be found. There are, however, few or no flat contradictions. These allegedly contradictory accounts are usually somewhat different descriptions which approach an event from various angles. One can easily see how these accounts could be harmonized if all the circumstances were known. One is reminded of the story of the blind men and the elephant. Each gave a true but partial description. The one who felt the elephant's leg thought the animal was like a tree; the one who felt the trunk thought the elephant was like a rope. Each thought the others were wrong, but the fact was that all of their descriptions were correct but partial.

We must remember that the Gospels were intended for different audiences, were possibly written in various languages, and quoted largely from the sayings of Jesus, who spoke Aramaic. When Jesus' words differ somewhat in the various accounts of a parable or other teaching, it is possible that actually the evangelists refer to two different sermons presented by Christ. Our Lord doubtless repeated His teaching many times to the various crowds in Palestine. When, however, the reports differ but refer to the same event, it is likely that part of the problem lies in the varying translations of the original Aramaic. One translation may be as correct as another and represent the original teaching equally well and yet differ somewhat in wording. Still another type of difficulty may be resolved if we remember that in early times quotation marks were not used to indicate whether a statement was an exact quotation or a summarization. A long sermon delivered by Christ may well have been abstracted in a certain way, emphasizing a particular line of thought, by one Evangelist, and in quite another way by a different author. An abstract is not necessarily incorrect. A faithful abstract of a long discourse is preferable to a few verbatim quotes that miss the main teaching. "Jesus said" need not always mean "Jesus said these words," but "the following is a faithful report of a whole discourse Jesus delivered." Some examples may be given of a few commonly cited New Testament problems.

The inscription on the Cross is sometimes mentioned as a problem. The four forms are as follows: "This is Jesus the King of the Jews" (Matt. 27:37); "The King of the Jews" (Mark 15:26); "This is the King of the Jews" (Luke 23:38); and "Jesus of Nazareth the King of the Jews" (John 19:19). It is clear that the accounts do not contradict each other: they simply emphasize different elements. The total inscription may even have been as follows: "This is Jesus of Nazareth from Galilee, the King of the Jews, charged with such and such crimes and condemned on such and such a date." More likely the varying accounts reflect different languages. It may well be that the official Latin form was the long one and the Greek and Hebrew were shorter variations, reflected in the shorter readings of Matthew, Mark and Luke.

Often mentioned in connection with these apparent contradictions are the varying accounts of Paul's conversion found in Acts 9, 22, and 26. It would be exceedingly strange if these accounts were contradictory, for it seems clear that Acts was written by a companion of Paul. This was admitted even by Harnack, the critical New Testament scholar of the last century. It seems unreasonable that there should be a basic contradiction in the writing of one man who undoubtedly had heard Paul tell the story repeatedly and had naturally given close attention to so important a fact. The only problem worth considering is the statement in Acts 9:7 that Paul's companions heard a voice, whereas Acts 22:9 says that they "heard not the voice of him that spake to me." Surely the problem cannot be considered serious. The individual words may contradict each other, but the words taken in context need not contradict at all. All the accounts give the impression that only Paul understood what was said. In this sense his companions did not hear because they did not hear that which was spoken. Even a blind man says, "I see," meaning "I understand." Paul's companions did not understand. In that sense they did not hear. Most worshipers in the rear of the church who say they "cannot hear the preacher" hear him talking but cannot hear what he says. Similarly, Paul's companions heard that a voice was speaking but did not hear what was said. This would seem to be answer enough. Some add that in Acts 9:7 the term "hear" is used with the genitive case, whereas in Acts 22:9 it is used with the accusative. This may reflect the difference in meaning of the two passages, but the two constructions are used rather interchangeably, and the solution seems to be apparent from the context aside from this detail of grammar.

A more serious contradiction is allegedly found in the accounts of the Last Supper. The Synoptic Gospels make it clear that Jesus ate the Passover meal (cf. only Luke 22:7, 8, 11, 15). But John says that He was condemned on "the preparation of the passover" and that He was taken down from the Cross in haste because it was the "preparation" (John 19:14, 31). Some have argued from John's account that Jesus was crucified on Thursday afternoon, the passover lamb was killed that same evening, and that Jesus remained in the grave all of Friday and all of Saturday. Some have argued that the Crucifixion took place on Wednesday afternoon. The contradiction is made explicit in the Revised Standard Version, prepared by critical scholars, which translates the genitive in John 19:14 thus: "Now it was the day of preparation *for* the Passover." This problem has been satisfactorily discussed before,[3] and the solution is simple. The point is that the Jewish preparation was a preparation for the Saturday Sabbath — it was Friday until sundown, for the Jewish day begins at sundown. This is made abundantly clear in Mark 15:42, which declares that "it was the preparation, that is, the day before the sabbath," when the body of Jesus was entombed, and "when the sabbath [singular] was past" (Mark 16:1) the women came to the tomb. Luke states with equal clarity that Jesus ate the Passover on the proper day as others did and died the following afternoon, which was the preparation. John's phrase becomes clear when we remember that the Feast of the Passover lasted an entire week. This is clear from Luke 22:1, where the Feast of Unleavened Bread is called the Passover and the same usage is witnessed in Acts 12:3, 4 (where "Easter" is "Passover" in the Greek). The preparation of the Passover, therefore, is simply the preparation for the Saturday Sabbath of the Passover week. John 19:14 merely indicates that it was Friday afternoon of that week. Curiously, this view has received recent support in the Jewish ostraca found in Egypt.[4] This illustrates how an apparent contradiction disappears before fuller information. The problem is not so acute but that a person with a little faith might have trusted that a resolution would be possible when all the facts were considered.

Another difficulty that has troubled some concerns Peter's denial and the crowing of the cock. In Matthew and Luke we read that before the cock crowed, Peter would deny his Lord thrice, and so it occurred. Mark states that Christ predicted that Peter was to deny Him three times before the cock crowed twice. In fulfillment, Mark says, after Peter's first denial the cock crowed, and after his third denial the cock crowed a second time. Perhaps it is not too difficult to imagine that the cock's crowing twice may have been generalized by Matthew and Luke to mean "shall not have finished crowing." But there is another interesting point suggesting a textual critical resolution of the problem. The Greek words in Mark which differ from those in Matthew and Luke are few. They could be dropped completely without altering the sentence structure. Furthermore, they are not found in Codex Sinaiticus and in several other highly respectable witnesses. It is quite possible that the confusion began as a result of a later tradition taken up into the text. One of the principles of textual criticism is that the harder reading is to be preferred. But with questionable external evidence for this particular reading, one may be pardoned for believing that it is not really preferable. If this position is held, the problem vanishes completely. It is rather strange that the Revised Standard Version does not even mention the textual variation in the verse from Mark's Gospel. It gives many less important footnotes of a critical nature but here, where a helpful footnote would have been justified, none is given.

Another problem is the request of James and John that they be the greatest in the Messianic kingdom. In Mark 10:35 the sons are said to have made the request; Matthew

20:20-28 declares that the mother made the request. This incident is typical of several others. Matthew 8:5 tells us that Jesus was approached by a centurion in behalf of his sick servant; in Luke 7:3 we read that the centurion sent his request through the elders of the Jews; in II Samuel 12:9 David is said to have killed Uriah; in II Samuel 11:17 the Ammonites are said to have killed him. The problems are minor. It is common to speak of what we have done through another as something we have done and for which we are held responsible. A friend may prepare my income-tax return in consultation with me, but I speak of it as the return I have prepared. Actually, Matthew 20:20-28 says that the mother came with her children.

Another problem frequently cited is the duplicate genealogies of Christ in Matthew 1 and Luke 3. This matter has been much discussed, and several views have been proposed. It was considered as early as the days of Origen, and the usual view from that time on has been that Luke gives us the genealogy of Mary. Indeed, the Talmud calls Mary the daughter of Heli.[5] Evidently Heli had no sons and Mary continued the family line in a way possible but not usual in the Jewish genealogies (cf. the daughters of Zelophehad in Num. 36). Lightfoot insists that the Greek says that Jesus (not Joseph) was the son of Heli — through Mary.[5] This maternal genealogy of Jesus is important, for it assures us that He was the Son of David according to the flesh (Rom. 1:3). The genealogy of Matthew is apparently not a pure genealogy, ending as it does in Jesus' foster-sonship. One point is of special interest. Two-thirds of the way through, mention is made of Salathiel, who "begat Zorobabel." Zerubbabel is called the "son of Shealtiel" in Ezra 3:2 and elsewhere. But in I Chronicles 3:19 the further detail is given that Jeconiah had eight sons (or more likely seven, since the word *Assir* should perhaps be translated "Jeconiah *the captive*"), including Salathiel. No sons of Salathiel are mentioned, and it is likely that in the turmoil of the Captivity he died childless. Pedaiah, his brother, however, had two sons, one of whom was

Zerubbabel. It appears that Zerubbabel was actually Sala-thiel's nephew, and that the word "son" is used with a wider significance, or possibly he was even adopted. Since this link in Matthew 1 shows that it is not a true gene-alogy, we note that Matthew's purpose in the chapter is not to present a line of descent of Jesus, but to set forth Jesus' right to the theocratic crown. This right would or-dinarily pass from father to son, but in the event that a man died without issue, it would pass to the next of kin, as in the case of Zerubbabel, or to a foster son, as in the case of Jesus.

Another minor problem concerns the hour of Jesus' cru-cifixion — the third hour when He hung on the Cross, ac-cording to Mark 15:25, and the sixth hour when Pilate said, "Behold your King!" according to John 19:14. Various solutions have been suggested, but the simplest and most natural seems to be that John was using the Roman method of reckoning time from midnight and that therefore Jesus was condemned about 6:00 A.M.; Mark was using the Jew-ish method of reckoning from daybreak and says that Jesus was on the Cross about 9:00 A.M. We today are accustomed to one official and uniform method of reckoning time, and yet we sometimes miss a train because of daylight saving time. Confusion was much more possible in antiquity, when standard time had not yet been established.

Judas' death is reported with some variations in Matthew 27:5 and in Acts 1:18. Matthew's account says that he hanged himself, and the book of Acts tells us that he fell prone and burst asunder. It must be remembered that the word "hanged himself" is found only this one time in the New Testament. It is used in the Old Testament and the Apocrypha (II Sam. 17:23 and Tobit 3:8). In the former instance it need not mean "hang one's self" but merely "commit suicide." In the latter case it can hardly mean "hang," but seems, rather, to mean "choke" or "strangle." The picture of Judas' sad end is quite consistent if the field were purchased with Judas' treason money and Judas in his wild despair committed suicide, being discovered later.

The account of Christ's triumphal entry also receives frequent criticism. Mark 11:7 mentions only a young ass which had never been used as a beast of burden. Matthew 21:2-7 says that this colt was with its mother, which doubtless was thoroughly accustomed to bearing burdens. That Jesus rode upon both animals would be a rather unlikely conclusion which no sober author like Matthew would be likely to draw, entirely apart from the matter of contradiction. Also, the point of using the young ass was to have an animal whereon no man had sat. The statement that Christ sat on them is only a way of saying that the two animals were led along in the parade and that Jesus sat in the place of honor — on the unbroken colt. We intend the same meaning when we say, "He rode on the floats in the parade." We mean that the person did not ride the horses, nor did he walk.

Another example may be cited which is taken from the New Testament but concerns the Old as well. In Stephen's speech (Acts 7:15, 16) it is said that the patriarchs were buried in the field which Abraham bought of the sons of Hamor in Shechem. It is clear from Joshua 24:32 that there was such a patriarchal burying place in Shechem, where Joseph and his descendants were buried. The difficulty is that Joshua says that Jacob had bought it. Jacob had bought land there, as Genesis 33:19 says. But Abraham had also been at Shechem and had built an altar there (Gen. 12:6, 7). And, of course, Abraham had bought Machpelah (Gen. 23). It is possible that a scribe copying Joshua confused the two transactions, or that a copyist of Luke at a very early date confused Jacob with Abraham because his transaction was the more famous. Or it is perhaps more likely that Jacob had repurchased a field which Abraham had previously bought or that Jacob bought an additional one to enlarge the family holdings. Jacob speaks of a further portion in a place not specified which he had obtained by conquest (Gen. 48:22). If there is actually a mistake in Acts or Joshua, it is probably a copyist's inadvertent error, for the facts were clear enough in the recognized documents, and the numerous verbatim quotations in Acts indicate that the author was careful and referred to his documents. But an inadvertent error by a copyist is readily understandable.

An adjacent difficulty in Stephen's speech is the mention of Jacob's family as seventy-five persons who went to Egypt (Acts 7:14); Genesis 46:8-27 lists only seventy. But this is not a contradiction: it is only a manner of reckoning. The fact is that the author of Acts regularly used the Septuagint version, since he was writing for Greeks familiar with it, and at this point he followed the Septuagint reckoning. The Septuagint here lists seventy-five people, for it counts Joseph's five grandsons, whereas the Hebrew does not. Both texts list the wives but do not count them. It should be noted that even this listing does not count all the people who went down into Egypt, for the various sons had wives and probably several daughters-in-law. Also it is specifically stated that of the seventy or seventy-five listed, Er and Onan had died in the land of Canaan. It is rather a general compilation of Jacob's family and lists seventy or seventy-five, depending on how one counts. Neither reckoning is an error. Interestingly, an unpublished Dead Sea fragment agrees with the Septuagint in Exodus 1:5 in using the number seventy-five. This was evidently the original reading.[6]

Turning again to the Old Testament, we find more instances of difficulties evidently due to textual error or to the varying styles of the authors. In II Kings 8:26 Ahaziah is said to have been twenty-two years old when he began to reign; II Chronicles 22:2 says that he was forty-two. The passage in Kings is clearly the correct one, for Ahaziah's father died at the age of forty. Moreover, some Greek manuscripts of the Septuagint and also the Syriac version read "twenty-two years" in Chronicles as well as in Kings. What has happened is clear enough. "Twenty and two" written with the use of Hebrew letters for numbers would be *Koph* and *Beth*. "Forty-two" would be *Mem* and *Beth*. In the old Phoenician alphabet used by the Hebrews until a short time before Christ, the *Koph* and *Mem* were rather similar. A confusion of the two numerals in copying would therefore be easy.

Such confusion of letters explains many discrepancies in names occurring in the Old Testament. For instance, Achan (Josh. 7:1) is called Achar (I Chron. 2:7), with a *Nun* miscopied as *Resh*. Hemdan (Gen. 36:26) is in the Hebrew consonants like Amram (I Chron. 1:41), except for the next to the last letter, where *Daleth* has become *Resh*. Anyone with experience in ancient Hebrew manuscripts knows that to the uninitiated, these two letters look almost exactly alike. Other names differ in vowels only. Haley, in his excellent book on such discrepancies, [7] quotes Davidson as listing 114 names which thus differ chiefly due to copyists' errors. This is a small proportion of the whole. Haley continues, "Here let it be observed that it is not simply *easy* to commit these errors; but, under the circumstances above described, it is impossible, except upon the hypothesis of an unintermitted miracle, to *avoid* committing them. No human skill and patience can preclude occasional slips of the copyist's pen and mistakes of his eye. Yet we regard all errors like those illustrated in the above examples as of very trivial consequence. No doctrine, precept, or promise of the Bible is affected by them in the slightest degree."

There are other cases of names which seem to the English reader to differ when the Hebrew student sees only a variant form. For instance, King Ahaziah of Judah (II Chron. 22:1) is called Jehoahaz in II Chronicles 21:17. The name means "The Lord [which may be spelled *Jah* or *Jeho* or a form similar to *Jehovah*] will hold fast." The two forms result when the divine element in the name is placed at the beginning or end. Similarly, Jeconiah is called Coniah or Jehoiachin. All three forms mean "the Lord will establish." They differ only in the position of the divine element and the form of the verbal element. Such examples could be multiplied. The names Ishbaal and Ishbosheth, and Meribbaal and Meribbosheth, illustrate a slightly different point. In this case the element naming the heathen god "Baal" has been exchanged in the text by the noun *bosheth*, meaning "shameful thing," a euphemism for Baal. Whether this was done by scrupulous Israelite contemporaries of these men or by overscrupulous scribes, we do not know, nor need we care. The two names are simply variants and not contradictions.

Another difficulty may be mentioned. It does not lie on the surface but is occasionally cited. Genesis 11:28 and 31 and Nehemiah 9:7 state that Abraham left Ur of the Chaldees with his family. In Genesis 24:4 and elsewhere it is said that the land of Laban and his relatives in Padan-aram is the country of Abraham and is the land of his kindred. There is a tendency among critical scholars to insist that this word *mowledheth* means not "kindred" but "birthplace." Buhl's *Hebrew Lexicon* gives the meaning as "home" (*Heimat*). References such as Esther 8:6 and Genesis 43:7 show it cannot mean "birthplace" exclusively. In any case, the objection breaks down. There is, however, a further point. In every one of the three places where Abraham is said to come from Ur of the Chaldees, the Septuagint says "land of the Chaldees." The Hebrew words for "Ur" and "land" are similar, and the mistake could be made easily by a later copyist who was aware of the fact that Ur was a Chaldean city in later times. But there is no insoluble difficulty in the passages when all are consulted together.

It is a temptation to continue the discussion of these alleged contradictions, but space forbids. These are, perhaps, the usual alleged contradictions, and their solution suggests the method of approach to many more such problems. For particulars a harmony of the Gospels, such as Robinson, [8] and a handbook on difficulties in the Bible, such as Haley [9] or Engelder, [10] can be consulted.

There are other problems for the Bible student besides these alleged contradictions. There are especially moral, doctrinal and historical problems. Here the field is large, and the literature on the subject must be consulted. The moral and doctrinal problems are usually not troublesome to one who has accepted the Head of all doctrine and the perfect Example of all morality. But the historical objections multiply with the reconstruction of ancient history after a pattern suggested by the study of comparative religions. It may safely be said that although dozens or scores of historical problems are raised by critical scholars, yet the alleged contradictions between the Bible and well-established historical fact can be counted on the fingers of one hand. Numbers of such historical contradictions have been alleged in the past, but they have a most peculiar way of vanishing before advancing historical research.

Engelder gives a number of alleged historical blunders[11] where the Bible has been found to be strictly true. The list could be enlarged. In the mid-nineteenth century it was doubted if Moses could write. This ghost has long been laid low. In 1889, Wellhausen insisted that Genesis 14 reflects an unbelievable campaign of four great kings against five petty kinglets near the Dead Sea. The historical background of the chapter is still not entirely clear because of our lack of information, but all now admit that such an invasion with the results stated is fully believable. The Hittites were once thought to be a petty kingdom. Engelder quotes an older English critic to the effect that the mention of the Hittites and Egyptians on equal terms was like linking England and the Choctaw Indians! No one would make this assertion today. Two great periods of the Hittite Empire are now known. As a matter of fact, the kings of the Hittites did deal with the Egyptians on equal terms. One excellent example that Engelder omits is the case of Sargon, king of Assyria, mentioned only in Isaiah 20:1. He was not mentioned in the secular literature nor in early archaeological findings. The eighth edition of the *Encyclopedia Brittanica* declared that this mention of Sargon was doubtless a mistake. In the meantime excavators began work at Khorsabad, and the next edition of the Brittanica contained a description of Sargon's magnificent palace and of Sargon's wars, including his campaigns to the far west.

A Biblical "mistake" concerning Belshazzar is no longer alleged. Early archaeological study revealed that Nabonidus was the last king of Babylon. However, no mention was made of Belshazzar. Then Dougherty of Yale became interested in the problem, searched out and collected the evidence, and wrote a book, *Nabonidus and Belshazzar*, in which he fully vindicated the Biblical account. [12] It appears that Nabonidus was indeed on the throne at the end of the kingdom of Babylon, but that he was in retirement — studying archaeology! Belshazzar was acting king. Oaths were taken in his name, which was true also of other kings. Doubtless having been killed during the conquest, he was vilified by the Persians. Nabonidus, not having an active part in the reign, was befriended by the Persians. All this shows why Belshazzar promised Daniel not the second but the third place in the realm. All these facts harmonize when a fuller archaeological picture is viewed.

New Testament historical problems are few and minor, probably because we know more about New Testament historical background and there is less opportunity for problems to arise as a result of misinformation. Sir William Ramsay is well known for his many books vindicating the New Testament in these matters. There are two major points that once were called unhistorical: one was the census taken when Quirinius was governor of Syria, at the time of the birth of Christ. Most would agree that Ramsay, on the basis of papyri and information discovered later, has completely vindicated the Bible in this instance. The second point concerns Acts 13:7, which calls Sergius Paulus the "proconsul" in Cyprus. It was thought for some time that Cyprus was an imperial province and that the proper title for its ruler was therefore "propraetor." More recent information shows that by Paul's day it had become a senatorial province, and Luke's title for Sergius Paulus is absolutely correct, as even liberal commentaries now admit. [13]

Naturally, not all the historical difficulties in the Bible

have vanished. Conservatives would not expect all problems to disappear as long as our knowledge of ancient history is as fragmentary and, in spots, as untrustworthy as it is. Every contradiction between a historical source and the Bible is not an error in the Bible. Contemporary historical sources are occasionally slanted to serve political and propaganda purposes. The records of the kings of antiquity would have us believe that scarcely one of them ever lost a battle! By comparison the Bible is clearly a book of truth and candor!

Probably the main difficulty remaining for Bible students concerns Darius the Mede, mentioned in Daniel 5:31 and the following verses. All of our historical records say that Cyrus the Persian was in control of the kingdom after the defeat of the Babylonians. Secular sources do not mention Darius the Mede. They do mention, however, a Gobryas, a general of Cyrus, and several have thought him to be Darius. Perhaps he was. Still, it is to be noted that the secular sources do not actually contradict the Bible by saying, for instance, that Darius was an Egyptian whom Belshazzar conquered. No, they merely omit all mention of Darius the Mede. This troubles us less when we realize that we know very little about the Median kingdom. Babylon fell under a combination of Scythians, Medes, and Persians, but soon only the Persians were in control. What happened to the Medes we scarcely know. It appears that at first they were stronger than the Persian element, but soon this situation changed. In other such cases a king occasionally deliberately falsified the records so as to cause his predecessor and antagonist to be forgotten (Thutmosis III erased the name of Hatshepsut from all royal inscriptions in Egypt). It may well be that the Persians *wanted* to forget the name of Darius the Mede. At all events, whatever the final solution may be, we are in no position to declare the Bible here to be in error. We simply need further light. For this, a man with a grain of faith can patiently wait.

The ethical and moral problems discovered in the Bible

are not merely problems related to the doctrine of verbal inspiration. There is a constant tendency to believe in the main teaching of the Bible but not in its detailed wording. In many of the moral problems the entire narrative is implicated. It is not a question of a theory of inspiration but whether or not the Bible is God's Word in any distinctive sense at all. These criticisms, in short, go so deep that they must be held to be untenable by those who would ascribe any honor or authority at all to the Lord Jesus Christ. Christ is the highest standard of morality this world has ever known. Yet He defended the Old Testament, and in these matters the New Testament is far more easily supported. This is sufficient for the Christian.

The problems which are alleged are not numerous. They concern chiefly the wars of Canaan, the polygamy of Abraham and others, the slavery of the Mosaic code, the matter of divorce, and the imprecations which a number of the Psalm writers level at their enemies. Perhaps a few remarks concerning these topics are in order.

In all of these matters it is well to remember that the social organization of ancient Israel was different from ours today. It was by God's command, a theocracy. It was a church-state. God had gathered the people of one nation in a land by themselves. This land was bordered by great nations, but because of its peculiar geography it could rather well isolate itself also from world affairs. Here in Palestine God promised to betroth Israel to Himself as a special nation. All in that nation were challenged by the Biblical faith. At numerous times of revival many, if not the great majority, were saved people obedient to God's holy law. He could do with them what He cannot do with any nation today, for this is the age of universal proclamation of the Gospel. No nation today can claim such promises as Israel had. No nation today can properly be called a Christian nation. Some nations at some times may have a majority of Christians, but in this age the Church and state are to be kept separate, as Christ Himself commanded in Matthew 22:21.

It follows from the foregoing that the law of ancient Israel included elements of a civil nature which today are quite outside the province of the Church. The priests, for instance, were the health officers of the congregation (Lev. 13, etc.). The priests and the prophets also directed the congregation in war. The great painting of Sir John Millais entitled *Victory, O Lord,* pictures Moses the prophet on the mount with Aaron the priest and Hur upholding his hands in supplication for victory over the Amalekites. In later years Saul received God's condemnation because he had not utterly destroyed the Amalekites as God had commanded him. Joshua, at God's command, exterminated the inhabitants of Jericho and of many other towns. God commanded the Israelites to war and to engage in total war. A chivalrous former age spoke of women and children as innocent. It is not clear that only men are guilty of the sins and actions that lead to war, but, in any case, we make no distinction today when in one night a vast area of Rotterdam or Cologne or Coventry or Hiroshima is blotted out. In all medieval warfare a city that resisted siege could be legitimately exterminated — men, women and children. And in ancient times, surrounding nations saved alive only those whom they felt would be valuable slaves. Israel, of course, was commanded to practice total war only in the initial conquest of Canaan. In other campaigns, noncombatants were spared (Deut. 20:12-18).

As to the practice of total war, it may be remembered that the Israelites did not actually conduct it extensively. They did so in the case of Jericho, Ai, and a few other cities. But they soon decided that the effort of conquest was too great and the possibility of slaves too attractive to wage total war, so they mingled with the peoples they had subjugated. Unfortunately, this had the result God had foreseen. Often a conquering people is conquered by the customs of the vanquished. In this case the evil customs of Canaan survived. Psalm 106:34-39 records the sad result of their misplaced mercy. They were mingled with the heathen. Finally, they joined in sacrificing their own innocent children to idols, thus shedding innocent blood as a result of sparing the guilty. Perhaps God's command of total war was wiser, after all!

But the objection continues: is it ever right to go to war? Total war may at times be a necessary expedient in battle, but are God's people ever justified in going to war? Is not the Old Testament picture of Jehovah as a "man of war" (Ex. 15:3) antithetic to the spirit of Christ, who commanded Peter to sheathe his sword in Gethsemane? Bishop G. Bromley Oxnam has given a blatant affirmative to this question. He approves the scene in Walpole's novel *Wintersmoon* in which the little boy argues that a God who would destroy the Canaanites was a "dirty bully." Oxnam will have nothing of such a deity.[14]

In this attitude, the Modernist is at least logical. He does not believe in the propriety of capital punishment, in the justice of any war, in the awfulness of sin, or the reality of hell. He holds no punishment of any kind to be just. The net result of this theology is to deny any justice in the character of God. God becomes the servant of human greed or lust. He may give grandfatherly advice against evil, but He does not possess the prerogative to punish in penal vindication of justice.

The objections to this position are twofold. First of all, the New Testament fully supports the Old Testament in its declaration that sin is real, that judgment is necessary, that there is a hell, and that God is just. It is often remarked that Jesus warns us about hell more than does the whole of the rest of the New Testament; cf. only Mark 9:42-50, Matthew 23:33, and Luke 16:25, 26. The general doctrine that evil should be punished is also clearly presented in the New Testament. Paul declares that this is the function of the state (Rom. 13:1-4). Jesus also gives to Caesar his own functions but does not hint that the burdensome, despotic, military government of the Caesars was evil (Matt. 22:21). The prominent and unrebuked position of soldiers in the Church is illustrated by Cornelius, the first Gentile convert (Acts 10), and the soldiers who came to John the Baptist (Luke 3:14). Some have argued for a pacifistic position because the early Christians would usually not serve in the Roman Army. But the other element in this situation is that later the Roman soldiers were required to show their loyalty by burning incense before the emperor's statue. This no Christian could do. The Christians were monotheists more than pacifists, and this kept them out of the army.

The second point to remember in connection with the Old Testament wars has already been considered. The Old Testament State Church had the functions of a state as well as a church. Today it would be wrong for the Church to fight, but warfare was as proper a function of the state then as it is now. God fought for Israel. He determined that the sinful and unworthy inhabitants of Canaan should be driven out. The Canaanites had fallen so low into immorality that even archaeological evidences show their degradation.[15] Their slaughter was a fitting retribution and punishment, just as Israel's partial defeat before Assyria was a punishment of God upon it (Isa. 10:6, 7). As a nation, Israel suffered many attacks from her predatory neighbors. God promised assistance in defense against these; but He did not promise that He would bless Israel in an empire-building conquest. David's victories reached the limit of the promised holy land. Beyond these, Israel did not go.

The wars of Canaan are thus a problem only for those who do not view the complete picture of the Deity as drawn by Christ and the entire New Testament. War, though manifestly a great tragedy, is none the less justified according to the Bible and according to the best judgment of men when evils and indignities rise to such magnitude that action becomes necessary. As Kipling put it, "Once more the nations go to meet and break and bind a crazed and driven foe." Patrick Henry chose war rather than the chains of slavery, and many others will echo his conviction that the slavery and indignity of enemy occupation, of concentration camps, and genocide can be worse even than the frightful nightmare of war. War is not to be minimized. But it is not the only evil among nations, and it comes as a scourge of God for human sin. There are times when it is justifiable.

Polygamy, slavery, and divorce can perhaps be considered together. In Israel all three were practiced. It is one thing, however, to say that polygamy was practiced, and quite another to say that God approved of it. The Bible does not picture Abraham, Moses, and David as angels. They were men — and sinful men. But they sought God's face for mercy, and He received them by grace. The Bible does not condone nor bless their polygamy. Indeed, Jesus appeals to the Old Testament as support for the principle of monogamy as being God's will for man (Matt. 19:4-6). The same is true of slavery. The Hebrews were an ancient nation. Slavery was common. They practiced it. That one man was as good as another in God's sight was plain in ancient Israel. One God was over all, and all should worship Him. Slavery in Israel was of two kinds: temporary and permanent. The temporary slave, which was doubtless the more common, was a seven-year indentured servant not unlike the man who in colonial days sold himself into a seven-year job that he might obtain needed cash. The permanent servant was one who refused freedom because of his advantageously secure position or he was a foreign bondman (Lev. 25:35-46). In any case, it was required that the slave should be well treated, for Israel had been a slave in Egypt, and consequently the Israelites should remember to treat slaves in a way different from their own hard bondage. In short, slavery was a custom of the times in ancient culture. God did not choose to eradicate it in His ancient nation. Neither did He approve of it. He bade the Israelites alleviate some of its grosser evils. Even in the New Testament we read that Paul returned the runaway slave Onesimus to Philemon, but with the admonition to treat him like a brother in Christ.

Volumes have been written in recent years about making the principles of Christ vital in society. Much of this discussion has been from the Modernist viewpoint and has degenerated into propaganda for a mere social gospel which is no gospel at all. Christian citizens should indeed favor strongly all types of laws that will insure justice and opportunities for all. But it is noteworthy that Paul never urged legislation in Rome to free the slaves or to better the lot of the downtrodden. Paul appears to have recognized that society is, after all, composed of individuals. He stressed the fact that when a man becomes a Christian he should put the principles of Christ's moral law into action not in the realm of politics so much as in his personal contacts with individuals. Be he slave or free, employer or employee, white-collar worker or ditch digger, king or slave, he should be God's man acting like a Christian in every personal relationship. A king who becomes a Christian should not pass a law to make everyone else a Christian. Nor should he expect everyone else suddenly to act like a Christian. Rather, he should be the world's best king, ruling in equity, justice, and mercy. He should not think he rules a Christian nation. But he should be a Christian king. In accordance with these principles, we can understand — without condoning its evils — the allowance of slavery in ancient Israel.

The same may be said of divorce. Indeed, this is exactly what Christ says: "Moses because of the hardness of your hearts suffered you to put away your wives: but from the beginning it was not so" (Matt. 19:8). In the theocracy, divorce was allowed, but it was not ideal. It was not prohibited — nor condoned.

Proof for the latter statement requires an explanation of Deuteronomy 24:1. This verse and Malachi 2:16 are the only Old Testament verses concerning divorce. Nor are there examples of the practice. The verses in Deuteronomy 24 have the distinction of being the oldest portion of the Septuagint translation yet found. They appeared on a fragment recovered from a mummy case in Egypt dating from about 150 B.C.[16] As argued previously in another connection,[17] the verse rightly translated simply indicates that if a person secures a divorce according to the social customs of the day, then he is prohibited from remarrying his wife after she has married another. Notice that this would forbid wife-trading for financial advantage. Wives in antiquity were paid for! But divorce is not condoned nor reasons for divorce set forth. It was allowed simply because in the theocracy God, on account of the hardness of their hearts, allowed some social customs to continue without His either approving or condemning them.

The matter of the imprecations in the Psalms may be treated like the question of pacifism. Is it right to execute justice in penal fashion? If so, then it is not wrong for David to pray God's wrath upon the incorrigibly wicked. Some of the imprecatory Psalms seem to concern the times of the Messiah, and the imprecations refer to His enemies. Thus Psalm 109:8 is applied to Judas by Peter in Acts 1:20, as is also Psalm 69:25. Psalm 137, however, includes a wish for the destruction of Babylon. Only a few of the Psalms fall into this category. The point is, simply, is it right to pray for God's avenging justice to fall on His enemies? This is not a problem peculiar to the Psalms. Jeremiah includes a similar section (Jer. 18:21-23), and Jesus' concluding woes on the Pharisees are of this nature (Matt. 23:32-39). In Revelation 6:9, 10 we read that the redeemed under the altar of God plead for God's avenging justice. It appears that the entire Bible agrees that such an imprecation is proper. Only a priori judgment could question the propriety of such statements. If difficulty there be in these portions of the Bible, it is the difficulty occasioned by the conflict between what we, as humans and sinners, may feel to be right and what God's revelation in the Bible and in the words of Christ indicates to be correct. There is no conflict of fact — only a conflict of feeling. In this realm surely we should not trust too greatly to human feelings.

In conclusion we cheerfully admit that many detailed criticisms have been leveled against the Bible in the course of ages of study by millions of people. Exceedingly few of these detailed criticisms are new. They have been answered repeatedly by those who knew and loved the Book. The fact that scholars and saints, rich men and poor, have loved and cherished the Bible and believed it in spite of all, is full proof that the criticisms can be satisfactorily answered. Any few remaining questions can be neglected by those with a grain of faith with the expectation that when all the evidence from literary and historical sources has been considered, the problem will have been shown to be solved. Since this has happened repeatedly, and since the Book as a whole is so noble in subject matter and accurate in detail, to by-pass a very few remaining problems does not require great faith. Charles Hodge is worth quoting on this point:

> It is enough to impress any mind with awe when it contemplates the Sacred Scriptures filled with the highest truths, speaking with authority in the name of God, and so miraculously free from the soiling touch of human fingers. The errors in matters of fact which skeptics search out bear no proportion to the whole. No sane man would deny that the Parthenon was built of marble, even if here and there a speck of sandstone should be detected in its structure. No less unreasonable is it to deny the inspiration of such a book as the Bible, because one sacred writer says that on a given occasion twenty-four, and another says that twenty-three thousand, men were slain. Surely a Christian may be allowed to tread such objections under his feet.
>
> Admitting that the Scriptures do contain, in a few instances, discrepancies which, with our present means of knowledge, we are unable satisfactorily to explain, they furnish no rational ground for denying their infallibility. . . . The Christian need not renounce his faith in the plenary inspiration of the Bible, although there may be some things about it in its present state which he cannot account for.[18]

It should be noted that Hodge in the above quotation does not admit that there are small, but real, errors in the Bible. This quotation has lately been used in some quarters as such an admission.[19] Actually, Hodge is rightly pointing out that the alleged errors are so minor that the Christian need not worry. There are some questions which we cannot answer "with our present means of knowledge." But they are so few and insignificant that faith can expect a complete answer when full information is available.

It is remarkable indeed that the Bible, having been written so long ago and having been produced in a culture extremely different from ours, does not contain many more problems in text and material than it does. The reason it is defensible at all is surely its supernatural origin. It is God's Word, and God's Word is truth. Beyond that it has been loved and revered by millions, including the noblest characters and best minds of earth, for nineteen centuries of our era and by others before that. To trust in the Bible is to take as our armor the sword of the Spirit, which is the Word of God. When Mr. Valiant for Truth, in the second part of *Pilgrim's Progress*, had finished his fight with three enemies and was recounting his struggles to Mr. Greatheart, the latter asked him to show him his sword. "So he showed it him. When he had taken in his hand and looked thereon a while, he said, 'Ha! it is a right Jerusalem blade.' And Mr. Valiant for Truth answered, 'It is so. Let a man have one of these blades, with a hand to wield it and skill to use it, and he may venture upon an angel with it. He need not fear its holding, if he can but tell how to lay on. Its edge will never blunt. It will cut flesh and bones and soul and spirit and all.' "

May we have more Valiants for Truth today! For that sword is still quick and powerful and waiting only to be wielded in the cause of the Lord.

PART II

THE CANONICITY OF THE OLD TESTAMENT

CHAPTER 6

HISTORY

It is rather strange that more attention has not been given in theological circles to questions of canonicity. Many books have been written on inspiration, but the doctrine of Scripture is not complete until the doctrine of the canon is also considered. Hodge, in his *Systematic Theology*, devotes one page to canonicity and thirty-six to inspiration. The percentage is all too typical. There are, of course, a few basic studies that are well known, such as B. F. Westcott's famous book *The Canon of the New Testament* and W. H. Green's *General Introduction to the Old Testament, Canon, and Text* (bound as separate volumes). These are of great value and are standard in their fields. But Westcott, who was a great scholar of the English Church, treats largely the history of the New Testament canon and assumes rather than proves that the canon was determined by the Church, which he, of course, assumes to have been episcopal in its organization. Green gives much valuable information regarding the Old Testament canon but devotes much of his space to analyzing the weaknesses of critical views rather than to a positive study of the principles of formation of the canon of the Old Testament.[1]

It is our purpose to consider the question of the principles involved in the collection of the books both of the Old Testament and the New Testament. Why were certain books accepted as canonical? Why should they be so accepted by us?

Most Christians are quite content to use the Bible just

131

as it is, that is, just as it has been used for centuries. The judgment of the Christian Church has been unanimous regarding the canon of the New Testament and equally so with regard to the canon of the Old Testament, except for the seven Apocryphal books accepted today by Roman Catholics but not by Protestants or by the ancient Church. There is no reason for us to be dissatisfied with our historic canon. The Church has accepted these books for various reasons, and we shall consider them. One very practical consideration, however, is their obvious inherent excellence. By and large, in these books the Christian recognizes the voice of God. This or that particular chapter, or one of the smaller books, can scarcely be validated by this method. But the Bible as a whole has been instinctively received and differentiated from all other books by earnest Christians of all groups through the ages. There are adequate reasons, however, behind these instinctive judgments.

The question of the canon has been raised anew in recent years because of the new Neo-orthodox theology. The old Modernism reduced the Bible to human proportions. It considered Scripture to be merely an interesting record of the religious aspirations of ancient Palestine and nothing more. It was to be compared with other literature, and the difference between it and contemporary books was minimized. The canon of the sacred books, according to this view, resolved itself into an interesting study of the Jews and their religious insights and eccentricities. It was not an important question, in any case.

But the New Modernism boasts that it is a theology of the Word. It emphasizes revelation[2] and attempts to account for the unique place of the Bible in Christian thought. The Bible is said to be the unique bearer of divine revelation. It is a "witness" to the Word of God, a "pointer" to the truth.[3] For this reason both the questions of inspiration and canonicity must be raised again. As abundant quotations evidence,[4] this theology does not hold to verbal inspiration nor to the literal truth of the Bible. Yet the uniqueness of the Bible is affirmed.

Now, since it is obvious that the Bible is composed of many ancient books, some long and some short, it is obvious that any view which holds the Bible to be unique must face the question as to why this particular collection should have been assembled. The usual Protestant answer has been that inspiration determines canonicity.[5] A book is in the canon because it has been recognized as being verbally inspired. The canon is, according to this view, a collection of authoritative books. The Roman Catholic view is not so greatly different as some suppose. The Vatican Council[6] insists that the authority of the Bible stems from the fact that God is its Author. The Church may certify the books, but the truth of the books depends upon the fact that God is their Author. The Bible, therefore, is an authoritative collection of authoritative books. Both of these views maintain that the books were collected and are unique because of their being the true and inspired Word of God. Their infallible truth is maintained.

If the literal truth of the Bible books is denied, as it is denied by the New Modernism, the chief criterion for the assemblage of the books is abandoned, and the problem of the canon returns with new force. This may explain the increased discussion of the subject today. Brunner, though elevating the Bible to some sort of unique position, does not hesitate to call in question the place of the fourth Gospel in the canon, or of Hebrews, or of James, or of several other of the sacred books. The appeal of the Neo-orthodox writers to Luther also raises these questions. They maintain that he did not have a firm belief in inspiration because he spoke of James as a "right strawy epistle." True, his words are usually taken out of context. He merely said that the Book of James was of less importance than the Gospels, as probably all would admit. None the less, Luther, as was pointed out above,[7] did perhaps question, at some points, the canonicity of James. In his position at the threshold of the new Reformation, this error was understandable. But such assertions force us to re-examine the bases of our doctrine carefully.

It is commonly assumed in unbelieving circles that the formation of the canon was a growth. It is held that the books were not written as authoritative, nor received by the authors' contemporaries as true and divine, but that their reception and veneration required time. The Old Testament books were written over a period of a thousand years and the New Testament written over a space of half a century, so it is obvious that the canon was a growth. The question is, however, was it the collection that grew by way of new accretions, or did the idea of canonicity grow by way of the veneration occasioned by time, etc.? Did the original authors believe their work to be divine? Or did they merely write excellent spiritual discourses which were later believed to be divine? If one agrees with the latter alternative, he believes the Bible to be merely a human book, and it would seem impossible to maintain its real uniqueness. The first alternative is the one which the Christian Church has always chosen. But what are the reasons for this view, and can they be sufficiently established?

Our answers will be partly exegetical and partly historical. What does the Bible claim for itself? How have the Bible books been regarded? The principles are similar, but the situations different, for the Old Testament and the New. In the case of the Old Testament, however, we have the testimony of Christ to assist in clarifying the picture, and we may therefore begin at that point.

The beginnings of the Old Testament are given plainly enough in the Bible, but we have no other early literature paralleling and referring to these ancient beginnings. There is much archaeological information bearing on the origins of the Jewish nation and confirming the historicity of the Bible in many points. But so far, ancient Hebrew literature is altogether wanting in this respect. Our information must come from later sources and from statements which the various Bible books make about each other.

Since 1947 our direct knowledge of the Old Testament in pre-Christian times has been greatly increased as a result

of the finding of the Dead Sea Scrolls. From 130 B.C. to
68 A.D. the Essene community on the northwest shore of
the Dead Sea was evidently busily engaged in copying
the Scriptures.[8] Their town of Qumran has been excavated,
and the bench and the table at which the scribes sat, even
their very inkwells and pens, have been found.[9] Several
caches of documents, stored by the scribes for safety in
near-by caves, have been discovered. There is, therefore,
no doubt regarding the general date of the documents,
and the abundance of material has allowed those who
specialize in paleography to arrange a sequence of handwriting styles so as to date, with considerable certainty,
manuscripts copied in these years. Paleographical knowledge regarding this era has thus been greatly advanced.[10]

Reports now indicate that all of our Old Testament books
are represented among the Dead Sea Scrolls. The best
known is the first scroll of Isaiah, a beautiful and complete copy of the book, whose date may now safely be
placed before 100 B.C. It is of great value, and, as previously explained,[11] its value is largely confirmatory of our
Hebrew consonantal text. Fragments of Ecclesiastes have
also been discovered[12] which are said to date from about
150 B.C. The significance of these scraps will be considered later. For the present we will note that they establish the fact that these books existed at an earlier date.
Also significant in the collection is a series of fragments
of the Books of Samuel. These are said to date from around
200 B.C.,[13] which would precede the Maccabean wars of
independence. A further fragment of special interest is a
portion of Leviticus which dates, according to Birnbaum,
from about 400 B.C. Yeivin is not convinced that this early
date is correct and argues for a date in the first century
B.C.[14] Further study may resolve the differences. If the
earlier date should be established, it would carry our manuscript evidence for portions of the Old Testament back
to the days of the writing prophets. The fragments of some
of the other books in which we are especially interested —
Daniel, Chronicles, etc. — do not seem, as yet, to have been

dated publicly. It will be difficult to restrain our curiosity until the results of the necessary detailed study become available.

The significance of these fragments is greater than their individual dates would indicate. They show an interest and a scribal activity which betoken the same love and reverence for Scripture that would be expected according to the orthodox view. The books exist not only in fragments, but there are fragments of many different copies. Preliminary reports indicate that parts of more than a dozen copies each of Deuteronomy, the Psalms, and Isaiah have been found. Daniel also is represented in several copies.[15] It is of interest to note that the three major books of Deuteronomy, Psalms, and Isaiah are also the ones most frequently represented in New Testament quotations. They were evidently favorites of the Jews just as of the New Testament Church and of us today.

We must admit that the fact that they were copied does not prove that they were regarded as in a sacred canon. But other considerations lead to this conclusion. The finds include a few other pieces of old Jewish literature. A number of books written in the inter-Testamental period, which have heretofore been known chiefly in Greek dress, were discovered at Qumran in Hebrew fragments. In Protestant circles we call these the Apocrypha (the seven books which Roman Catholics receive and Protestants do not) and the Pseudepigrapha (so called because of their pseudonymous attribution to great men of antiquity, such as Moses, Enoch, etc.). The books of such a nature so far identified are Enoch, the Book of Jubilees, Ecclesiasticus, and possibly the book of Lamech.[16] Also there are a few writings peculiar to the community where they have been found. One is the Manual of Discipline, a kind of monastic rule for the community, another is a commentary on chapters 1 and 2 of Habakkuk, another is the War of the Children of Light with the Children of Darkness, another is a group of Thanksgiving Psalms, and another is a portion of the Zadokite Fragment, also called the Damascus Document.[17]

In the 1890's two copies of the latter document had been found in the Cairo Genizah — a storage room of the great Cairo Synagogue — by Schechter.[18] It was correctly appraised by Schechter as a copy of an ancient work, and his views have been fully confirmed by the discovery of a portion of the document among the Dead Sea Scrolls. We are therefore at liberty to use the Genizah pieces with the others to learn more about the Qumran community.

These extra-Biblical finds give us an insight into the view of Scripture held by this ancient community. The very abundance of the Scriptural material is in itself significant, and also to be noticed is the fact that several of the Scriptural copies antedate the founding of the community — which occurred in the middle or late second century. These writers were copying the *old* books. The Dead Sea Manual of Discipline apparently dates from the late second century B.C.[19] It is therefore of great historical value. It refers to what "God commanded through Moses and through all His servants the prophets."[20] There are other references to the law of Moses, and two quotations from Isaiah with the introductory phrase "it is written."[21] The Zadokite Fragments are longer and add considerably to our information. They also refer twice to the Law and the Prophets.[22] There are many references such as "the Book of the Law," "Moses said," etc. The formula "it is written" is applied to Deuteronomy, Isaiah, Numbers, Leviticus, and even to Proverbs.[23] Other references to Scripture books as authoritative, with the phrase "God said," etc., referring to a Scripture citation, include passages from Isaiah, Malachi, Amos, Zechariah, Hosea, Deuteronomy, Numbers, and Micah. The fact that a commentary on the text of Habakkuk appears is an evidence in the same direction. Fragments of commentaries on Micah and Isaiah are also now reported. Apocryphal, and especially the pseudepigraphical, literature is alluded to, but never quoted as authoritative. Jubilees is mentioned by name in the Zadokite Fragments.[24] These facts are not surprising. The books used by the sect make no claim of inspiration for themselves. In this they follow the practice of the Apocryphal books already known, some of which are from this same period. Before these discoveries, we had no copies of such literature from so early a date, and the wealth of evidence from the Dead Sea caves is impressive.

To assess the significance of these new discoveries we must consider the usual view of the rise of the Old Testament canon as held by critical scholars.[25] The first point held is that the Scriptural books were written at various times through the history of Israel by the schools of writers designated by the symbols "J," "E," "D," and "P," and by unknown prophets and singers. These books were not written nor at once received as inspired, but gradually came to be held in reverence. The Pentateuch, comprising the J, E, D, and P Documents, was not pieced together by the major redactors until about 400 B.C., about fifty years after the P Document (the latest one) was completed. Approximate dates for the writing down of these documents are held to be 950 B.C. for J, 850 B.C. for E, 625 B.C. for D, and 450 B.C. for P.

Why the finished law was finally reverenced as sacred is an unsolved mystery to critical scholars. Wildeboer says that the Jews came to regard *ancient* books as sacred. Hitzig says that books written in the *Hebrew language* were revered.[26] Both of these theories clearly oppose the facts. The Apocryphal books were written· in Hebrew during the period from 200 - 50 B.C., and yet they were not revered by the Jews of Palestine, who did revere the others. Also, some of these Apocryphal books are fully as old as the dates claimed by critics for some of the canonical books, but they were left out of the canon.

The formation of the Pentateuch by about 400 B.C., and its eventual canonization through increasing veneration by the Jewish nation, was followed, according to the critics, by the collection, through the next two centuries, of a second canon of lesser esteem, consisting of the Prophets. The present Hebrew Bibles have three divisions of books: the Law, the Prophets, and the Writings; or Torah, Nebiim, and Kethubim, to use the Hebrew names. The second division, the Prophets, consists of Joshua, Judges, I and II Samuel, I and II Kings (the Former Prophets), and Isaiah, Jeremiah, Ezekiel, and the twelve Minor Prophets (the Latter Prophets). The other Old Testament books are in the Writings. The canon of the Prophets, according to the critical view, developed between 400 and 200 B.C. These dates are set by the situation with regard to the Pentateuch on one hand, and the Writings on the other. If prophetical books had been highly esteemed before 400, they would have found their way into the canon of the Law. Any books found in the canon of the Writings, it is said, were not written and venerated before 200 B.C.

This date of about 200 B.C. was established by critics as a turning point in the history of the canon by the date they assigned to Daniel. This book, so widely discussed, has been confidently assigned to 168 B.C. by three generations of critics.[27] It is argued that since this is the fixed date of Daniel — a book so obviously prophetic in character — it would certainly have been inserted into the canon of the Prophets if that canon had still been in a plastic state. The fact that Daniel appears in the canon of the Writings demonstrates, they say, that the canon of the Prophets was closed before the Maccabean wars. The following period, extending to the Council of Jamnia in 90 A.D., was the era of the solidification of the canon of the Writings. It will be remembered that there are Talmud references to questions raised in that council concerning the canonicity of Esther and Ecclesiastes and the Song of Solomon.

This entire imposing structure of the development of the Old Testament canon, supported by the most highly esteemed critical scholars, must now be seen to fall under the weight of evidence, some new and some old. The most impressive new evidence comes from the Qumran finds. In the second century B.C. there was evidently no difference in reverence accorded to books of the various divisions of the canon. Deuteronomy was loved and copied and regarded as authoritative, as were Isaiah, the Psalms, and Proverbs. According to the theory, the Psalms, if highly esteemed in 200 B.C., should have been found in the canon of the Prophets. Although, so far, copies of the Psalms are not claimed to date from 200 B.C., yet a portion of Ecclesiastes (one of the lesser books in the third division of the Writings) is declared to date from 150 B.C. Indeed, its publisher concludes that the discovery of the copy argues that the book must have originated some time sooner — perhaps, he says, in the mid-third century or the late fourth B.C.[28] If Ecclesiastes were copied — and evidently copied because treasured — in the mid-second century, the canonization of the Writings must have come close upon the heels of the canonization of the Prophets. Indeed, they must have been almost synchronous if the Prophets were not canonized until 200 B.C.

The use of Habakkuk as the basis for a commentary in approximately 100 B.C., the presence of a copy of Samuel dating from about 200 B.C., and the multitudinous copies of Isaiah affirm that the Prophetic canon was no novelty in 200 B.C. The evidence from the old portion of Ecclesiastes, the many copies of the Psalms, and references to Proverbs as authoritative Scriptures[29] declare the same for the canon of the Writings. The only argument of any weight for a late date for the canon of the Writings is derived from the date and the position of Daniel, and this we should now examine.[30]

Two points form the basis for the entire critical construction of the development of the canon: first, the Maccabean date of Daniel, and, second, its inclusion in the third division of the canon, the Writings. Orthodox scholars have for years denied the first position. The second position may be considered first because more readily disproved on the basis of present evidence; we shall speak later concerning the Maccabean date of the book.

That Daniel is now in the third division of our Hebrew Bibles is quite clear, but its ancient position in the canon was not necessarily the same. There are only two old lists of the books of the Hebrew canon which shed light upon this question. The first list is in the tract Baba Bathra of the Babylonian Talmud. Baba Bathra dates, in its present form, from approximately the fourth century A.D., though its sources may be somewhat earlier (how much earlier it is difficult to know). This tract lists the books of the Hebrew canon as follows — the Prophets (the books of the Law are not enumerated here, but their names are clear from many other references): Joshua, Judges, Samuel, Kings, Jeremiah, Ezekiel, Isaiah, The Twelve; the Hagiographa (or Writings): Ruth, Psalms, Job, Proverbs, Ecclesiastes, Song of Songs, Lamentations, Daniel, Esther, Ezra, Chronicles. Comments on this quite unusual order follow in the context.[31]

The second ancient list of the books of the Hebrew canon is in the work of the Jewish historian Josephus. Josephus lists the books in connection with his statement on inspiration referred to previously. He says, "For we have not an innumerable multitude of books among us disagreeing from and contradicting one another (as the Greeks have), but only twenty-two books, which contain the records of all the past times, which are justly believed to be divine. And of these, five belong to Moses, which contain his laws, and the tradition of mankind till his death. This interval of time was little short of three thousand years. But as to the time from the death of Moses till the reign of Artaxerxes, king of Persia, who reigned after Xerxes, the prophets, who were after Moses, wrote down what was done in their times in thirteen books. The remaining four books contain hymns to God, and precepts for the conduct of human life." All agree that Josephus' twenty-two books are our thirty-nine in a different counting.[32] Note that instead of putting eleven books in the Writings, Josephus includes only four. From his description of the books in the third division it is obvious that Daniel was among the Prophets, the second division, in his day.

Josephus' testimony is of more value than that of the Talmud for two reasons. First, it was given some two

centuries earlier. These centuries were centuries of up-
heaval for the Jews. Josephus saw their dispersion after
70 A.D. He wrote unaffected by the decisions of the Council
of Jamnia, of about 90 A.D. The importance of this council
has been overemphasized by some. We have no contemporary information concerning its membership or decisions. All our information comes from the later pages
of the Talmud, which itself was a product of the Judaism
which dominated the council. It is possible that since
this council discussed (and favored) the canonicity of
Ecclesiastes, etc., it may also have decided upon an official
classification of the Hebrew books (though according to
Baba Bathra the order was not invariable or at least was
different in details from that found in our Hebrew Bibles
today). The classification in the times before Jamnia may
have been quite different. Indeed, the witness of Josephus,
reaching back into pre-Jamnia days, gives us a very different grouping.

The second reason for valuing Josephus' testimony is his
own declaration in his autobiography that his friend (for
Josephus was pro-Roman) Titus, when he conquered Jerusalem in 70 A.D., took the golden furniture for himself (re-
liefs of the candlestick and table of shewbread may still
be seen on the Arch of Titus at Rome) but gave the sacred
scrolls to Josephus. Josephus would thus likely be in an
excellent position to know the official views of the Temple
concerning the order of the books.[33]

There is additional evidence supporting this vital conclusion. The other evidence is not so much that Daniel
was included among the Prophets but that the threefold
division was not so rigid as is usually supposed. Probably
the careful historian should not regard Josephus as contradicting the Talmud in regard to which books belong in
which category, but should rather regard each witness as
giving legitimate alternate views, one of which became
stereotyped for all later Judaism. The variation in the
numbers of the Old Testament books, according to different ancient reckonings, supports this suggestion. Eusebius,

at A.D. 325, says that there are 22 Hebrew books. Jerome says 22 or 24. Origen, at 250 B.C., says 22. Tertullian, at A.D. 200, says 24. Melito, at A.D. 170, enumerates 22. [34] Josephus' count is 22. The Talmud figure is 24. This variation is occasioned by the positions of Lamentations and Ruth. If these books are joined to Jeremiah and Judges respectively, the number is 22. If they are separated, the number is 24. But in the present Hebrew canon, Jeremiah and Judges are among the Prophets; Ruth and Lamentations are among the Writings. Therefore, to unite or separate these small books and their larger partners is actually to shift them from section to section. Such shifting was clearly done without compunction in the first three centuries of our era. In short, this evidence, together with the evidence from Josephus, proves that we have to do not with a rigid tripartite division of the canon but with a threefold classification — and a fluid one at that — of the sacred books. Such a loose threefold classification cannot be made the basis of a three-stage development of the canon. For that, there is no evidence. [35]

Confirmation of this position is readily found in the classification of the books in the Septuagint manuscripts. This argument has been rendered less sure by the fact that our major Greek manuscripts of the Old Testament come from the fourth and fifth centuries A.D. None of them follow a threefold division. They show a twofold division in that they all place the five books of Moses together and the remainder are in various orders. The value of this evidence is not easy to assess. It would fully confirm, as far as it proves anything, the position taken above, that the threefold classification was quite loose and used for convenience only. The Septuagint, partly as a result of the Dead Sea discoveries, is lately assuming new importance. The type of text given in the Septuagint is recognized to be as old as the second century B.C., [36] even in books in the Prophetic division of the Hebrew canon. The Septuagint is old and reflects a sound tradition. However, the extant copies of it are not extremely old, and these copies may reflect, indeed, do reflect, later ideas of canonization. For instance, they include the Apocryphal books, yet not always the same ones,[37] nor in the same places. They are totally unconscious of any threefold classification. A new manuscript of the Septuagint has been discovered among the later, post-Christian scrolls; unfortunately, however, it is not extensive.[38]

Concerning the order of the books in the canon used by the early Christians, there is reliable evidence in the early listings of and references to the Scriptures. The earliest and most informative is that by Bishop Melito of Sardis, who, about 170 A.D., took a trip to Palestine to ascertain accurately the books of the Old Testament. He lists the books of our Protestant canon, agreeing with the Hebrew enumeration, but he does not have the threefold classification.

That there was a general threefold classification is clear from several ancient references. But there is no emphasis upon its rigidity. This is clear, likewise, from the evidence of the New Testament itself. In Luke 24:44 reference is made to the "law of Moses, and . . . the prophets, and . . . the psalms," which are in the context called "the scriptures." Against this threefold classification are to be considered frequent New Testament references to the Old Testament as simply the Law and the Prophets (Matt. 5:17, Luke 16:16, 17) or Moses and the Prophets. There are approximately a dozen such references. In Luke 24:27 the expression used is "all the prophets." The Scriptures are referred to in the context as "all that the prophets have spoken." Moses, of course, was a prophet. David also, who wrote many of the Psalms, was recognized as a prophet (throughout the New Testament and also in one passage in the Old Testament, Nehemiah 12:24, 36, where the equivalent, "man of God," is used). So the entire collection could be called the word of "the prophets." Also the entire work could be called "the law." In John 10:34 a quotation from the Eighty-second Psalm is said to be written "in your law." And in Matthew 5:18 the term "the law" is rather obviously the collection called in the context "the law and the prophets." As far as the New Testament is concerned, the threefold classification receives no emphasis whatsoever. The usual division is the twofold division occasioned by the authorship itself, "Moses and the prophets."

Previous to the New Testament the references to the threefold classification of the canon are scanty. The main one is found in the prologue to the Apocryphal book of Ecclesiasticus. The brief prologue, dated, by reference to the king of Egypt, in 132 B.C., speaks of "the law and the prophets and the others that have followed in their steps"; "the law, and the prophets, and the other books of our fathers"; "the law . . . and the prophets, and the rest of the books." In the last instance, the author of the prologue, who was the translator of the book, excuses his translation, saying that even the "law itself and the prophets, and the rest of the books" sound quite different and, he implies, somewhat barbarous, in Greek dress. The variety of nomenclature for the third division has been cited to argue that its canon was not yet closed. But the quotation would seem, rather, to be a proof that the Septuagint translation was finished before 130 B.C. At least it seems clear that the author believed that such books as had been written and were properly in the canon had all been translated. These, we would certainly argue, included all the books of our Hebrew Old Testament. This conclusion has, of course, been denied by those who believed that some of the Old Testament books were not then written. The canonical Ecclesiastes was dated by some as late as Herodian times, as indicated above.[39] The Dead Sea finds now disprove all such skepticism and show that all the books were written, copied, and apparently revered at Qumran. They render much more certain the conclusion we have advanced that the entire Hebrew canon had been translated into Greek before 130 B.C. How much earlier we have no way of knowing, but Ben Sirach, the author of the prologue, does not indicate that it was a particularly recent event. Thus we have in the second century B.C. a clear witness to a three-fold division.

New evidence concerning the division of the books comes from the Dead Sea literature. The Manual of Discipline, etc., and the Zadokite document, whose antiquity is now assured, refer to the Scriptures as embraced in two divisions, "Moses and the prophets," just as does the New Testament. There is no hint of a threefold classification nor of a lesser canonicity attaching to any of our single books or to the second division as a whole. Isaiah (both the early chapters and the later chapters) are quoted as by Isaiah and are referred to by the formula "it is written," just as are Deuteronomy, Psalms, and Proverbs.[40] No book outside of the present Hebrew canon is so quoted. The view of the Old Testament held in the Qumran community was evidently the same as the New Testament view and the view here presented. There is no evidence for a three-stage canonization at around 400 B.C., 200 B.C., and 100 A.D. Rather, there is positive evidence against it.

The Dead Sea literature is virtually contemporaneous with the prologue to Ecclesiasticus. The latter refers to the Old Testament in three parts. The Dead Sea materials refer to the same Old Testament in two parts. This is precisely the situation in the New Testament material two centuries later. It follows that the prologue to Ecclesiasticus does not witness, by the variation in its designation of the third portion, to a developing canon the third part of which was still incomplete. Rather, the variation shows a generality of reference to the Old Testament books as a whole which arises from the fact that the three divisions were not rigidly separate. Not until the fourth century A.D., and then only in Jewish circles, do we see the full establishment of the threefold division used in our Hebrew Bibles. In the intervening centuries our Old Testament books were variously classified, although all were revered.

Such a view — that our Old Testament books were classified at an early time as simply the Law and the Prophets —

seems to be the only one that adequately explains all the facts. It explains the varying practice in the New Testament. It explains the same variety of expression in the second century B.C. It explains the fact that the Septuagint, arising in the second century B.C., shows only a general division into Law and Prophets. It explains a few scattered references to a twofold division in ancient Jewish sources.[41] But such a view effectively dispels the idea that the Old Testament canon grew in three stages.

Actually, there were weaknesses in the developmental view which were not recognized. It is obvious that on the basis of any theory, many of the books now found in the division of the Prophets had been written before the date of 400, when the canon of the Law was thought to have been closed. Indeed, the P Document (dated in the days of the Captivity because its emphasis on the Temple and its worship was so similar to Ezekiel's), and also the Book of Ezekiel, were both said to have been written during the Captivity. One may well wonder what will now happen to the P Document if Ezekiel is divided and ascribed to later hands.[42] But in any case, how would the P Document find its way into the canon of the Law when its great counterpart, Ezekiel, did not?

Again, if it be held even now by critics that Ecclesiastes was written before 250 B.C., we must notice that the alleged three stages of canonization do not agree with dates of authorship, but only with dates of acceptance. Many of the Psalms are now held to be pre-Exilic, and none are thought to be very late,[43] yet they are in the division of the Writings, not in the Prophets or even in the Law. Is it logical to believe that these great and loved songs were actually used in the worship of Solomon's Temple and yet were excluded from the sacred Scriptures in 400 B.C. or 200 B.C.? Other hymns and poems are found in the Law. Why not these? Acceptance of the three-stage canonization theory now is seen to involve many difficulties. Books like the Psalms or Isaiah or Ezekiel were written early but not canonized until later. Other writings, like the P

Document, are thought to have been written late and canonized within fifty years. Ecclesiastes was written before 200 B.C., during the period of canonization of the Prophets, but is excluded therefrom; and yet Daniel's position outside of the canon of the Prophets is said to prove that its date was after 200 B.C. Fragments of Daniel have been found among the Dead Sea material, but have not yet been dated. It would seem that in the critical theory the view one may hold of the acceptance of a book need not be closely associated with its date. Even if much of the critical view be allowed and Daniel's date be accepted as 168 B.C., this cannot prove that the canon of the Prophets was closed before that. Daniel conceivably could have been written at 168 B.C., the canon of the Prophets closed at 100 B.C., and Daniel held to be sacred and canonical at 75 B.C.! This is all supposition contrary to fact, for we know on the basis of direct evidence that all the books were written and accepted by the end of the second century B.C., but the hypothesis shows the fallacy behind the concept of the three-state canonization theory. It can no longer be held. And therefore all conclusions based on it should be abandoned.

The date of Daniel, whether Maccabean or not, is to be decided on other grounds. Much effort has been expended on studying its language and history with a view to determining its date. Dr. R. D. Wilson devoted much of his life to the study of this question and concluded that the linguistic argument against its early date was fallacious.[44] There are, it is true, three or four Greek words in Daniel — the names of musical instruments. These by no means prove an authorship during the period of Greek supremacy — 333 B.C. and following. The Greek language was spread by Greek merchants and colonists long before this. A Greek coin, the drachma, is mentioned in Ezra 2:69 and Nehemiah 7:70, 72 as used in Persian times. For years this reference was doubted. The Gesenius-Buhl *Hebrew Lexicon*, written in 1915, remarks, "The compiler has confounded the daric (a Persian coin) with the drachma."[45] The Revised Standard Version in these three references replaces the Hebrew word "drachma" with the name of a Persian coin, "daric," thus seeming to assume a mistake in the text. This is done without manuscript evidence or footnote. Actually, the Revisers introduced a mistake that is not in the text! The recent (1951) Kohler-Baumgartner *Lexicon* rightly translates the term "drachmas." In the meantime, Dr. Albright, in excavations at Beth-Zur, had discovered a Greek[46] drachma in the Persian layer, fully confirming the references in Ezra and Nehemiah and showing the early spread of Greek influences. Futhermore, Greek inscriptions have been found in the Persian palaces at Persepolis, so there is no longer any need to be troubled about three Greek words in Daniel. They do not prove a late date. Indeed, it is gratifying to find the conclusion of Wilson supported by the most extensive recent study of the Aramaic language. Rosenthal concludes that the Aramaic of the Persian Period (the Royal Aramaic, or *Reichsaramaische*) is so unified that the date or origins of Daniel cannot be proved from its language.[47]

As to the historical argument for the late date of the Book of Daniel, that question is somewhat more involved. The historicity and accuracy, even in small details, of the references to Belshazzar have been amply confirmed by Doughty.[48] The references to Darius the Mede are a problem possibly because contemporary scholarship knows virtually nothing about the part the Medes played in the overthrow of Babylon. Some have thought that Cyrus' general, Gobryas, is the one called Darius the Mede, but there may be a character referred to here who is as yet unknown in secular history.[49] The main argument for the Maccabean date is that the history of the Babylonian, Persian, and Grecian Empires is given in accurate detail until the days of Antiochus Epiphanes, the "vile person" of Daniel 11:21, and thereafter the prediction becomes hazy. This argument, of course, assumes that detailed predictive prophecy is impossible. If, on the other hand, one holds that predictive prophecy is possible and that it was

God's purpose to predict the orgies of Antiochus Epiphanes and then cease, one can still readily maintain the early date of the writing.

But it is not a fact that the predictions become hazy after Antiochus Epiphanes. The coming of prince Messiah is predicted in Daniel 9:25 as occurring sixty-nine weeks (or heptads — periods of seven) after the commandment to restore and build Jerusalem. There are three main views of this interesting passage, and as they bear upon the character and date of Daniel, they must be discussed.

The critical view is that the *terminus a quo* must be found in Cyrus' restoration of the Jews. In 539 B.C. he sent back a remnant. Some would even say that God's heavenly decree expressed to Jeremiah in 605 B.C. may be taken as a starting point. Subtracting 69 times 7 or 483 years gives the date 56 B.C. or 122 B.C. respectively. In both cases the "prophet," writing about 168 B.C., missed the date of the Maccabean deliverance by a considerable margin, but it is said that extreme accuracy cannot be expected in ancient chronologies. This view can scarcely be said to solve all problems. There is no statement in the context of Daniel 9:25 that the prediction runs to Antiochus Epiphanes' times. It is definitely not stated that the deliverance was to take place at the coming of the Messiah at the end of the sixty-ninth week or even in the midst of the seventieth week, which critics apply to the Temple rededication of 165 B.C. after three and one-half years of Antiochus' defilement. In short, the entire critical view is built upon the assumption that the time interval must run from Cyrus' restoration or thereabouts.

The fact is that an equally logical *terminus a quo* is to be found in the restorations under Ezra or Nehemiah — which were of similar purpose and only twelve years apart. The Temple had been rebuilt and its worship re-established for many a year. But Jerusalem's wall was still broken down and the city itself, with the exception, probably, of the estates of the rich, lay in ruins. The purpose of Ezra and Nehemiah was to rebuild the city, and they received permission from the kings of Persia to do precisely that. Nehemiah's commission is very explicit (Neh. 2:5). Ezra had a similar purpose and work (Ezra 7:8, 9). Now, 483 years from Ezra's date of 456 B.C. is 26 A.D. (26 rather than 27, for there is no year 0 A.D.), the time, as nearly as we can tell, when John the Baptist proclaimed to the people of Judea, "Behold the Lamb of God, which taketh away the sin of the world." There would seem to be no need to look further or to say that the author of Daniel is vague in his predictions of events which occurred after the days of the Maccabees.

There is a widely used variation of this computation. The decree given to Nehemiah is so explicit that the date of 444 is chosen as the starting point. It is then claimed that the 483 years are "prophetic years" which are thought to consist of only 360 days. Evidence for this is believed to be found in Revelation 12:6, 12:14, and 13:5, where 1,260 days is apparently equated to three and one-half years, or 42 months. One year would then be 360 days. Four hundred and eighty-three of these years would therefore be only 483 x 360/365¼ solar years, or 476 years. Subtracting 476 from 444 B.C., we have 31 A.D., which is satisfactorily close to the date of Christ's crucifixion, the exact date of which is not known. To the present writer this variation appears artificial because the Hebrew year, though it varied between twelve and thirteen lunar months, using a leap month occasionally, actually averaged 365¼ days, for the Passover festival was always held in the spring of the year. A detailed argument supporting this view can be found in most commentaries on Daniel written from the premillennial viewpoint.[50]

A third approach to this prophecy is often found in amillennial circles. It expresses an uncertainty concerning the time elements involved. It simply considers the "seven" weeks and "sixty-two weeks" to be periods of indefinite extent whose starting points are not known with certainty. This view is presented by Keil and given in detail with references to the literature by E. J. Young.[51] Not only does this view do away with any possible evidential use of this prophecy, but it seems to fail to recognize that other such prophecies were given and interpreted literally in the Books of Jeremiah and Daniel (Jer. 25:11, 12; Dan. 9:2). There is no hint in the text that the seventy-week passage is to be interpreted in any other way than literally. It says that the Messiah will come in sixty-nine sevens — 483 years — and then it gives details concerning certain troubles which will take place during a seventieth week. This seventieth week is divided in half in the reckoning, and at its mid-point the sacrifices shall cease and the abomination of desolation shall be seen (Dan. 9:27). In Daniel 12:11 this last half-week period (called in 12:7 "a time, times, and an half") is said to be 1,290 days, which is just a trifle more than three and one-half literal years. It seems clear that careful attention to the prophecy itself in the context shows it to be a literal prediction of the coming of the Messiah to Israel, which was literally fulfilled. If this should be granted, any historical objection to the early date of Daniel deriving from its literal predictions of the various empires must fall to the ground. No one would date the Book of Daniel later than 27 A.D.!

A further point is even more widely appreciated and is often discussed. The critical view that the four empires are Babylon, Media, Persia, and Greece, terminating with Antiochus Epiphanes, runs counter to the language of the book itself, where Media in the prophecies is always mentioned in connection with Persia as a unified empire. Surely a fair exegesis of Daniel 7, with its parallels in chapter 8:20, 21, shows that the second kingdom is twofold and resembles Medo-Persia, whereas the third kingdom is fourfold and can refer only to Alexander the Great and his four successors. The fourth kingdom must therefore be Rome. Young's commentary gives an adequate discussion of the details of the exegesis.

We therefore conclude that there is no valid evidence against Daniel's also having been written at an early date. Its presence in the third division of the present Hebrew

Bible is not to be explained on the basis of the three-stage canonization theory. Nor is it to be ascribed to the character of the author as being a prophet in gift but not in office, as Green supposes.

Rather, it is to be said simply that in ancient times Daniel was not among the Writings where it is found today. Indeed, the entire three-stage canonization theory is to be denied. The age of Daniel is to be determined on the basis of other criteria. Possibly the newly discovered fragments will be of some help. At all events, there is no evidence whatever in favor of the three-stage developmental view. Careful attention to the ancient evidences, and now the new evidence from the Dead Sea Scrolls, disproves the three-stage view. With that view disproved, we are left to other evidence to determine how the canon grew. Data here will bear upon the principle of canonicity and will be given in the following chapter.

CHAPTER 7

THE DETERMINING PRINCIPLE OF THE
OLD TESTAMENT CANON

What, then, was the origin of the canon of the Old Testament? The fact is that there is no early evidence outside of the books themselves. The evidence clearly indicates that a fully developed canon existed in the second century B.C. That this canon was accepted and approved by Christ and the apostles in the New Testament is clear from the New Testament statements. There should be no difference of opinion among those who honor Christ and the Gospel as to what books belong in the Old Testament. There remains, however, the interesting and important question as to the principles used, in antiquity, for placing certain books in the canon and excluding others.

Some ancient Hebrew books were certainly excluded. The evidence refutes the view that all old Hebrew books were eventually considered sacred. The abundance of literature in the inter-Testamental period is becoming amazing in its richness. And the ancient Hebrews certainly, like their Egyptian and Mesopotamian neighbors, had a literature. A curious illustration of this fact is given by the recently discovered portion of the Gilgamesh epic in a dump heap of the excavation of Megiddo.[1] The Hebrews obviously enjoyed the common literary heritage of the Near East. The Bible itself makes frequent references to this other literature such as the Book of Jasher, the Chronicle of the Kings, etc. The only reason that some of these pieces have not survived is that the Hebrews apparently wrote most of their longer works on Egyptian papyrus rather than on clay tablets as the Assyrians did. The Hebrew-Phoenician alphabet was the most facile literary tool in the ancient Near East. But it could not be used on clay.[2] Clay tablets would have endured in Palestine. Papyrus documents have lasted in Egypt. But Egyptian papyrus and skins will not survive in the Palestinian climate except in the hot, dry Jordan valley. It is precisely this accidental (or providential!) feature that has preserved for us the Qumran Scrolls — and none from other sections of Palestine. The Hebrews had a literature. But they also had a selected and sacred literature. What was the basis of its canonization? The answer of Protestants has usually been that inspiration determines canonicity. Those books were venerated and received which were held to be inspired. This answer, however, only puts the problem one step farther back. What was the test of inspiration?

We have shown[3] that the old critical criteria of mere age or of being written in Hebrew are not valid. Books which critics have said were written only about 200 B.C. were received as authoritative by 150 B.C., and some very worthy books like Ecclesiasticus, similar to Scripture in subject matter and also written in Hebrew, were excluded from the Hebrew canon. Why the difference?

A view that has been suggested by some is that the canonization was done by an ecclesiastical council. This view has some attraction partly because the Christian Church considered such matters in later councils and partly because the Jewish Council of Jamnia, of about 90 A.D., debated the canonicity of a few of the Old Testament books — if we are to believe the later reports about this council. Two remarks may be made concerning this theory. First, there is no evidence of an appeal to such a council to establish the canonicity of a book. When the rabbis of Jamnia considered Ecclesiastes, they appealed to the decisions of previous rabbis, not to a council. Indeed, there are no references to any such council in pre-Christian Jewish history or in the Bible itself. The closest approach is the appeal to the tradition of the men of the Great Synagogue found in the tractate *Pirke Aboth*.[4] But here the reference is not to a council but to a great generation of rabbis who followed Ezra. And the argument of *Pirke Aboth* ("Sayings of the Fathers") is that the chain of tradition goes back without a break through the rabbis, through the men of the Great Synagogue, through Ezra and previous rabbis, back through the seventy elders who assisted Moses and to Moses himself, to whom God spoke on Sinai. The ultimate in the tradition is not a council, but a man to whom God spoke — a prophet.

Here is the key to the authority which the Old Testament claims for itself and which is still recognized in the traditions of Israel. The Jewish theologians attempt to distinguish what is authoritative from what is merely advisable by calling the former teachings those which are *Mi Sini* — "from Sinai." Moses, the great prophet, was privileged to speak with God face to face. What he said and what was preserved from him in writing was authoritative. It was the word of God.

The Pentateuch rings with the claim that Moses wrote,[5] wrote a book, and wrote it according as God spoke. He was directed to write in a book (or, more properly, in *the book*), Exodus 17:14 and 34:27, and in Exodus 24:4-7 and 34:28 he is represented as writing. These passages refer to the wars, the Ten Commandments, the treatment of the Canaanites, and the various festivals. Numbers 33:2 declares that he "wrote their goings out according to their journeys by the commandment of the Lord," that is, apparently, a kind of daily journal. Deuteronomy is, if possible, even more express on the point, in such passages as 31:9, 22, and 24, enjoining that the "book," the "song," the "law" be read and rehearsed and preserved.

In Genesis there is no specific claim that Moses was its author, as there is in Exodus, Leviticus, Numbers, and Deuteronomy. There is doubtless no special significance in this fact except that it accords well with the traditional view that Moses wrote his first book as history and the remaining four as a record of events contemporary with him. It all was included in the term *Torah*, "law of Moses."

The following books bear large testimony to the fact that the Pentateuch was written by Moses and was received as God's true authoritative revelation, because of Moses' special relation to God as the prophet of Israel par excellence. Any concordance will give information regarding this. Joshua many times speaks of Moses as God's "servant," "the man of God" to whom God gave commandments. He mentions the law of Moses (1:7; 8:32) and the book of the law of Moses (8:31; 23:6) and indicates that Israel is bound by that book. The reference in Joshua 8:31 includes a reference to Exodus 20:25 as in the law of Moses. In Joshua 3:4 the same emphasis is given, namely, that Israel was to obey the commandments of the Lord given by Moses.

The history of the kings gives us many such references. David charged Solomon to keep God's laws "as it is written in the law of Moses" (I Kings 2:3). Amaziah acted "according unto that which is written in the book of the law of Moses" (II Kings 14:6), and there follows a quotation from the Book of Deuteronomy (which critics have dated in the reign of Josiah, almost two hundred years after Amaziah). Hezekiah kept the "commandments, which the Lord commanded Moses" (II Kings 18:6). Manasseh, his wicked son, however, did not do "according to all the law that my servant Moses commanded them" (II Kings 21:8). Josiah, as is well known, instituted a reformation following the discovery in the Temple of the book of the law — a book which clearly included directions for the Passover — by Hilkiah the priest. Critics have been almost unanimous in holding that this discovery was a hoax. They insist that it was not the Pentateuch which was here rediscovered, but the D Document, which, they say, consists largely of Deuteronomy, and this was palmed off on Josiah as the work of Moses. There is, of course, not a hint of all this in the text. Rather, this book is explicitly called "the law of Moses" (II Kings 23:25). If the D Document was a forgery given the name "the law of Moses," what about the two older documents J and E, which were current long before Josiah? Were they not yet so called? If not, how did they manage to acquire this title? And if they were known as Mosaic, how is it that the new forgery was so happily hailed as *the* law of Moses? No, the consistent tradition of Israel's historical books is that the law of Moses was an authoritative book during the entire kingdom because God had spoken through Moses.

The other historical documents give the same view. Chronicles refers in similar fashion to the above kings and their obedience or disobedience to the "law of Moses," also called the "law of the Lord" (II Chron. 17:9 — Jehoshaphat; II Chron. 23:18 — Joash; II Chron. 25:4 — Amaziah; II Chron. 30:16 — Hezekiah; II Chron. 33:8 — Manasseh; II Chron. 34:14, 35:12 — Josiah).

Ezra and Nehemiah have too many references of this sort to present in detail. Ezra was a "ready scribe in the law of Moses, which the Lord God of Israel had given" (7:6), as his book and all later tradition insists.

The Psalmist declares that God "made known his ways unto Moses, his acts unto the children of Israel" (Ps. 103:7) and follows with a quotation from Exodus 34:6, 7. The encomiums of the law of the Lord in Psalms and Proverbs are many and well known. Isaiah directs his people to "the law and to the testimony" (8:20) and complains that they are "children that will not hear the law of the Lord" (30:9). Jeremiah also reproves Israel because those who "handle the law" — the priests — have departed from God. He says that the law, the written law, was openly flouted (Jer. 8:8), though his adversaries maintained that "the law shall not perish from the priests, nor counsel from the wise, nor the word from the prophet" (Jer. 18:18). Ezekiel, in a rather obvious reference to this verse in Jeremiah, declares that actually "the law shall perish from the priest, and counsel from the ancients," and "a vision of the prophet" shall fail (Ezek. 7:26). Daniel is very explicit in confessing departure from "the law of Moses" (Dan. 9:11, 13). Hosea mentions the written law of the Lord

(Hos. 8:12; 4:6) and proceeds to allude to the Pentateuch more than six times (11:1, 8; 12:3, 4, 12, 13), and to the Book of Judges once (10:9), and probably includes a quotation from Exodus and Deuteronomy (Hos. 12:4 with Ex 20:1 and Deut. 32:39). Amos also contends that Judah has "despised the law of the Lord" and gives a bill of particulars. Micah probably quotes from Deuteronomy (Mic. 6:8 with Deut. 10:12). Zephaniah, like Jeremiah, accuses the priests of having "done violence to the law" (Zeph. 3:4). Haggai questions the priests "concerning the law" and brings up a point from the laws of cleanliness (Hag. 2:12, 13). Zechariah declares that the people have refused to "hear the law, and the words which the Lord of hosts hath sent in his spirit by the former prophets" (Zech. 7:12). Malachi, after saying that the priests, the sons of Levi, have not honored God's law (2:5-8), ends the ancient volume with an appeal: "Remember ye the law of Moses my servant, which I commanded unto him in Horeb" (Mal. 4:4). Note that references in Jeremiah, Ezekiel, Zephaniah, and Malachi indicate that the guardians and expounders of the law were supposed to be the priests of Israel. This coincides with Moses' instructions (Deut. 31:9-13, 26) and Ezra's activities. The law of God governed both king and priest and was supposed to be ever at the heart of the nation's life.

It is clear from the foregoing that regardless of what one may himself believe concerning the Pentateuch, ancient Israel believed that Moses wrote it as the spokesman for God. There is no dissenting voice. And is it not clear that this is precisely why ancient Israel received it as authoritative, i. e., canonical? It was not canonized because of its antiquity, linguistic phenomena, beautiful style, royal imposition, or ecclesiastical decision. The principle for canonizing the Pentateuch which guided ancient Israel, as far as we have any evidence at all, is, Was it from God's great spokesman, Moses? The human author, admitted by all to be a spokesman for the divine Author, guaranteed the writing.

But Moses, before his death, indicated that others would arise to carry on his work. Moses, the man of God, was the prophet par excellence in ancient Israel. But he predicted that the Lord would raise up a prophet to whom the people should hearken (Deut. 18:15-19) and warned them against false prophets, giving them tests whereby one could discriminate (Deut. 13:1-5; 18:20-22). It has been held by Jews and Christians alike that the great Prophet prediction of Deuteronomy 18:15 refers to the Messiah (John 1:21; Acts 3:23), but it is also clear that the institution of prophecy in Israel, alive already in Moses' day (Num. 11:29), was a very important continuing institution. It is generally said to be typical of Christ, the great Revealer of God's will, who is Prophet, Priest, and King.

It has been usually supposed that the institution of prophecy was unique to Israel. The Bible, however, does not appear to say so. There were both priests and kings throughout the ancient Near East, and why should there not have been prophets! Still, there are no examples of such in Egypt and until recently none in Mesopotamia. In the Mari archives a figure has been identified recently as a possible prophet.[6] However, it makes very little difference. It is clear that there were numerous false prophets in Judah and in Israel. Indeed, at Ahab's court the ratio was 850 to 1! Evidently Baalism had, or invented, prophets in abundance.

The occurrence of false prophets, however, does not make invalid the messages of the true. A counterfeit coin can be easily detected by comparing it with the genuine. There were prophets in Israel from Abraham (Gen. 20:7) to Malachi. What was their work, their characteristics, and how were they regarded?

The Hebrew noun *nabhi*, "prophet," is of somewhat uncertain derivation and its etymology is of no great help in our problem. The synonym "seer" (I Sam. 9:9) clearly refers to the prophet's vision, by trance or otherwise, of divine things. Moses saw God revealed. Other prophets were to receive the revelation in visions, dreams, or dark speeches (Num. 12:6-8). But the great characteristic of the prophet was that God would speak to and through him. The situation in Exodus 7:1 is illustrative. Moses argued that he was not eloquent. God gave him Aaron as a mouthpiece and said that their relationship should be like that of God and a prophet. Moses would give Aaron the commands. Aaron would be merely the transmitter. Incidentally, it is never said that Aaron actually spoke before Pharaoh. Though Moses and Aaron were together, the speaking is attributed to Moses — though it is possible that it was done through Aaron. In similar fashion the word and writings of prophets are called the word of God in the New Testament and in the Dead Sea literature.

The work of a prophet, as described in Deuteronomy 13 and 18, is simply to speak all that God commands. A false prophet speaks his own ideas, which may include speaking in the name and for the advancement of other gods. The commands of God may include prediction. Deuteronomy 18:22 mentions false prediction as an evidence of a false prophet. The Word of God may include religious exhortation. Deuteronomy 13 declares that no amount of evidence is to be allowed to persuade Israel against the religion of the Lord their God, who had already revealed Himself in such signal ways in the great redemption from Egypt. Religious truth and predictive truth are here given as a prophet's work and the test of his veracity.

There are many interesting examples of duels between the true prophets of Israel and the false, but that in I Kings 22:13-37 is one of the most interesting. Ahab was persuading Jehoshaphat to come with him against Ramoth-gilead. Jehoshaphat asked that the Lord's will be ascertained. Ahab's prophets, four hundred strong, were very agreeable to his wish. But close attention to the text shows that they prophesied in the name of the Lord, not in the name of the LORD (Jehovah). They were, of course, Baal worshipers and had used a neutral name for deity which still did not satisfy Jehoshaphat. Deuteronomy 13 would have revealed their apostasy. Finally, Micaiah, the only available prophet of the LORD, was brought. Ahab told Jehoshaphat of the enmity between him and Micaiah. Micaiah never prophesied anything good about Ahab! Meanwhile, Ahab's prophets, seeing what was desired, changed their terminology (though not their message), and Zedekiah, the son of Chenaanah, employed a very colorful method of winning the king's favor, this time, of course, using the name of the LORD. Micaiah was asked to vote with the majority, but rugged man of God that he was, he answered, "As the LORD liveth, what the LORD saith unto me, that will I speak." And in accordance with his prophecy, Ahab died the next day in spite of his clever strategy of disguise to avert the dangers of battle.

Here is the Old Testament view of a true prophet: "What the Lord saith unto me, that will I speak." Jeremiah spoke thus to his people (Jer. 26:8-15). The authorities did not like this and took steps to execute him. Jeremiah submitted to their plans, but declared that he was innocent of all guilt: "of a truth the LORD hath sent me unto you to speak all these words in your ears." A sequel is found in Jeremiah 28, where Jeremiah's prophecy of doom was relieved by the prophet Hananiah's assurance in the name of the LORD that in two years Nebuchadnezzar would fall. What was Jeremiah to say? Had the Lord changed His purpose? Jeremiah said, "Amen"; he hoped so. But when a prophet prophesied peace — when all was evil around him — the prediction should be believed only when it occurred! That night Jeremiah received a further confirmatory revelation from the Lord, and the next day he faced Hananiah with his lie. Then Jeremiah added the dreadful prediction that within the year the false prophet, who "makest this people to trust in a lie," would die. In two months Hananiah was dead. Jeremiah's long-range predictions also were literally fulfilled, e.g., Jerusalem's doom and the ending of the Babylonian captivity in seventy years.

It is frequently stated that a prophet's work was not so

much foretelling as forthtelling. That is, prediction was not so much his work as was preaching. There is real truth in this assertion. The books of the prophets, as we have them, consist mainly of sermons and histories rather than predictions. Yet we should never forget that there are predictions in abundance. God revealed the future to Abraham (Gen. 15:3), Moses (Num. 14:33), Samuel (I Sam. 15:28), David (II Sam. 7:12ff.), Solomon (I Kings 3:13, 14), Isaiah (7:8; 44:28), Jeremiah (25:11; 22:30), Ezekiel (26:3-14), Daniel (8:19-26), and many of the Minor Prophets. These are but a few of the hundreds of predictions — some short range, some long range — which dot the pages of the Old Testament.

Even when a prophet did not predict, but declared in sermonic style the will of God for Israel, his constant claim was that he spoke the word of God. Isaiah 40 - 52 includes the remarkable Cyrus prediction in chapters 43 and 44, but most of it concerns ethics and doctrinal teaching. Yet many times the expression "thus saith the Lord" appears. In fact, it is almost a refrain. Jeremiah's six great messages, which constitute Jeremiah 2:1 to 15:21, contain only general prediction, yet each is prefaced with a formula such as "the word that came to Jeremiah from the Lord, saying" and they are punctuated by the refrain "thus saith the Lord of hosts." A prophet foretold events and forthtold truth because he spoke what God revealed to him. This was the continual claim of the Old Testament prophets, and although there were false prophets who led the people astray and apostate people who did not regard the word of the Lord, yet by and large the prophets' messages were received by the faithful for what they were — God's authoritative word.

It seems that prophecy was the only institution in Israel for imparting new revelation of God's Word. Moses, the great prophet, had written the basic code for Israel's life, state, and religion. All else must agree with that. The priests, as we have seen, were to teach that book, but priests do not concern themselves with new revelations.

It is true that a priest with the ephod could ascertain God's will in certain situations. David asked Abiathar to bring the ephod, and then he asked two questions. The answer to both was affirmative. The question of the legitimacy of certain priests in Zerubbabel's day was delayed until a priest should arise with the Urim and Thummim — jewel-stones of the ephod — who could decide the questions (Ezra 2:63; Neh. 7:65). Saul got no word from the Lord "by dreams, nor by Urim, nor by prophets" (I Sam. 28:6). It appears that the priests with the ephod bearing the Urim and Thummim could give a "Yes" or "No" reply, but a consideration of the hundreds of Old Testament references to priests indicates that their power to give a word of the Lord seldom if ever extended beyond that. The proclaiming of God's will was left to the prophets.

A priest, of course, could be a prophet. Any man could be used by the Lord to prophesy — even Saul. Ezekiel is expressly called a priest, yet in his commission he was called to be a prophet to Israel (Ezek. 2:2-5). The division of labor is neatly given in Jeremiah 18:18, which records the people's declaration that "the law shall not perish from the priest, nor counsel from the wise, nor the word from the prophet." Revelations from God were recognized to be the function and prerogative of prophets in Israel. When the prophets prophesied, they were to be believed — if the standard tests did not show them to be false prophets — as speaking God's revelation. Kings were humbled by the prophet's messages. Battles were won or lost at their word. The Temple was not built by David, was built by Solomon, and rebuilt by Zerubbabel, all at the word of the Lord through the prophets. And through them the people were rebuked, encouraged, and directed in the way of the Lord.

But the prophets also wrote books. We have seen that Moses was the great prototype in this, but his successors also committed their words to writing. All are familiar with Jeremiah's activity in this regard. Jeremiah 36 records that the Lord commanded Jeremiah to write in a roll of

a book "all the words that I have spoken unto thee against
Israel, and against Judah, and against all the nations, from
the day I spake unto thee, from the days of Josiah, even
unto this day." Jeremiah did so, dictating the work to
Baruch, just as Paul used Tertius years later as a secretary
(Rom. 16:22). Baruch read the scroll before the people
and finally it was read to King Jehoiakim, who promptly
cut it up with a penknife and burned it on the hearth,
whereupon Jeremiah rewrote the book and added words.
The books of the Minor Prophets are all inscribed with
the names of the prophetic authors. In this connection it
should be emphasized that Amos does not disclaim the
gift of prophecy when he says, "I was no prophet, neither
was I a prophet's son" (Amos 7:14). Rather, as the context
shows, he says to Amaziah, the false priest of Bethel, that
he was not a prophet by profession; he had been a shepherd,
and the Lord had called him and given him a commission,
saying, "Go, prophesy." With a commission like this he
could not forbear merely because of the possible displeasure
of Jeroboam, the king of Israel.

Ezekiel also was commanded by God to write the description and ordinances of the Temple (Ezek. 43:11), as
given in his closing chapters. Isaiah was commanded to
write the vision of Mahershalalhashbaz (Isa. 8:1), and regardless of what one may believe about the Isaianic authorship of the book which bears his name, it is obvious that
Isaiah the prophet was credited with a written vision as
early as any evidence which we have. We refer not only
to the abundant New Testament citations, but also to the
Zadokite Documents, noted above, and the Book of Chronicles (II Chron. 26:22; 32:32), which is a witness dating
to at least 200 B.C. and probably considerably earlier.

It would have been strange indeed if prophets who
ministered in Israel from Moses to Ezra had not committed
many of their messages to writing. Joshua wrote (Josh.
24:26); Samuel wrote (I Sam. 10:25). Time after time
the Books of Kings refer to what was written in the books
of the chronicles of the kings of Israel and of Judah. The

well-known *Samaria Ostraca* reveal that the tax officers
wrote various kinds of inventories in the eighth or ninth
century B.C. Solomon complains that the production of
books was endless (Eccl. 12:12)! Happily, we have abandoned the idea that the Israelites or any of the neighboring
peoples were semibarbarous or primitive people, not advanced in such arts as writing. It would have been most
strange, we repeat, if the prophets had not written.

The most direct testimony, however, comes from the
Books of Chronicles. The value of this evidence will be
estimated variously according to one's view of its origin.
Those who receive the Bible as authoritative on the basis
of our Lord's certification and other reasons will accept
these verses at face value. Critics are inclined to minimize
the Books of Chronicles, ascribing to them a date of 200
B.C. or later. In any case, they indicate the tradition of
Israel as early as the second century B.C. As we have shown,
their presence in the Jewish canon of the Writings does
not preclude their earlier authorship, and fragments of
them are also now reported among the Qumran Scrolls.[7]

A chain of verses in Chronicles gives us the tradition of
a series of writing prophets in Israel. First Chronicles 29:
29 says that the history of David was written in the books
of the prophets Samuel, Nathan, and Gad. In II Chronicles
9:29 the history of Solomon is said to have been written
by the prophets Nathan, Ahijah, and Iddo. In II Chronicles 12:15 the work of Rehoboam is said to have been
written by the prophets Shemaiah and Iddo. Abijah's history
was added by Iddo (II Chron. 13:22); Jehoshaphat's by
Jehu the prophet, the son of Hanani (II Chron. 20:34);
Hezekiah's by Isaiah the prophet (II Chron. 32:32); Manasseh's by unnamed "seers" (II Chron. 33:19). The other
kings are said to have their deeds recorded in the "book
of the kings of Israel and Judah" (II Chron. 35:27), although the names of the authors are not specified. We
have listed here a chain of writing prophets from before
the days of David to virtually the end of the kingdom of
Judah. The old traditions of Israel preserved for us in

the Books of Chronicles clearly include a succession of writing prophets.

It would seem to be obvious that the writings of these prophets would be accorded the same credence as were their spoken words. The incident in Jeremiah 36 indicates as much. Jehoiakim, the king who despised Jeremiah, cut up and burned Jeremiah's scroll. But the men who defended Jeremiah also defended his writing. The reference of Daniel to Jeremiah 25:11f. is also instructive. Daniel had studied "the books" (The Hebrew has the article). But he evidently believed the Book of Jeremiah because he knew it was "the word of the Lord" which "came to Jeremiah the prophet" (Dan. 9:2). Also the situation in Jeremiah 26:18f. is of interest. A verse is quoted from the Book of Micah, but is cited as authoritative not merely because it is in a sacred book, but because Micah the Morasthite had prophesied (125 years earlier), saying, "Thus saith the Lord of hosts." Credence was given to the written word because it was given by the prophet. In this the Israelites merely followed the teaching that had begun with the law of Moses. The law was accorded the respect of the author, and he was known as God's messenger. Similarly, succeeding prophets were received upon due authentication, and their written works were received with the same respect, being received therefore as the Word of God. As far as the witness contained in the books themselves is concerned, this reception was immediate. Joshua received Moses' books as inspired, Isaiah is quoted verbatim by his contemporary Micah — or vice versa — (Mic. 4:1-4 with Isa. 2:2-4), and Daniel accepts Jeremiah, his elder contemporary, as presenting gospel truth (Dan. 9:2).

This concept that there was a recognized succession of writing prophets in Israel may be used to solve an old problem. A frequent objection to the traditional view of the authorship of the books is that Moses could hardly have written the account of his own death which appears in Deuteronomy 34:1-12. This matter has been much discussed, but the acute observations of Girdlestone do not

seem to be well known.[8] It is true that Moses could scarcely
have written the last twelve verses of the Pentateuch. They
concern his death and do not appear to be or claim to
be prophetic, but, rather, historical. It is equally true, however, that Joshua could scarcely have written the last five
verses of his book, which deal with his own death and
later events. As to Judges, we should remember that in
the old listings of books, Ruth is attached to Judges, and
Ruth ends with a genealogy of David which would necessarily have been added after David's rise to power. Samuel
and Kings are a unit and record the history of Israel to
the Captivity. But the last four verses could have been
added only after the Babylonian captivity was far advanced
— indeed, after 561 B.C. These verses parallel the last four
verses in the Book of Jeremiah. Indeed, the whole of the
last chapter of II Kings parallels material found in Jeremiah
52, 39, 40, and 41. It is barely possible that Jeremiah, who
began to prophesy in the thirteenth year of King Josiah —
626 B.C. — wrote these last four verses while in exile in
Egypt, but as the period from 626-561 is sixty-five years,
it is more likely that they were added by a successor.
Similarly, the Books of Chronicles, which parallel the histories of Samuel and Kings, end with two verses which
were added after 539 B.C., after the material of the body
of the book, and the verses are identical to the beginning
of the Book of Ezra. Ezra begins his book, after writing
these two verses, by giving the intervening history of
Zerubbabel's time in Ezra 1:1 - 6:22 before presenting his
own message. It thus appears that in every case from the
Pentateuchal history to the post-Exilic writings a historical
book is given a colophon or footnote that unites it in continuous narrative fashion to the succeeding book. Deuteronomy 34:1-12 is not an exception, but part of a regularly
observable phenomenon, and this is important for our purposes because it betrays the sense of continuity in Israel's
written records. The chain of prophets evidently wrote a
chain of histories from Genesis to Nehemiah, and the writings of these prophets were accepted, one by one, through

the centuries until, when the spirit of prophecy departed
from Israel, the canon was complete.

That this was the view of the inter-Testamental period
is witnessed not only by I Maccabees, in which the de-
filed stones of the Temple are commanded to be put aside
"until a prophet should arise" (I Macc. 4:46; cf. 9:27; 14:
41), but also now by the Dead Sea Manual of Discipline,
which looks forward to the time of the "coming of a
Prophet and the anointed ones of Aaron and Israel."[9] In
the meantime, the Torah and the previously mentioned
words of the prophets and the rule of the community shall
obtain. Much the same idea is expressed somewhat later
by the statements of Josephus, who declared that the
prophets wrote from the days of Moses to Artaxerxes; he
also stated, "It is true our history hath been written since
Artaxerxes very particularly but hath not been esteemed
of the like authority with the former by our forefathers,
because there hath not been an exact succession of prophets
since that time."[10] Similar is the Talmudic reference, "After
the latter prophets Haggai, Zechariah, and Malachi, the
Holy Spirit departed from Israel."[11]

One objection to the above formulation is that the books
of the Old Testament were not, as a matter of fact, written
by Moses and such a succession of prophets ceasing in
approximately 400 B.C. Consideration of this view of higher
criticism has been given briefly above, but it is actually
the province of special introduction to the books concerned.
All such theories are based upon internal evidence. As far
back as our information goes, which is now into the second
century B.C., the traditional view of the authorship of the
various books is maintained. It is a serious question if
this consistent tradition, held ever after, can be lightly set
aside. The Zadokite Document and Dead Sea Scrolls are
in their attitude to the Old Testament books so very similar to all later tradition, both New Testament and Talmudic, that it seems that only an extreme skepticism would
not feel that this tradition was actually established in the
days of the Great Synagogue of Ezra's day, which would

be a natural time for such views to be stereotyped. And if the tradition arose as early as that, it certainly should be given large credence and doubted only on positive evidence. It is possible that further publication of the Qumran Fragments and additional discoveries may clarify the evidence even more.

There is another objection that comes from the side of those who hold the traditional view of the authorship of the Old Testament books and who accept their inspiration and the authority of Christ in these matters. They say that one cannot prove that all the Old Testament books were of prophetic authorship. Thus Young, who does not observe that the present threefold Hebrew canon is not the ancient one, argues in his very valuable *Introduction*,[12] that the authors of the second division were men who held the office of a prophet and their authorship guaranteed canonicity to these books. With regard to the books of the third division, however, he does not claim to know what caused them to be canonized or who collected them. They were written by inspired men who did not hold the office of a prophet. Some of them, like David and Daniel, had the gift of prophecy, but not the office. No council collected these books, but in God's providence, His people recognized His Word and made the collection of inspired writings in our Old Testament canon.

Several remarks may be made regarding this view of the canonization of the Old Testament. First, it proceeds without regard to the facts concerning the threefold classification, which have been discussed in detail above. Second, it invents a distinction between the office of a prophet and the gift of a prophet. (Green had made it more imposing but no less objectionable by using the Latin terms *munus* and *donus*.) This view has been criticized severely, as Green acknowledges, and it is difficult to see how it will survive. Ezekiel was both priest and prophet; David was both prophet and king; Moses wrote the five books of the Law and also a Psalm which is found in the Writings, etc. Third, we should remember that the view does not disprove the prophetic authorship of the anonymous books; rather, it merely makes an assumption that the books which are not expressly attributed to prophets were not actually prophetic in authorship.

This last assumption can be challenged in two ways. The first is that the regular New Testament phrase used to refer to the whole Old Testament outside of the Pentateuch is simply "the prophets." This terminology is used a dozen times in the New Testament. Half of these expressions came from the lips of Christ Himself. Ezra, Samuel, Job, Isaiah, and Daniel are all grouped together by Christ in the category "prophets." Of course, Daniel and David are specifically called prophets in the New Testament without a suggestion of any distinction between "gift" and "office" (Matt. 24:15; Acts 2:30). But more than this, all the books, without distinction, are said to be "the prophets." Compare Matthew 26:56 and other passages where the expression "the scriptures of the prophets" refers to the Old Testament. This is not the usage only of the New Testament, but also of the Qumran Scrolls. The Manual of Discipline speaks of what God "commanded through Moses and through all his servants the prophets."[13] And again, in interpreting Isaiah 40:3 (which is quoted with the formula "it is written"), it says: "That means studying the Torah which He commanded through Moses, so as to do according to all that was revealed time after time and according to that which the prophets revealed through His Holy Spirit."[14] It is important to observe that although the Discipline refers most often to the Torah as the basis of instruction (some nine times, two of which specify the Torah of Moses), yet the word of the prophets is considered a revelation equally authoritative. The same phrase "it is written" applied twice to Isaiah is applied also to Exodus,[15] and as the above words show, the prophets were said to give God's revelation.

The longer Zadokite Fragments present the same picture. The author objects to some who rebelled "against the commandments of God given by the hand of Moses

and also by the hand of the holy anointed ones and prophesied falsehood."[16] In another place one of the two manuscripts of this work refers to the "books of the law" and
the "books of the prophets."[17] The Books of Ezekiel and
Isaiah are quoted as from the Lord through the hand of
the prophet.[18] The expression "it is written" is applied in-
discriminately to all sections of the Old Testament — to
Deuteronomy, Isaiah, Numbers, Leviticus, and Proverbs.[19]
Other authoritative expressions, such as "He said," "God
said," etc., cite quotations from Isaiah, Malachi, Amos,
Zechariah, Hosea, Deuteronomy, Numbers, and Micah. One
problem should be mentioned. The Book of Jubilees is
mentioned by name, but is not, however, cited as authoritative. "And the exact statement of the epochs of Israel's
blindness to all these, behold, it can be learnt in the Book
of the Divisions of Times into their Jubilees and Weeks."[20]
The book was evidently a favorite. A fragment of it was
found in the Ain Feshka cave, as Rabin notes. But it is
not cited as authoritative or prophetic. A last item of
interest is found in the Habakkuk commentary, where it is
said that "the last generation will hear from the mouth
of the priest whom He has given unto the children of
Israel for a teacher to give the meaning of all the words
of His servants the prophets . . . by whom God has related all that is to come upon His people."[21]

All this evidence shows that in the two pre-Christian
centuries in which our evidence begins, and also throughout the writings of the New Testament, all of the books
outside of the Law are called collectively "the Prophets,"
with no attempt to elevate some over others in authority.
We do not know the author of Esther, Chronicles, or Job,
but they are found among the Prophets, and there is no
reason to object to claiming their authors also as prophets.

A second remark is that most of these books probably
were actually written by prophets. We think at once of
the Major and Minor Prophets and the Davidic Psalms.
Though David, obviously a prophet and repeatedly so
called in the New Testament, is so referred to in only one

section of the Old Testament — Nehemiah 12:24, 36: "David the man of God" — Asaph, responsible for a dozen Psalms, is also called a seer (II Chron. 29:30). This, plus the Pentateuch, accounts for nearly two-thirds of the Old Testament.

A further point is that consideration of the authorship of the various books and the work of a prophet will show that much of the rest of the Old Testament was also written by prophets. Consider the Books of Samuel and Kings. Samuel wrote "the manner of the kingdom" and "laid it up before the Lord" (I Sam. 10:25) evidently as Moses (Deut. 31:26) and Joshua (Josh. 24:26) had done. Samuel wrote a sacred book, though its extent is not here defined. Now, the chain of references in the Books of Chronicles already given indicates that a virtually continuous history of the kings of Israel and Judah was written by successive prophets working during those centuries. We have such a history in the books of Samuel-Kings. Now, is it not most natural to suppose that Samuel-Kings is the history written by these prophets rather than to think that the prophets wrote one history which was lost and that an anonymous author or authors wrote a second one which has been preserved? Knowing the reverence accorded to prophecy in Israel, we surely find it easier to accept the first alternative.

As to the work of Joshua, Solomon, and others, can it be considered the labor of a prophet? We find no mention of a ceremony of induction for a prophet. He was not crowned like a king or consecrated like a priest. His was the spiritual and divine anointing. God told Moses that He would speak with a prophet in a vision or a dream or in dark speeches or might permit him to see the similitude of the Lord, but God would speak with Moses mouth to mouth (Num. 12:8). And thus God spoke to the prophets. We think at once of the call to the child Samuel, of the vision in the Temple granted to Isaiah, of the dream described in Daniel 7, etc. We should then be able to identify a prophet by the fact that he was a recipient of such revelation.

By these criteria, Solomon was a prophet. God spoke to him in dreams on two known occasions. Joshua also met Jehovah in similitude by Jericho and received from Him the instructions concerning the capture of the city. Likewise, God told Joshua, in some unspecified manner, about the trespass of Achan and promised final victory at Ai, etc. Critical opinion, of course, refuses to Joshua the authorship of his book and has maintained that Proverbs, Ecclesiastes, and the Song of Solomon were written years after the death of the great king. Driver long ago argued that the Hebrew of Ecclesiastes bears resemblance to the Mishna, which is post-Christian in its present form. He favored a date of 200 B.C.[22] or later. Extremists had placed the date as late as Roman times. These views are now effectively disproved by the Dead Sea Fragments and, moreover, the alleged linguistic bases and certain other alleged internal evidences also are shown to have been faulty. We are left with no positive arguments against the traditional Solomonic authorship of Ecclesiastes, the Song of Solomon, and the bulk of the Book of Proverbs — at least to chapter 25. This is the clear implication of the introductions of these three books, and orthodox scholars have usually argued for the Solomonic authorship.

With this in mind, we have left for consideration only the books of Judges, Ruth, Chronicles, Ezra, Nehemiah, Esther, and Job, the longest of which, Chronicles, has much material in it of obvious prophetic origin and many lengthy passages which parallel Samuel-Kings. The total of these seven books is just a little more than one-sixth of the Old Testament, and it should be remembered that there is no evidence that the authors of these books, known or unknown, were not prophets.

We have here a practical and reasonable test of canonicity that could have been applied by all the generations of the Jews and, except for a few places where evidence now is more slender, can be readily applied even today.

What was prophetic was regarded as the Word of God. What was not prophetic was, as we know from I Maccabees 4:46, etc., not regarded as the Word of God. The canon grew as the prophets succeeded one another in their ministry; it was finished, as Josephus says, when the Holy Spirit ceased speaking through prophets in Israel. Moses, the great precursor of the prophetic line, specified tests to be applied in determining the reality of prophecy. We must consider not only the explicit tests described in Deuteronomy 13 and 18 but also the great model of true prophecy found in the writings of Moses himself. Anything not in agreement with the fountain of truth was *ipso facto* a false prophecy. But when all these tests were applied and a prophet was acknowledged to be true, his words and writings were received forthwith by the faithful as from God, i.e., canonical.

Only a few lesser problems need detain us. Were all of the prophetic writings preserved? Of course we cannot say. Most of these inspired speeches of the prophets have perished. A number of their inspired writings may also have been lost. In the vicissitudes of his prison experiences, a number of Jeremiah's works, for example, may have been destroyed by enemies or lost by accident. Some of his writings may have been so strictly applicable to the siege of Jerusalem alone that he made no effort to preserve them. But the writings that we have were providentially preserved from destruction. We may therefore add to our tests for canonicity the factor of divine providence in preserving for us such writings as God wished us to have through succeeding generations. We have no knowledge of a sifting of a prophet's work by his contemporaries or successors. It was not that people chose what they wished to preserve. This would place the burden of forming a canon on uninspired people, rather than leaving it in the hands of God's inspired teachers. The prophet himself may have exercised some discrimination in this regard — indeed, Jeremiah directed that one of his messages, though probably only a copy, be thrown in the river Euphrates

(Jer. 51:63f.). But as far as our evidence goes, the contemporary and succeeding believers in Israel venerated, treasured, and preserved all the prophetic writings. It is not necessary to suppose that there was a class of other authors, inspired but nonprophetic, who formed an extra group of men, not witnessed to in the narratives, who gave revelation to Israel.

Another point we should consider is this: were the prophets continuously inspired, and was every word they spoke or wrote the word of God? This is not a question to be answered too quickly. God could have given continuous inspiration or temporary. The prophets could have written only official instructions or could also have written ephemeral, merely human, memoranda. The question for the Christian is: what does the Bible say they did?

In the first place, revelation to the prophets was not continuous. We have referred to Jeremiah's controversy with Hananiah (Jer. 28). Jeremiah had given a prophetic word. Hananiah claimed to give an additional but contradictory revelation. Jeremiah evidently doubted Hananiah, but had no positive reply until God gave him an additional message. We may note, however, that though the revelation was not continuous, the inspiration could have been. Jeremiah made no mistake in the interim. Another example of occasional revelation is found in I Kings 13. The man of God from Judah delivered his message against the idolatrous altar of Bethel and started home as he was bidden. An old prophet brought him back to his house, saying that he had received a new and contradictory revelation, "but," the account adds, "he lied unto him." Later the old prophet really received a revelation from the Lord, which was in due course fulfilled, and the first prophet died as a result of listening to the old prophet's lie. We can learn from this example that revelation is not continuous. Neither is inspiration continuous, for the old prophet told a clear untruth and did so knowingly. It was evidently possible for a prophet to lie in speaking and presumably also in writing. We may note, however, that the old prophet knew what he was doing.

Examples are quite rare, however, of a true prophet who departed from the Lord's word. Solomon, it is said (I Kings 11:4-9), in his old age was rejected by the Lord because of his idolatry. The extent of his apostasy is not specified. The narrative states that he "went not fully after the Lord." He built high places for heathen gods, but there is an intimation in the context that he did this chiefly for his wives. He sinned in allowing such worship and in so far as he joined with his wives in their worship. This period of Solomon's compromise is a sad chapter. But he and the people evidently knew that the Spirit of the Lord was no longer using him as a prophet. He had violated the tests of a true prophet (Deut. 13:2) and was publicly denounced by Ahijah (I Kings 11:29-39). He was a castaway, and writings produced during this period would have had no reception by the faithful. In short, writings of a true prophet, during such a time as he remained true to his Lord, were received as God's Word. This rule would eliminate such a man as King Saul who, as far as we know, prophesied on only a couple of occasions. The Spirit of God had left Saul, and Israel knew that his word was not to be regarded.

It is sometimes thought that a prophet's chance utterances should not be regarded as inspired. Did the Spirit's activity descend to mundane matters? Perhaps one cannot be altogether certain on this point, but it is well to be somewhat cautious. Men are often poor judges of what is, or is not, inconsequential. In the New Testament, Paul gives directions about his cloak (II Tim. 4:13) which some might feel are unworthy of inclusion in the sacred canon. But this detail is in close proximity to important doctrinal truth and, as a matter of fact, has a very important bearing on the question of whether or not Paul was imprisoned a second time. Many matters which seem at the time inconsequential to us are so providentially arranged as to be of great import later. Saul searched for his father's asses that had been lost (I Sam. 9). He finally went to Samuel, the seer, to inquire about the animals. He was told that they had already been found, and then Samuel anointed him king over Israel. This particular mundane question received a divine answer and led to matters of great moment. The Bible records many matters of seemingly small consequence. As we have argued in the first part of this work, these details are all true, whether they concern genealogies or lost asses or mislaid cloaks.

It would be difficult indeed to maintain that a prophet is inspired only when he speaks of spiritual truths or major matters. It would be more logical to believe that a prophet is inspired in his specific teaching ministry. If it is the prophet who exercises the right to indicate what of his own work is to be preserved, the decision is on the shoulders of a man through whom God has spoken. If his successors or contemporaries pick and choose what they feel is inspired or what is worth preserving, an all-important task is left to the hands of uninspired and very fallible men. Of course, critical views would hold that no man is the organ of supernatural revelation and the bearer of God's infallible Word, so their tests for canonicity are vastly different. But to those who have believed the prophets, the logical view is that the function of the hearers of the message is not to pick and choose what seems true or valuable, but, rather, to submit to and to accept what the divine mouthpiece has spoken. Thus any decision as to what ought to be preserved should come from the prophet. A decision as to what can be preserved through the vicissitudes of history may be left in the hands of divine providence.

Thus our conclusion would be that the words of a prophet in his teaching ministry were the very words of God and were received as such. His writings were of equal credence and none were to be rejected by his contemporaries or successors. These views are, in fact, taught and illustrated in the Bible. Moses wrote at the command of God, collected his work into a law, and arranged for its preservation. Succeeding men, most of whom were clearly prophets and all of whom may have been prophets, added to the sacred scrolls, being conscious of the continuity of the record. All of this was received by contemporaries, as far as any positive evidence indicates, as equal in authority to the speaking prophetic voice. In the days following the close of the Old Testament canon it was regarded quite soon as a complete and authoritative body of literature. The Lord Jesus Christ's seal of approval upon this literature, in the form which it then and now has, is guarantee enough of its canonicity and truth for those who find in Him the Way, the Truth, and the Life. But when Christ approved of the Old Testament books, He was not promulgating new doctrine. Rather, He was in full agreement with the Jews of His time and was actually approving the teachings which the people of God had held through generations reaching back to the great basic revelations of God to Moses on the Holy Mount — to Moses, the prophet who was to foreshadow Christ Himself, that Prophet who should come into the world.

CHAPTER 8

THE EXTENT OF THE OLD TESTAMENT CANON

We come to a subject less controverted in Protestant circles and which can therefore be treated somewhat more briefly, with references to abundant literature for more extensive study. What are the books which belong in the Old Testament? The Protestant churches have always agreed with the Jews that the thirty-nine books regularly appearing in our English Old Testament are canonical. The Roman Catholic Church, since the Council of Trent (1546 A.D.), receives also as canonical Tobit, Judith, Wisdom, Ecclesiasticus (also called Sira or Ben Sirach), Baruch, I and II Maccabees, and certain additions to the Books of Esther and Daniel. We may briefly review the evidence for the origin, acceptance, and authority of these books.

Two lines of approach may be followed, the one historical and the other an appeal to authority. By both methods it can be seen that these Apocryphal books cannot properly be included in the sacred canon. We may add, however, that it is not our purpose totally to disparage these books. They are not Scripture. They are, however, books of considerable antiquity and of real value. They, like the Dead Sea Scrolls, are monuments to Jewish literary activity of the inter-Testamentary period. They partially fill the large historical gap between Malachi and Matthew, and they illustrate the religious situation at that time among the chosen people of God.

If our previous conclusions regarding the basis of canonicity be accepted, we can readily dispose of these writings.

They were all composed after the period when prophecy was recognized to have departed from Israel. They are all anonymous except two — first, Ecclesiasticus, which makes no claim that its author was a prophet or that the Lord spoke by him.[1] Nor does the grandson, Jesus ben Sirach, who translated the work into Greek and added the prologue in 132 B.C., make any such claim. Indeed, his words can only be understood as excluding his grandfather's composition from the category of Scripture, which is referred to as an entity and already translated into Greek as a unit. Second, the short Book of Baruch, which purports to be by Jeremiah's secretary, can in no case be accepted as genuine. Baruch is said to be in Babylon (1:1), though Jeremiah 43:6 says that he went to Egypt with Jeremiah. The book says that the Temple vessels were returned from Babylon, though Ezra and Nehemiah give quite a different picture. It speaks of Belshazzar as Nebuchadnezzar's son, as does Daniel. But in Daniel the time element with regard to Belshazzar is correct, whereas the Book of Baruch gives a date which is much too early. The book also predicts that the Captivity was to last seven generations (6:3), which contradicts both Jeremiah's prediction and Ezra's fulfillment. These and other discrepancies prove that the book is not genuine. If it should be by Baruch as it claims to be, it would be uncanonical in any case because untrue!

The two Books of the Maccabees make no claim to prophetic authorship. They record in detail the events of the glorious wars of independence of 165 B.C. and following, when the five Maccabean brothers fought against the armies of Syria with brilliant success. First Maccabees is generally regarded as more historically trustworthy than the second book. First Maccabees 4:46, 9:27, and 14:41 have been quoted above to show the current feeling that a prophet was not available for consultation. The Spirit of prophecy had long since departed. The entire historical situation is avowedly that of the second century B.C. and quite different from that of any canonical book.

The scenes of Tobit and Judith are laid in the days of the

Assyrian and Babylonian captivities and thus lie within the time of the writing prophets. But as Green says, "The Books of Tobit and Judith abound in geographical, chronological, and historical mistakes, so as not only to vitiate the truth of the narratives which they contain, but to make it doubtful whether they even rest upon a basis of fact."[2] It is said, for example, that in Tobit's youth the ten tribes revolted under Jeroboam (1:4, 5), which was in about 925 B.C., but that he was alive after the captivity of the ten tribes, which took place in 725 B.C. Yet he died when he was 158 years old (14:11). Judith speaks of Nebuchadnezzar as reigning in Nineveh instead of Babylon (1:1) and contains many other internal problems. The books neither claim to be the work of prophets nor could they be defended as such. The description "false prophets" would better characterize their authors.

Nor were they received as prophetic and inspired. Reference to Rabin's extensive indexes in his edition of the Zadokite Fragments[3] will show that although the canonical Scriptures are quoted repeatedly with such authoritative phrases as "it is written," "God said," "as He spoke by the hand of the prophet," etc., never once are the Apocryphal books so quoted. Several similarities in wording may indicate that some of these books were known to the Qumran community and, indeed, fragments of Ecclesiasticus have been found as well as portions of Jubilees and possibly the Testament of the Twelve Patriarchs.[4] These other books, called technically *pseudepigrapha*, are also not quoted as authoritative in the Zadokite Fragments. The shorter Manual of Discipline and the Habakkuk commentary give less evidence, but it is in the same direction. In short, in the pre-Christian era these writings were known, but were not among those accepted as authoritative in Palestine.

Nor were they accepted by Christ and His apostles. The evidence is plain that Christ accepted the common Jewish canon, which is determinative to this day for Protestants. This is clear, first of all, from the use the New Testament makes of the Old. There are, it is generally reckoned, about six hundred quotations of the Old Testament in the New, some, of course, being more lengthy and explicit than others. There are still other allusions of wording and events. These citations, many of which contain the express introduction "it is written," "God said," "through the prophet," "Scripture saith," etc., show clearly that the books were esteemed divine. The extent of authority accorded to the Old Testament by Christ and the apostles has already been shown in Part I. They regarded it as absolute truth. But the extent of the canon of that sacred book is shown by the fact that all of the Old Testament books are quoted except Ezra, Nehemiah, Esther, Ecclesiastes, and the Song of Solomon.[5] These are doubtless omitted not by design but because they are shorter and there was, because of the nature of their contents, less occasion to quote them. They all fall, it happens, in the third division of the Writings, but they surely are not neglected on that account. The Book of Psalms, which heads the third division, is quoted more frequently than any other Old Testament book!

On the other hand, the seven Apocryphal books and the minor Apocryphal additions are never quoted in any way. Alleged allusions to them are extremely few and doubtful. There may be some "coincidences of thought and expression," as Green puts it, but the full evidence given by him is strongly against the contention that any authoritative view of the Apocrypha was held by the New Testament authors.[6] The other books called pseudepigrapha also were not received. The only disputable passage in this connection is Jude 14 and 15, which refers to a quotation from Enoch, the seventh from Adam. It may be that this quotation is from the book by that name, though the text of Enoch is not too certain and this quotation could possibly be a post-Christian interpolation. In any event, as Green says, Jude does not by this sanction the Book of Enoch any more than Paul sanctions the writings of the Greek poets Aratus, Menander, and Epimenides, from each of which he quotes a sentence (Acts 17:28, I Cor. 15:33; Titus 1:12).[7]

The net result of such study, with which virtually all

agree, is that Christ and the apostles used and believed the group of books accepted into the Hebrew canon, and none others. For those who find their authority in Christ and His apostles, this would seem to be enough.

Further confirmation is, however, readily available. Historical study of the canon of the Jews of Palestine and of the early Christian Church points in the same direction. As to the Jewish canon, the evidence given in the Talmud and in Josephus *Against Apion* has been referred to above.[8] Also the writings of Philo, an Alexandrian Jew who wrote about 40 A.D., give important evidence, although he has not left a list of received books. The listing in Baba Bathra totals twenty-four books, which was the figure arrived at when Ruth and Lamentations stood alone. As we in our English Bibles count I and II Samuel and I and II Kings and I and II Chronicles separately, Ezra and Nehemiah separately, and the Minor Prophets as twelve books, not one, we enumerate these same twenty-four books as thirty-nine. But the books are the same.

Josephus' catalog lists the five books of the Law, then thirteen books of the Prophets, then four books containing hymns to God and counsels to men for the conduct of life. This gives the total of twenty-two, which is evidently reached by associating Ruth with Judges and Lamentations with Jeremiah. The four books in the third classification unquestionably include Psalms and Proverbs; and Ecclesiastes and Song of Solomon are most naturally taken as the other two. All the others outside the Pentateuch are classified by him among the Prophets. Green remarks, "It will be observed that Josephus here departs from the current classification, and adopts one of his own suited to his immediate purpose."[9] It is difficult to see how Green can be so sure that Josephus "departs from the current classification" when we have no way of knowing what the "current classification" was! The Talmudic reference is later and itself differs in some points from the order of our present Hebrew Bibles. But in any case, Josephus is in exact accord with the Talmudic tradition that the books which we count as the thirty-nine were the ones received among the Jews as fully divine.

Philo, the learned Jew of Alexandria, is of great interest in relation to the study of philosophy and Jewish thought. But for our purposes he is of special interest because he is our only representative of the views of first-century Egyptian Jewry. The evidence from his writings as to the extent of the canon comes from his quotations from the Old Testament and His comments upon various parts of it. Green refers[10] to detailed studies by Eichorn which show that Philo refers to or uses as authoritative all the books of the Jewish canon except Esther, Ezekiel, Daniel, Ecclesiastes, and the Song of Solomon. Again, these few books are not denied but simply neglected for lack of occasion to use them. On the other hand, the Apocryphal books are never mentioned nor quoted. It seems abundantly clear that Philo did not recognize them as among the sacred writings.

The above data would seem to be conclusive since excellent witnesses are available from Christ and the New Testament as well as from Palestinian Jewry and Egyptian Jewry. But two problems arise: one concerning a narrower and one a broader canon. On the one hand, some have felt that the Sadducees believed only the Pentateuch; on the other hand, it is regularly said that the Septuagint included the Apocrypha. These points may be briefly examined.

Unfortunately, very little is known directly concerning the sect of the Sadducees. The Talmudic references are all much later than the vital first-century period and may well be colored by later Jewish opinion. The New Testament couples the Pharisees and Sadducees together several times in speaking of their opposition to Jesus, but never in discussion of questions of canonicity. Indeed, as far as we can see, Jesus Christ never differed with His contemporaries on this question, though He never hesitated to condemn them on other matters when necessary. From Acts 23:8 we learn that the Sadducees did not believe in a resurrection, nor in angels, nor in spirits. But this does not imply a limited canon, for the existence of angels and spirits is clearly taught in the

Pentateuch. It is simply evident that the Sadducees were masters of mis-exegesis. Evidently they denied the traditions of the Pharisees just as they opposed the Pharisees themselves wherever they could, but there is no solid evidence of a variant canon. As to the sect of the Essenes, Green quotes Havernick to the effect that the Essenes probably "accepted the same canon as the people at large, though they also had other books written by members of their own sect which were held in high esteem."[11] This conclusion has been fully confirmed by the new Dead Sea discoveries, which seem to represent the work of a division of the Essenes of whom we had known very little except what was said by Josephus and Philo.

The more important question concerns the canon of Alexandria. Granted that the Septuagint, an Egyptian production, contains the Apocryphal books, does this imply that the Alexandrian canon was larger than the Palestinian? This question also has been mentioned above.[12] That our present Septuagint copies have a variant canon really proves nothing about the Alexandrian canon of 50 A. D., much less the Alexandrian canon of around 200 B. C., when the Septuagint was translated, for in those vital centuries there were three major factors which surely affected such questions.

In the first place, the Roman destruction of Jerusalem in 70 A. D. ended the thousand-year centralization of the Jews at Jerusalem and ushered in the dispersion of Israel, which has only now been somewhat reversed by the rise of the contemporary infant state of Israel. As long as Jerusalem was preserved, the Egyptian Jews — like the Ethiopian eunuch — returned to the holy sanctuary to worship. Jerusalem at Passover time was crowded with pilgrims. The canon would naturally be defined at Jerusalem for all the Jewish world. After the fall of Jerusalem, all this was changed. Diversification then had less of a check upon it. If someone loved certain more recent writings, no authority existed to say that these writings should not be exalted also.

Secondly, the Septuagint soon passed into Christian hands.

Great multitudes of Jews became Christians in those early days, as the Book of Acts makes clear. Those who did not, reacted the more violently against the new sect. The break seems to have become most sharply defined at the fall of Jerusalem when Jews, expecting Messianic deliverance, held out to the bitter end. Christian Jews, however, forewarned by such passages as Luke 21:20, fled to Pella, deserting the city but delivering themselves. They thus completely broke with Israel according to the flesh. Through these early decades the Christians appealed to the Old Testament prophecies to win Jews, and they were successful in winning many. The Christians throughout the Roman Empire naturally used the Greek, as the New Testament language evidences. They therefore naturally appealed to the Greek Old Testament. The Jews in self-defense argued that some of the Messianic passages were mistranslated. New Jewish Greek translations were made, but on the whole the Jews retreated into the Hebrew while the Christians took over the Septuagint. And the Christians did not have the regulative effect of ancient history to help them retain a proper view of the canon. This argument can be pressed too far because we can actually prove that the early Christian canon was in accord with the Jewish. But they were not so meticulous in defending it as the Jews had become as a result of centuries of self-defense. These other ancient worthy books were used, though not regarded as fully canonical. Eventually some of them found their way into our copies, but the copies do not show absolute uniformity.

The major factor may have been one of the accidents of history which are so unpredictable in their effects. The old Jewish copies had been kept in rolls. Shortly after Christ, the codex, or bound volume, was invented. Scrolls cannot be made large enough to hold the entire Old Testament or even a major part. The Pentateuchal division into five books was thus possibly occasioned partly by mechanical requirements. With respect to scrolls, the listing of books is vital; the order is not. Nor is it important what scrolls are mingled in a box or on library shelves. The wide variations of order in our earlier Septuagint copies[13] may reflect this situation. Today the printer can gauge accurately the number of pages needed in a book and can plan to bind it accordingly. But in those days the book had to be bound first — or at least cut and planned — and then it was filled. What should one do if he planned a book of a thousand pages? Obviously, he should make it large enough so that he would not have twenty pages of material left for the last page! But if he had fifty blank pages of precious leather at the end, what should he do? Naturally, he would fill it with helpful devotional material. Thus the tendency would be to associate other good books with the sacred books until eventually some of the good books attained a deuterocanonical status, that is, were received into a second rank.

This at least is what happened, for we know from considerable testimony of the first four centuries that the Apocryphal books were not then received into the canon. The evidence may be summarized again. Melito, bishop of Sardis, at about 170 A.D. went to Judea to ascertain the true number of the Old Testament books. His list may be repeated for interest, since it is the first list available from Christian sources; "Five books of Moses, Genesis, Exodus, Leviticus, Numbers, Deuteronomy, Joshua, Judges, Ruth, four of Kingdoms, two of Chronicles, Psalms of David, Proverbs of Solomon, which is also Wisdom, Ecclesiastes, Song of Songs, Job; the Prophets, Isaiah, Jeremiah, the twelve in one book, Daniel, Ezekiel, Ezra."[14] Lamentations was, of course, part of Jeremiah and Nehemiah of Ezra. Esther is curiously omitted and the reason is not clear. A few other catalogs also omit Esther, so it was likely not a mere slip. It is clear from other evidence that at this time Esther was fully recognized. The best explanation is that since in the Septuagint, Esther begins with the Apocryphal additions, Melito, probably reading only the first verses of each book, could not recognize it among the books which the Jews told him were canonical — Jewish books were named by their first words. However, except for this strange discrepancy, which surely has some explanation, Melito agrees exactly with the Jewish canon — not, however, with any known Jewish order. Other witnesses of this time, like Justin Martyr, and the Peshitto Syriac version (which had the Apocrypha only later), agree in using only the canonical books.

The next list is given by Origen, the scholar of Egypt.[15] Origen was not only a scholar; he had access to information and books which have long since perished. His library became the nucleus of the Eusebian Library at Caesarea, which possessed the treasures of Christian antiquity, but was destroyed by the Mohammedans in later centuries. Origen's list includes all the thirty-nine canonical books (grouped so as to number twenty-two, with Ruth and Lamentations attached to Judges and Jeremiah), but he omits the Minor Prophets. This is a slip of a copyist because the number given is twenty-two, although the books listed total only twenty-one. Following the list, he says, "And apart from these are the Books of Maccabees." Origen thus agrees with the Jewish canon precisely and explicitly, except that he declares that the Book of Jeremiah includes also Lamentations and the Epistle of Jeremiah (found in the Apocrypha as chapter 6 of Baruch). This probably is merely Origen's mistake, for he says that he follows the Hebrew canon, and all evidence excludes this epistle from that canon. Some have thought that he meant not the Apocryphal addition but a portion of the canonical book, but it is perhaps easier to assume a simple mistake. Tertullian of Carthage at about 200 does not give us a list, but tells us the books number twenty-four, which is the number of the Hebrew canon reckoned with Ruth and Lamentations independent.

In the fourth century eight prominent Church fathers, Athanasius of Alexandria, Cyril of Jerusalem, Epiphanius of Cyprus, Amphilocius of Asia Minor, and Gregory Nazianzus of Cappadocia, Hilary of France, Rufinus of Italy, and Jerome have left us lists all of which agree with the Hebrew canon except for very minor variations regarding Esther, Baruch, and the Epistle of Jeremiah. Athanasius gives the clue to the difficulty about Esther which was mentioned above. He says, "Esther is noncanonical and begins with Mordecai's dream." He refers, thus, to the Apocryphal addition with which Esther begins in the Septuagint copies. But "Esther is canonical among the Hebrews; and as Ruth is reckoned as one book with Judges, so Esther with some other book."[16] Perhaps Athanasius is wrong about details, but he probably gives the reason for Esther's curious omission from a few of these lists. We may add the testimony of Basil the Great of Cappadocia, who speaks of the twenty-two Old Testament books,[17] and the great Chrysostom, who declares himself for the Hebrew canon.[18]

This would seem to be evidence enough to convince the most skeptical that the ancient Church, regardless of some of its habits of Bible publication, held strictly — when it considered carefully — the. Hebrew canon and that alone. We may remark that in Episcopal circles and in many Protestant pulpit Bibles of a generation ago, the Apocrypha are printed, although no Protestant group has ever held them to be canonical.

The single voice of antiquity in favor of the Apocrypha is that of Augustine and the Councils of Hippo (A.D. 393) and Carthage (397), which he dominated. Augustine has left a list of the canonical books numbering forty-four and including the Apocryphal books. He places Tobit, Esther, Judith, and I and II Maccabees and Esdras after Job, and Wisdom and Ecclesiasticus after Ecclesiastes, using an order differing from both the Hebrew and Septuagint.[19] Notice that he omits Baruch and inserts what in English editions of the Apocrypha is called I Esdras, a book not received by the Roman Catholic Church. Other writings of Augustine seem to show clearly that he distinguished the canonicity of the Jewish Scriptures from the secondary canonicity of the Apocrypha. Several quotations are given by Green,[20] but these must suffice: "The account of the times since the restoration of the Temple is not found in the Holy Scriptures which are called canonical, but in others, among which are also the books of the Maccabees, which the Jews do not, but which the Church does, esteem canonical on account of the violent and extraordinary sufferings of certain martyrs."[21] It is rather clear that the books of Maccabees were not canonical in the strict sense. Elsewhere he insists that they are not prophetic, and speaking of books like Judith, he says, "They are not found in the canon which the people of God received, because it is one thing to be able to write as men with the diligence of historians, and another as prophets with divine inspiration; the former pertained to the increase of knowledge; the latter to authority in religion, in which authority the canon is kept."[22]

We have here summed up all the important witnesses in the Early Church to about 400 A. D. With one voice they insist that the strict Jewish canon is the only one to be received with full credence. Various Apocryphal books were known, however, quoted from, and included in later codices. This proves only that they were regarded as worthy and helpful — which we also grant. For the same reason, until the present century many Protestant Bibles also included them. Probably more Christians should read these Apocryphal books occasionally, especially Maccabees. Of special interest is the fact that Jerome, who was the translator of the Latin Vulgate, used to this day in Roman Catholic circles, expressly ruled the Apocryphal books out of the canon. He was prevailed upon to translate Judith and Tobit, which he did very hastily, apparently, without great respect for them. The other Apocryphal books were taken from the older Latin translations.

Through the Middle Ages the looser view of Augustine was presumably known and the practice of including the Apocryphal books in Bibles was followed. The irony of history is that during this period, when Hebrew was forgotten and Greek little used in the West, the Latin Bible of Jerome, including the Apocrypha, was used to establish in usual usage the Apocryphal books which Jerome denied!

But also throughout this period the stricter views of Jerome were well known in scholarly and official circles. Gregory the Great, pope in approximately 600 A. D., in quoting

I Maccabees, says, "We address a testimony from books, though not canonical, yet published for the edification of the Church."[23] And the learned Cardinal Ximenes, in the preface to his Complutensian Polyglot, "dedicated to Pope Leo X and approved by him,"[24] states that the Apocryphal books printed therein were not in the canon but used for edification. This was just before the Reformation.

The Council of Trent, which is the fountain of Roman Catholic teaching for modern times, took a different view. Unmindful of evidence, of former popes and scholars, of the Fathers of the Church and the witness of Christ and the apostles, it decreed on April 8, 1546: "The Synod . . . receives and venerates . . . all the books both of the Old and of the New Testament — seeing that one God is the Author of both — as also the said traditions as well as those appertaining to faith and to morals, as having been dictated (dictatas), either by Christ's own word of mouth, or by the Holy Ghost." The list of books is then given, including the Apocrypha, and the decree concludes, "If anyone receive not as sacred and canonical the said books entire with all their parts, as they have been used to be read in the Catholic Church and as they are contained in the Old Latin Vulgate edition, and knowingly and deliberately contemn the traditions aforesaid, let him be anathema."[25]

Protestants, of course, object to such a decree. Some elements in it, nevertheless, are good: it ascribes the authority to God as the Author and declares that the Holy Spirit spoke (dictatas — "spoke" — is surely intended, rather than mechanical dictation, as in modern office practice) the words. But the elevation of unwritten tradition to an equal place with zealously preserved sacred writings is an affront to intelligence. That traditions such as the bodily assumption of Mary could be unknown in all ancient writings, debated hotly in the Middle Ages, and thereafter, by multitudes of Roman Catholics, actually denied by popes, and finally proclaimed as infallible truth for the first time in 1950 A.D., is preposterous. The elevation of the Apocrypha is far less serious, for it at least does not grow! But to insist that these writings be received upon pain of (presumably) divine anathema is hard doctrine to receive, when we remember that for more than fifteen hundred years no Roman Catholic was called upon to believe it.

It seems rather clear that the Council of Trent adopted this item for reasons of expediency rather than evidence. The revival of Hebrew studies since the Renaissance had brought scholars in touch with the Hebrew canon of the Old Testament, and Protestants had almost uniformly come to accept this and this alone. It is human to react and think that an opponent whom one thinks to be wrong in one point is wrong in all. Also, the Church at Rome had chosen its lessons for public worship from the Apocrypha as well as the other books. This was only in accord with wide-spread usage, but to change would seem to imply a mistake on the part of the Bishop of Rome, and this would have been fatal to papal pretension.

It should be said that in the Greek Catholic Church the Confession of Cyril Lucar of 1631 and the authorized Russian Catechism agree with the Hebrew canon; the Confession of Dositheus of 1622, who opposed Lucar for his Reformation leanings, adopts the Apocrypha.

Finally, the Roman Church in its argument in favor of purgatory, had need of the verses in II Maccabees 12:40-45, where it is recorded that Judas prayed for the dead. This is exceedingly inadequate support for the imposing doctrine of purgatory, but it was all the (alleged) Scripture they had and they were naturally loath to surrender it. It is more convenient to support an untenable position with poor argument than to surrender the position. Orientals are not the only ones who prefer to "save face."

CONCLUSION

The author was once asked by an earnest Christian woman why Protestants do not receive the Apocrypha. He gave in outline the arguments presented above—that the Jews did not receive it, that Christ and the apostles did not receive it, that the Early Church did not receive it, and that the Roman Catholics adopted it only in Reformation times in reaction to Protestantism and to bolster their shaky position with respect to certain dogmas. It was evident that the inquirer appreciated the argument, but was not in a position readily to receive or judge the evidence. Finally he advised her to go home and read the Apocrypha for herself. He predicted that she would enjoy portions of it, but would be struck by its inconsistencies when compared with the canonical Scriptures and by its evidently legendary and unnatural material. Months later she returned and declared that she was fully convinced — she had read it! More Christians should read the Apocrypha as interesting old history. To do so would settle many questions regarding canonicity. Perhaps we may suppose that Roman Catholics can retain the Apocrypha in their Bibles only because they do not, generally speaking, read and study their Bibles faithfully.

This argument from internal evidence has been discussed at length by Green, but we need not present a detailed treatment of it. He remarks rightly enough, however, that it is only an auxiliary argument. "The limits of the canon must be determined mainly by external evidence; for it is a historical question . . . historical questions can only be determined by historical evidence."[26] Fortunately, the historical evidence is plain upon the pages of the New Testament and in the teaching of Christ, so that the humblest Christian can satisfy himself as to the correctness of the Old Testament canon as held in all the Protestant churches.

One conclusion, on the basis of the historical evidence, that the Apocrypha should be rejected fully supports our view as to why the canonical books should be accepted. Just as the canonical books should be accepted on the authority of their authors as prophets of God, so also the Apocryphal books should be rejected, as the Westminster Confession says, and are not "to be otherwise approved or made use of than other human writings" (1, 3), for they are human writings. No "thus saith the Lord" is found in them. They were written after prophecy had been withdrawn from Israel. Their authors are conscious of that fact and speak accordingly. They claim no divinity and, as far as we have any information, were never so received by their contemporaries or even their immediate successors. The proof is complete. What God spoke and had committed to writing was to be received. What He did not immediately speak or have committed to writing was not to be received as authoritative. "For the prophecy came not in old time by the will of man: but holy men of God ["men of God," according to another text, i.e., prophets] spake as they were moved by the Holy Ghost" (II Pet. 1:21).

Part III

THE CANON OF THE NEW TESTAMENT

CHAPTER 9

INTRODUCTION

It is no mark of a spiritual Christianity to deprecate the Old Testament. Christ and the apostles never did so, nor have the men who have been greatly used of God through the centuries of Church history. But it is proper and Biblical to elevate the New Testament. "God, who at sundry times in divers manners spake in time past unto the fathers by the prophets, hath in these last days spoken unto us by His Son" (Heb. 1:1). The prophets had a wonderful place in God's economy of redemption, and Moses was chief among them. But Moses was a servant in God's house, whereas Christ is a son over His own house (Heb. 3:6). "The law was given by Moses, but grace and truth came by Jesus Christ" (John 1:17). The material in the New Testament is fuller than the Old Testament in its declaration of the explanation of the things of our redemption. Because the New Testament message transcends the State-Church of Israel, and reaches out to the ends of the earth, including the Gentiles, it is of more direct importance for us than the Old Testament could ever be. It is, as a natural consequence, more widely and extensively read among Christians. Questions of canonicity, therefore, are of even greater importance in the New Testament field than in the Old. What books shall we receive as the very Word of God? There are some other examples of first-century literature and many examples of second-century Christian literature which are of value, and which probably should be more widely studied among Christians. Should any of these be accorded a place

beside that of our commonly received twenty-seven books?
What is the test of canonicity in the New Testament field?

Again we say, as in the Old Testament, the test of canonicity is inspiration. The Early Church put into its canon, and we receive, those books which were regarded as inspired, and no others. We have already argued in Part I the subject of inspiration. God did inspire some men to write certain books. The statement is often made these days that the Bible is a divine library. Some would emphasize that it is a collection of books rather than a single volume. It is, of course, obvious that it is a collection, a library. But the Church has always emphasized that it is a *divine* library, and although several hands produced it, one Spirit inspired it all. Human books were not received as sacred by the decree of a Church and thus, by ecclesiastical error or superstition, bound together for perpetual veneration. Rather, divine books were recognized as sacred, different from all others, and therefore were associated together as the New Testament of our Lord and Saviour Jesus Christ. What we said in connection with the Old Testament applies to the New Testament as well. It is a collection of authorized books.

But how shall we know, in this case, which books are inspired? The test of prophetic authorship discussed in relation to the Old Testament must here be at least modified. The certification of Christ and the apostles, which is so convenient to determine authoritatively the limits of the Old Testament canon, here fails. There was no New Testament book to receive Christ's imprimatur, nor has any apostle left us a list of twenty-seven titles to be received inviolable. Furthermore, here also the tests which critics have applied in the Old Testament to explain the veneration accorded those books cannot be advanced. Antiquity did not decide the matter, for I Clement was written within the lifetime of the Apostle John. But the writings of Clement, Ignatius, Polycarp, etc., were never received as canonical. Likewise, there is no language difference like that which is believed by some to have operated in the development of the canon of the Old Testament. Here, clearly, all, or virtually all, of the early Christian literature (both canonical and otherwise) was written in Greek.[1] There was some other principle for determining the canon — a principle which, judging from its great accomplishment, must have been a strong one. For it is strange that the sacred Old Testament canon was so quickly and so easily matched by certain writings which were chosen above others and accepted, without serious argument, as fully God's Word and quite on a par with the great Law and the Prophets cherished by so many for so long. What was that powerful principle?

Whatever the principle was that led to the selection of the books now in our canon, it operated rather well. All of the divisions of Christianity — Roman, Protestant, Eastern Orthodox — agree on the New Testament canon, and although occasionally individuals may have expressed some doubts as to certain books, there has not been serious debate since the days of Athanasius, who prepared a list of the books accepted in his day. We do not refer to the question of canonicity raised on the grounds of extreme skepticism. If one doubts that any book is inerrant truth, as do Brunner, Niebuhr, and others,[2] then one may find it possible to question the canonicity of John's Gospel, etc. But actually the real question then is: can there be a canon at all? If certain books are not the inerrant truth, then it is a question if any authority of the Bible can be maintained. If it is not unique in truth — especially when it makes large claims that it is — then is it unique at all? The Church has always answered that it is the Word of God and absolutely true, being inspired by "God (who is truth itself), the Author thereof," as the Westminster Confession puts it. Belief in verbal inspiration necessitates a canonization of books so inspired. And by one means or another, the Church has satisfied itself that these books are inspired and therefore canonical.

Indeed, the Church came to a very high degree of unanimity on these matters in the very early years. The origin of most of the Old Testament books lies in dim antiquity, and we are dependent on what a book claims for itself and what other Old Testament books say concerning it. It seems clear that the New Testament books arose in the latter half of the first century A.D., and almost all of them were clearly known, reverenced, canonized, and collected well before a hundred years had passed. Though the evidence is not too complete regarding the first half of the second century, good evidence exists that within fifty years of their writing, the Gospels (which make up about a half of the whole) and the major Pauline Epistles were fully accepted as canonical. No great delay seems to have been needed; no imposing ecclesiastical council seems to have acted; yet the books, as soon as evidence was available, had been accepted as divine.

The history of this acceptance has been given extensively by the learned Westcott,[3] and little remains to be said on that subject. An outline of his main positions will suffice at this point. Later we shall traverse these centuries again, not so much to see the dates by which the books were received, but to show the reasons for this reception as they were given by the early Fathers.

Westcott chooses, as the first stage in his study, the years from 70 A.D. to 170 A.D., approximately a century after the martyrdom of Peter and Paul and some seventy years after the death of John. This is the age of greatest interest in determining the extent of the canon, as well as in determining the principles adopted by the churches in its acceptance. It is also, unfortunately, the period when the evidence is less complete. To fill up this lack, Westcott covers the field with great care, judiciously weighing each fragment of evidence no matter how small. Some material bearing on the period has come to light since Westcott's day (his first edition was published in 1835), but its effect has been only confirmatory.[4] In the time after 170 A.D. we have the full light of later Christian scholarship extensively preserved in the writings of Irenaeus, Tertullian, Clement of Alexandria, Origen, and numerous later authors.

The period from 70 to 170 A.D. Westcott further subdivides, according to the general practice, into the age of the Apostolic Fathers, 70-120 A.D., and the age of the Greek Apologists, 120-170 A.D. Again, the earlier age deserves our close attention because it is only one generation removed from the apostles. But the later age also is of great importance, for Polycarp was doubtless not the only Christian who lived to a ripe old age. As he, in his own lifetime, connected the Apostle John and Irenaeus, so others of less noble proportion also for a long time surely preserved in the Christian community a vital link with the early ages. In the middle of the second century there were very likely many people alive who had heard the Apostle John.

The testimony of the first period is given by the three great bishops and martyrs, Clement, Ignatius, and Polycarp. Basilides, the Gnostic heretic, also seems to have lived within this period.[5] Clement, the bishop of Rome about 95 A.D., wrote to the Church at Corinth one letter which is admitted to be genuine. Other items attributed to him by later men are also of value, but not for this period. Clement's letter deserves to be read by Christians. It contains some slight reference to fables, but is, on the whole, a fine exhortation to Christian faith and life. Westcott shows that I Clement contains allusions to five of Paul's Epistles (I Cor., Eph., I Tim., Titus) as well as to James, John's Gospel, and the Epistle to the Hebrews. His reference to I Corinthians is especially instructive, for it is the first reference to a New Testament book as authoritative: "Take up the Epistle of the blessed Paul the Apostle . . . in truth he spiritually charged you . . ." (Lightfoot translates, "Of a truth he charged you in the Spirit.")[6] His clear reference to the Epistle to the Hebrews is of special interest, since that letter was later denied in some quarters. Of one passage Lightfoot remarks, "The whole passage is borrowed from the opening of the Epistle to Hebrews, from which expressions, arguments, and quotations alike are taken."[7] The extent of Clement's testimony to the Gospels is plain, but the question is whether he refers to them as from written Gospels or only from current unwritten tradition. With regard to chapter 13 of Clement (Luke 6:36, 38; Matt. 6:12-15), Lightfoot says, "As Clement's quotations are often very loose, we need not go beyond the canonical Gospels for the source of this passage."[8] Westcott is somewhat more cautious and points out that in this case and in chapter 46 of Clement Jesus' words are quoted with the introduction "the Lord said," not "saith." The past tense, he argues, speaks in favor of Clement's taking this quotation from tradition, not from a current Gospel.[9] But Westcott admits that the usage of Barnabas does not sustain this fine distinction. Clement's references, including reference to the star that appeared at Jesus' birth (Clement chap. 16), are most naturally referred to the Gospel of Matthew.

Ignatius, the bishop of Antioch, who was martyred during the reign of Trajan (therefore before 117 A.D.), has left us seven letters and is another very important witness which goes back virtually to the days of the apostles. His letters appear in a shorter and larger form in the Greek. Goodspeed summarizes the view of the contemporary scholars concerning them as follows: "The seven Ignatian letters have had an extraordinary history, having been reduced in Syriac to three greatly abbreviated ones and, on the other hand, in Greek and Latin have been increased as a collection by the addition of six or more spurious letters, or individually expanded and interpolated, still accompanied by several spurious letters. But the list of seven given in Eusebius in A.D. 326, and known to us in the shorter Greek form, it is now generally agreed, is the original Ignatian corpus."[10] It is this shorter Greek form that Westcott cites. Like Clement, Ignatius refers once to a Pauline Epistle by name: "Ye are initiated into mysteries with St. Paul, the sanctified, the martyred, worthy of all blessing ... who in every part of his letter [some would translate "in every letter"] makes mention of you in Christ Jesus."[11] Ephesians is not the only Epistle with which Ignatius is familiar. Westcott shows references also to I Corinthians, Philippians, I Thessalonians (?), and Philemon (?). Numerous similarities in thought and expression also show the influence of John's Gospel. C. R. Gregory adds Matthew to the list: "The author clearly knows our New Testament in general. The Gospels of Matthew and John appear to have been either his favorites or the ones better known to him. He knew the Epistles of Paul well."[12] Westcott gives this same evidence with what seems unnecessary reserve. He points out that the facts and teachings of Christ found in the Gospels also occur rather extensively in the writings of Ignatius. The Gospel source seems the best explanation, for material not given in our Gospels is not included, as it would naturally be if Ignatius were selecting from extensive unwritten tradition. Westcott mentions the birth narratives, the Virgin Mary, the Davidic ancestry, the birth star (Magnes. 7; Smyr. 1; Trall. 9; Eph. 19, 20), the Crucifixion with details, the Resurrection and Christ's eating with the disciples (Magnes, 9; Smyr. 3), and also several discourses appearing in Matthew's Gospel.[13] One other passage should be mentioned, though its interpretation is difficult. Warfield translates the passage thus: "When I heard some saying, 'Unless I find it in the Old [Books] I will not believe the Gospel,' on my saying, 'It is written,' they answered, 'That is the question.' To me, however, Jesus Christ is the Old [Books]; His cross and death and resurrection, and the faith which is by Him, the undefiled Old [Books] — by which I wish, by your prayers, to be justified. The priests indeed are good, but the High Priest is better." He argues that Ignatius "appeals to the Gospel as Scripture."[14] Westcott's translation is similar. He says, "Jesus Christ is [the substance of all] records; my inviolable records are His cross and death and resurrection and the faith through Him."[15] Westcott understands Ignatius to mean that the "Gospel" which is superior to the Old Testament is the gospel message, not the New Testament. It should be allowed, however, that Ignatius evidently considered the Old Testament as not complete (though absolutely true) and found in the fact of Christ's life and death — facts which we know he knew from the written Gospels — a superior "record." The words at least are clearly consonant with the view that he recognized New Testament writings as on a higher level than the Old.

The third vital witness to this early age is Polycarp. Polycarp, the great martyr who maintained that he had served Christ eighty years and could not in his old age deny Christ his King, has left us a precious letter written shortly after the martyrdom of Ignatius, therefore in the vicinity of 117 or 108, depending on one's view of the date of that event. Polycarp, who had heard the apostle John, was martyred in 155-156 A.D.[16] Of him Westcott says: "The short epistle of Polycarp contains far more references to the writings of the New Testament than any other work of the first age. . . Polycarp's use of Scriptural language is so frequent that it is wholly unreasonable to doubt that he was acquainted with the chief parts of our canon; and the mode in which this familiarity is shown serves to justify the conclusion that the Scriptural language of other books in which it occurs more scantily implies a similar knowledge of the apostolic writings."[17] He, like his two predecessors, refers to an Epistle of Paul in terms surely implying authority: "The blessed and glorious Paul . . . wrote letters to you (the Philippians) into which, if ye look diligently, ye will be able to be built up in the faith given to you."[18] Other books with which Polycarp shows a familiarity, according to Westcott, are Matthew, Acts, Romans, I and II Corinthians, Galatians, Ephesians, I and II Thessalonians, I and II Timothy, I and II Peter, and I John.[19] Is it not a thrilling experience to have an epistle admitted to be authentic, and from the pen of one who had heard the Apostle John, thus witness so extensively to books which form the core and make up almost half of our New Testament? If the word "martyr" means basically "witness," surely Polycarp excels.

Another witness stands just on the edge of our period and, oddly enough, comes from the side of the Gnostic heresy. Basilides, the Alexandrian Gnostic, is placed by Westcott between Clement and Polycarp. Clement of Alexandria says that he wrote in the days of Hadrian (117-139). Eusebius declares that his works were produced "not long after the times of the apostles."[20] As mentioned above,[21] the writings of Gnosticism constitute a more reliable witness now because of the recent discovery of more than forty Gnostic works, heretofore known only by title, in Chenoboskian, Egypt. Preliminary reports affirm that they support the description of Gnosticism given by Irenaeus, Hippolytus, etc. Here we have the first unquestionable instance of a New Testament book's being quoted as Scripture in terms equating it with Old Testament authority. The instances are given in Hippolytus: "The Scripture saith 'Not in words taught of human wisdom, but in those taught of the Spirit'" (I Cor. 2:13). (The Greek text is identical to our Greek New Testament.) Again, "In accordance with what has been written, he says, 'And the creation groaneth.'" etc. (Rom. 8:22).[22] Westcott remarks, "If it seems strange that the first direct proofs of a belief in the inspiration of the New Testament are derived from such a source, it may be remembered that it is more likely that the apologist of a suspicious system should support his argument by quotations from an authority acknowledged by his opponents than that a Christian teacher writing to fellow believers should insist on those testimonies with which he might suppose his readers to be familiar."[23] In addition to these Epistles of I Corinthians and Romans, Basilides also clearly refers to Matthew, Luke, John, II Corinthians, Ephesians, Colossians, and possibly I Timothy and I Peter. As Westcott justly observes, Basilides did not originate this view of the authority of the New Testament. As a heretic, he had already departed from earlier teaching; but if we go back of him only one generation, we are in the age of the apostles! Basilides' heresy evidently did not consist in rejecting Scripture, but in interpreting it to his own ends.

Another group of heretics which should be considered here, although their date is less certain, are the Ophites.[24] They were the first to use the term "Gnostics," "professing themselves only to know (Ginosko) the deep things," as Hippolytus says. They maintained that their doctrine came from James, the Lord's brother, through Mariamne, and therefore they would supposedly be from the immediate post-apostolic age. The term "Ophites" means "serpent worshipers," but of their particular teachings, beyond their general Gnostic ideas, we know little. As quoted by Hippolytus, they clearly refer to Matthew, Luke, and John, and also to Romans, I and II Corinthians, Ephesians, Galatians, and probably to Hebrews and Revelation. That they, as Gnostics, had other books goes without saying. Gnosticism professed to have esoteric doctrine, and often used Apocryphal Gospels, etc., as well as peculiar Gnostic books. The Ophites used the Gospels of the Egyptians, and of Thomas, but there is no proof that even they considered these in any sense canonical.

The last witness from this early age is the Epistle of Barnabas. It was held in high regard in antiquity and even declared by a few as from the pen of Paul's companion, although this is rather clearly erroneous.[25] But that it was written at an early date seems clear. Westcott says that it was a product "of the first age." Lightfoot sets the date at 70-132 A.D.[26] Gregory places the date at 130 A.D.[27] Goodspeed says that it was written about 130 in its earliest form but was expanded between 150 and 175, though there is no historical witness for this.[28] Barnabas is of prime interest for us because he is the first orthodox writer to quote a book of the New Testament as Scripture. Barnabas, chapter 4, quotes from Matthew 20:16 with the phrase "as it is written" prefixed. In addition to this there may be a reference to I and II Timothy.

With this we conclude the survey of the scanty but precious literature of the first thirty years after the death of the last apostle. And what is the conclusion? Simply that, in a casual but revealing manner, the bulk of the writings of the New Testament were already, in this early age, known, and used, as profitable. Each of the first three orthodox authors recommends at least one of the Pauline Epistles (a different one each time) by name, and by Basilides, the heretic, two are specifically called "Scripture." Barnabas similarly refers to Matthew. All the Gospels except Mark (and this so closely parallels Matthew in material that it, too, may be included) are utilized, as are all of the Pauline Epistles and Hebrews (not to prejudge its authorship). In addition, James, I John, I Peter, and probably II Peter, and Revelation are witnessed to, leaving only the two small Epistles of John and the single chapter of Jude without attestation. With regard to these latter books, it should be pointed out that there is no negative evidence in this respect but only a silence which may well be accidental. This would be especially true in the case of the slight evidence for Revelation, which it seems was scarcely written when Clement wrote and was extant for only twenty-five years when this period closes.

In view of these facts, developed in detail by Westcott, it is difficult to see why anything other than preconception moves him to insist that "the idea of the inspiration of the New Testament, in the sense in which it is maintained now, was the growth of time. . . . The Old Testament was for two or three generations a complete Bible, both doctrinally and historically, when interpreted in the light of the Gospel. Many of the most farsighted teachers, we may believe, prepared the way for the formation of a collection of apostolic writings co-ordinate with the writings of the prophets, but the result to which they looked forward was achieved gradually, even as the Old Testament itself was formed by slow degrees."[29] We have given extensive evidence in Part II to show that the Old Testament canon did not arise by slow degrees. If Daniel's word be accepted at all, he trusted implicitly the writing of Jeremiah, his elder contemporary (Dan. 9:1). The contention that for two or three generations after Christ there was no new writing which challenged the completeness of the Old Testament is not in accordance with the facts that Westcott has so ably marshaled. Before the close of the first thirty years after the death of the apostle John, there are three quotations of different New Testament books (including a Gospel) as Scripture, and by twenty years after John's death, three other Epistles of Paul are referred to by name in a manner implying the fullest authority — there is no contradictory voice. These same writers, though they — Ignatius especially

— exalt the bishopric to a high degree, nevertheless make a sharp line of demarcation between their own writings and those of Peter and Paul, who are extolled as apostles and in other ways. Westcott ascribes this to "providential instinct," the "intuition of the Church, derived from no reasoning." [30] Is it not, on the other hand, possible that so large a conclusion was actually based upon a divinely taught principle which would operate immediately and effectively, as it seems it did, in fact? Is it not possible that the first generation after the apostles had been taught by the apostles themselves the doctrine of the inspiration of the apostolic writings? The development of this idea must wait until we approach the teaching of the New Testament itself on this subject.

With respect to the next period, 120-170 A.D., this discussion can be briefer because the evidence is more abundant. Still, we are not in the era of the great masters nor the virtual triumph of the new faith. But extensive writings by numerous authors of this period are available. A number of these are of lesser importance because they merely confirm views already established.

The survey of the period may begin with the name of a famous heretic, Marcion. Westcott draws attention to the fact that we are indebted to heretics for the first citation of the New Testament as Scripture; for the first list of books held canonical, Marcion's list; and for the first commentary on an apostolic writing by Heracleon. He remarks that it is impossible to believe that these heretics formulated the orthodox view of Scripture; rather, they arose as departures from the norm and endeavored to justify their vagaries by appeals to the acknowledged standards.[31]

Marcion is referred to by Justin, who died in 148 A.D., and other references indicate that he wrote in approximately 140 or before. The son of a bishop, he departed from the current teaching and was castigated by Justin, Polycarp, Epiphanius, Tertullian, and many later authors of all areas. His aim was to restore the doctrine of Paul after its corruption by the first apostles. Apparently he knew of the work of the other apostles, but, taking his cue from Galatians 2:14, he denied their value. In this he was strenuously resisted and condemned for mutilating the Gospel.[32] Mutilate he did. His canon consisted of two divisions, the Gospel, containing an abbreviated copy of Luke, and the Apostolicon, containing ten Epistles of Paul in the following unusual order: Galatians, I and II Corinthians, Romans, I and II Thessalonians, Ephesians (called Laodiceans), Colossians, Philippians, and Philemon. Acts is curiously omitted, but it should be remembered that the first twelve chapters deal largely with Peter's ministry, which was anathema to Marcion. Westcott adds a sage observation: "The canon of Marcion is of importance as shewing the principle by which the New Testament was formed. Marcion accepted St. Paul's writings as a final and decisive test of St. Paul's teaching; in like manner, the Catholic Church received the writings which were sanctioned by apostolic authority as combining to convey the different elements of Christianity."[33] As we have noted, this combination of the authority of Peter and Paul occurs clearly already in Clement. Obviously, here is the basis for the determination of the inspiration of a book in question.

Papias, the bishop in Asia Minor, is familiar to all students of New Testament introduction. His work, dated at about 140 by Goodspeed[34] and others, exists, unfortunately, only in fragments, quoted mainly by Eusebius. He wrote an *Exposition of the Oracles of the Lord* which seems clearly to have been a kind of commentary on the Gospels and used, especially, oral traditions from the apostles to give additional light. He is famous for his explanation of how Matthew wrote in Aramaic and Mark was "Peter's interpreter." He probably knew John's Gospel, and certainly I John, I Peter, and Revelation.[35] His views on Mark are significant and must be discussed later. It is interesting to note also his curious omission of everything Pauline. The reason for this is quite puzzling. He presents the opposite side to Marcion's opinions. There is no evidence as to whether this is due to his Jewish background, or to a reaction to Marcion, or to personal choice. In any case, his failure to use the Pauline corpus was not because it was not widely acknowledged. That Paul's work was accepted from the very first we have shown.

Irenaeus quotes the *Remains of the Elders* — others who, like Papias, stood next to the apostles. They round out Papias' omissions and mention to Matthew, John, I and II Corinthians, Romans (said explicitly to be by Paul), Ephesians, I Peter (?).[36] The letter to Diognetus presents a similar sampling, but possibly from a somewhat earlier age, written during the reign of Hadrian (117-139 A.D.).[37]

In consideration of the heretics of this period around 140 A.D. the Gnostic Valentinus should be mentioned. "He cites the Epistle of the Ephesians as 'Scripture' and refers clearly to the Gospel of St. Matthew, St. Luke, and St. John, to the Epistles to the Romans and the first to the Corinthians, perhaps also to the Epistle to the Hebrews and the first Epistle of St. John."[38] Of more importance, in our connection, is his disciple Heraclion, already mentioned as the first commentator on the New Testament (except for Papias' lost *Expositions*). He refers to Matthew and various Pauline Epistles, but the character of his commentary is what makes it of special interest. The smallest details of text or number, whether occurring in the discourses of Christ or in the Evangelists' narratives, were regarded as divinely intended. In short, the same principles were applied to the New Testament as were well known in Old Testament study — and for the same reason, both collections were divine.[39] Other heretics we may merely mention. The Simonions, named after Simon Magus, quote I Corinthians as Scripture, but Cerinthus, who was supposed to have prompted John to flee from the bathhouse lest he be overwhelmed along with the heretic by some disaster, rejected Paul's writings in company with the Ebionites. [40]

The extensive writing of Justin is of great interest for this study. Justin was martyred in 148 A.D.[41], and his writings were composed not long before. However, his activities as a Christian philosopher and evangelist had continued for some time, judging from his many travels and labors. The Scriptures to which he clearly refers are Matthew, Mark, Luke, John, Romans, I and II Corinthians, Colossians, II Thessalonians, Hebrews, and Revelation. His importance lies in the fact that he refers to a well-defined corpus of sacred books. Westcott remarks that Justin's quotations constitute a problem because of their inexactness. "Some fancied that Justin made use of one or more of the original sources from which the canonical Gospels derived. Others with greater precision identified his *Memoirs of the Apostles* with the Gospel according to the Hebrews. Others again suggested that he made use of a harmony . . ." etc.[42] After sixty-seven pages of painstaking examination, Westcott concludes, "It appears, then, to be established, both by external and internal evidence, that Justin's 'Gospels' can be identified with those of St. Matthew, St. Mark, St. Luke. His references to St. John are more open to question; but this, as has been already remarked, follows from the character of the fourth Gospel."[43] If it be granted that Justin's *Memoirs* are the canonical Gospels, our study is considerably advanced. More than seventeen times he refers to them as the "memoirs" or the "memoirs of the apostles." He used phrases such as these: "The apostles, in the memoirs composed by them which are called Gospels, have thus delivered unto us what was enjoined upon them."[44] "For in the memoirs which I say were drawn up by His apostles and those who followed (*parakolouthesanton*, παρακολουθησαντων*) them, [it is recorded] that His sweat fell down like drops of blood"[45] — a detail found only in Luke. In similar fashion he refers to a detail found only in Mark.[46] The Four Gospels are clearly, for Justin, an authoritative corpus. He refers to them as giving the basis of baptism, "and for this [rite] we have learned from the apostles this reason."[47] He cites the infancy narratives as authoritative, "and the angel of God who was sent to the same virgin at that time brought her good news, saying [here he quotes Luke 1:32 and Matthew 1:21] — as they who have recorded all that concerns our Saviour Jesus Christ

have taught, whom we believed . . ."[48] Justin provides
one of our early descriptions of a primitive church service:
"On the day called Sunday, all who live in cities or in
the country gather together to one place, and the memoirs
of the apostles or the writings of the prophets are read,
as long as time permits; then, when the reader has ceased,
the president verbally instructs, and exhorts to the imitation of these good things."[49] Here surely he is a witness
to the equation of the New Testament Gospels with the
Old Testament volume in authority and ecclesiastical use.
The Gospels were particularly treasured as containing the
records of the life of Christ, but we know well from the
sources that the Epistles were no less authoritative. Another quotation is in the same direction. "As he [Abraham]
believed on the voice of God and it was reckoned to him
for righteousness, in the same way we also, when we believed the voice of God which was spoken again by the
apostles of Christ and the voice was proclaimed to us by
the prophets even to dying [for our belief], renounced all
that is in the world."[50] The quotation clearly says that as
Abraham believed God, so do we. But the voice of God
which we believe even to the death is spoken by the
apostles and prophets. Now, the only witness of the apostles
which Justin used was the canonical Scriptures, and the
only voice of the prophets which he knew was the Old
Testament. He clearly puts the New Testament and the
Old Testament on a par here, as in the preceding quotation.

Of great interest is the next witness, the Muratorian
Canon. Published by Muratori, this fragment from the
seventh or eighth century had long lain in the Ambrosian
Library of Milan. The portion of the manuscript dealing
with the Canon claims to have been written by a contemporary of Pius (127-142 or 142-157), and the date of
the Canon is admitted to be close to 170 A.D.[51] The first
lines are gone, and it begins with mention of Luke, the
third Gospel. The Gospels are said to be a unity: "Though
various ideas are taught in each of the Gospels, it makes

no difference to the faith of believers, since in all of them all things are declared by one leading Spirit." Westcott notes, "The Fragment lends no support to the theory which supposes that they were gradually separated from the mass of similar books."[52] Acts follows, with thirteen Epistles of Paul introduced with short comments. The author takes occasion to deny certain spurious books, and then adds Jude, II and III John, and Revelation. He mentions the Apocalypse of Peter as received by some but doubted by others. Strangely omitted are Hebrews, James, and I John. More to be expected is the omission of II Peter, which has less attestation in early days. Westcott argues[53] that the omission of Hebrews, James, and I John can best be explained by assuming a "chasm" in the manuscript. In any case, these three Epistles are well enough attested from other sources. We then have a history of the New Testament books as an authoritative collection almost exactly like our New Testament from someone who wrote less than seventy years after the death of the last apostle and who may well have talked with Polycarp himself or others who knew the apostles.

There are several minor witnesses — minor for our purposes — from this same time which may be merely named. These include the second Epistle of Clement, which, though not by Clement, is very old and belongs to about the middle of the second century. Dionysius, bishop of Corinth, worked sometime between 150 and 176 A.D. The allegory called *The Shepherd of Hermas*, dated before 170 A.D., quotes the Gospels as on a par with the Law. Finally, Hegesippus, who worked between 157 and 190 A.D., leaves us a little information in fragments that remain. Details concerning these authors are given in Westcott or any complete source book. They add nothing to the total picture but confirm it by showing the use of all four Gospels, Acts, I Corinthians, Ephesians, I and II Thessalonians, James, I Peter, and Revelation. Hegesippus indeed used Apocryphal sources, but evidently employed them to assist in embellishing his five books, which apparently were a theological exposition

of the Gospel. He seemingly used canonical books alone as
authoritative. He recognized that "some of the books were
forged in his own time by certain heretics."[54]

The final witnesses from this period are fully discussed
by Westcott, but their dates are somewhat uncertain. They
are the actual translations of the New Testament into Syriac
and Latin. The age of the common Syriac version called
the Peshitto is not known with certainty, but for various
reasons it seems to fall into the mid-second century. All
the various sects of Syrian Christians received this version,
and since a division occurred in the fourth century, the
version must already have been deeply rooted by that time.
Also, the Armenian daughter version was made from it in
approximately 400 A.D. Finally, the Syriac Church itself
is very old, claiming to be planted by the apostle Thad-
daeus in the time of King Abgar of Edessa. Edessa itself
was the center of an important school in the second century, and it is difficult to believe that the version was not
connected with the flourishing church. Westcott refers
briefly to the manuscript of an older Syriac version of the
Gospels edited by Cureton in 1858. Since then another
copy has been found by Agnes S. Lewis in 1892 in the
monastery of St. Catherine of Mt. Sinai. The relation of
this old text to the Peshitto is not clear. Nestle[55] dates the
Peshitto in the fifth century and the old Syriac Gospels
in the second. He seems to be too late for the Peshitto.
At all events, this version — and, by inference, the Syriac
churches — at an early date had all the books of our canon
translated into a corpus except II and III John, II Peter,
Jude, and Revelation. There were no additions. Of this
Westcott remarks, "Many writings, we know, were current
in the East under apostolic titles, but no one received the
sanction of the Church; and this fact alone is sufficient to
show that the canon was not fixed without careful criticism."[56] It should be noted, however, that geographical,
political, and language barriers between the East and the

West made it difficult to check the authenticity of some of the disputed books. Because a false Apocalypse of Peter was abroad, a second Epistle of Peter was not to be lightly accepted.

The Old Latin version was clearly in use in the second century, because, among other things, Tertullian bears witness to it. Africa was the center of Old Latin Christianity, for in Rome the Church used Greek until around 200. But in the Carthage area the Church was planted early and was a flourishing communion until it was literally wiped out in the wars of the fifth century and later. From this area and time comes the Old Latin version, which was later replaced by Jerome's Vulgate. This Old Latin version has our canon except for the omission of II Peter, James, and Hebrews. Hebrews was added before the time of Tertullian[57] but always had to make its way because of doubtful authorship. Second Peter, as is well known, is the most poorly attested book of the New Testament. The omission of James is less easy to explain. It is possible that it actually was in the Old Latin, but that our evidence is faulty.

Combining the two versions of the extreme East and extreme West at the early date of 170, we have just what we should expect from abundant other evidence — the present canon of the New Testament with no additions and the omission only of II Peter.

A few remarks on the evidence so far are in order. It is quite striking that the formation of the canon of the New Testament did not consist in the selection by chance or purpose of a few books out of a welter that had early gained recognition. Quite the opposite. There was no large number that gained recognition only to lose it. In fact, there was not even one that gained any noticeable degree of recognition only to lose it. Certain books like the Gospels and the bulk of the Epistles of Paul gained, we may say, immediate recognition. Other books were accepted in certain areas and not yet in others. Finally they were universally accepted. The last one to pass the test — or tests — was II Peter. What was that test? We have not investigated this question specifically as the evidence from the Fathers has passed in review, but this must be done after considering the Biblical teaching involved.

CHAPTER 10

DETERMINING PRINCIPLES OF THE NEW TESTAMENT CANON

The final answer to our question — what is the test of inspiration and therefore of canonicity? — must come from the Bible itself. And this is not necessarily circular reasoning. The major portions of the New Testament can be accepted, for the sake of the argument, as historical records, excellently attested, giving us testimony as to the teachings of Christ and the apostles.

There is no reason for doubt in the minds of Christians that the four Gospels belong in the canon, as do the Epistles of Paul. There was some debate in the early centuries concerning the later portions of the volume — some of the general Epistles. But most of the books were never doubted. The principles laid down in the unquestioned books and in the undoubted teaching of Christ and the apostles can be used to assist in deciding questions where the evidence is more scanty. If, for instance, we can find why I Corinthians was accepted, we can perhaps tell why III John should or should not be accepted. If in the teaching of Christ we can discover principles bearing on the acceptance of any writings, we can bring them to bear on the acceptance of II Peter. The New Testament is both our authoritative source book of doctrine and also our earliest and best source book on the life of Christ, His teaching, and the work of His immediate followers.

The first conclusion that can be established from the undoubted and earliest records is that portions at least of the New Testament were written with the expectation that they were to be received and obeyed. Critics wince at this statement. Although there is nothing inherently unbelievable in such a view, even the orthodox occasionally question it. Westcott himself says, "It cannot, however, be denied that the idea of the inspiration of the New Testament in the sense in which it is maintained now was the growth of time. . . . If it be true that a prophet is not without honor except in his own country, it is equally true that he is not received in his own age . . . years must elapse before we can feel that the words of one who talked with men were indeed the words of God."[1] This interesting quotation is full of prejudgments, not facts. The idea that human words take time to be received as divine would go ill with the idea of an immediate reception of Christ's words and obedience thereto — the mark of the wise man who built his house upon a rock (Matt. 7:24f.). He declared in the Olivet Discourse that His words would never pass away (Matt. 24:35; Luke 21:33). It is as obvious as anything can be that the apostles, by virtue of Christ's resurrection, early came to full belief in His words and acted upon them — to the death. The words of apostles also were received by their contemporaries as authoritative. A clear proof is I Thessalonians 2:13, where Paul commends the Thessalonians for doing just that. A further bit of evidence has come to light since Westcott's day. Among papyri from the rubbish heaps of Egypt has been found a fragment of John's Gospel, the John Rylands papyrus already referred to.[2] Students of its style of writing declare that it dates from the first half of the second century, approximately 125 A.D., we may say. Remembering that John lived to a great age and that his Gospel may well be a product of the last decade of the first century, we see here an example of the writing of John copied in a distant land, and copied apparently because already within thirty-five years of the author's death it was revered exactly as in later times. Surely not many years need to elapse to accomplish the result Westcott mentions. Indeed, none need to elapse. If men see the finger of God in their midst, immediate acceptance of the writing is a natural consequence.

The writings of the apostles make the claim that they are authoritative and inspired. Perhaps the clearest instance of this is I Corinthians 14:37. In Corinth, Paul early had opened to him a great door and effectual, but he also found that there were many adversaries. His first Epistle to the Corinthians begins with a discussion of the sad divisions in the Church. Those divisions included a party strife which had, among other things, the effect of deprecating Paul's authority. He was not a man of pride who wanted to lord it over the flock personally, and he was quite willing to be counted a partner with Apollos and others in God's vineyard. But there were other issues at stake which Paul could not properly relinquish. They also questioned his authority. He responds by asserting his authority more strongly in these Epistles than in any other. He implores them to turn back to following him, his ways, and his teaching, lest he come to them with a rod (I Cor. 4:16-21). He commands church discipline (I Cor. 11:2). Then he deals, in chapters 12-14, with spiritual gifts and rebukes their disorders. He outlines for them the limits of propriety in the worship service. This command he seals with the declaration that the Word of God had come from him to them, not vice-versa, and declares (14:37) that what he, Paul, writes are the commandments of the Lord and are to be obeyed by those who exercise spiritual gifts at Corinth. The verse is positive and clear. Paul wrote to be obeyed, and wrote in the name of the Lord.

The same note of command is clear in II Corinthians, especially chapters 10-13. The force of chapter 10 may be lost to some because of the use of the first person plural. He speaks of "our authority, which the Lord hath given us for edification, and not for your destruction," verse 8, but he begins the section "Now I Paul," verse 1, and verses 9 and 10 continue in the singular, speaking of Paul's own letters. The threat of verse 11 is softened by the use

of the plural "we," but the reference to letters versus bodily
presence shows again that it is Paul speaking of himself.
And he continues, in verse 10, to denounce those who
oppose him who measure themselves by a human standard,
whereas "we" — Paul — can boast of things according to the
measure of the rule which God hath distributed to "us."
This measure is superior to the Corinthians. They are duty
bound to obey him, Paul, "whom the Lord commendeth,"
verse 18. The sharpness of the chapter is softened somewhat by the editorial "we," but the rapid interchange of
singular and plural shows that it is Paul's own authority
that is intended. He proceeds, in chapter 11:5, to show
that his was an apostolic authority, and not a secondary
one, either. Those who have thus opposed him are not
Apollos and Peter, with whom he feels all kinship, but they
are false apostles (11:13), posing as the apostles of Christ.
He continues by reciting his labors and privations and
also his spiritual revelations (for 12:1-5 rather clearly speaks
of Paul himself) and returns to the theme that he is not
behind the "chiefest apostles" (12:11) and that the Corinthians should know this, for the signs of an apostle were
wrought by him in miraculous power at Corinth (12:12).
So he writes to warn them that in bodily presence also
they, if they will, will see the "proof of Christ speaking
in me" (13:3), and he has written this letter, which if
they obey, they will make it unnecessary for him to use
sharpness, "according to the power which the Lord hath
given me to edification, and not to destruction" (13:10)
(he employs exactly the same words which he used in
10:8, near the beginning of this section, except that here
the singular is used, not the editorial "we.") He wrote as
an apostle. He claims the authority of an apostle. He
claims that the Lord has given him this authority. He
declares that he can give proof of "Christ speaking in me,"
and claims that he wrought the miracle signs of an apostle
at Corinth. These are large claims. But they only reinforce
the declaration of I Corinthians 14:37 that when Paul wrote
he consciously wrote "the commandments of the Lord."

In accord with this interpretation, the apostle, in I Corinthians 2:10-13, gives us further information regarding his claims to an inspiration of the Spirit. The force of the passage again has been obscured somewhat by Paul's use of the first person plural "we." As the sequence in II Corinthians 10 clearly shows, the apostle was in the habit of using an editorial "we" to allow his comments and claims to authority to be couched in language both polite and acceptable. But that the "we" in I Corinthians 2:12 really refers to Paul is clear from the context, for he has claimed that his own speech was in the demonstration of the Spirit and of power (I Cor. 2:4). That the "we" refers to Paul himself is also shown by the sequence of the argument in I Corinthians 4:3, where the thought of being "spiritually discerned" is applied to Paul himself, who declares that he does not regard human judgment (the same word as in I Corinthians 2:14). His judge is the Lord. Again, in chapter 4, the sequence varies between the plural "us" and the singular "me": verse 9, "us the apostles," and verse 16, "be ye followers of me." It seems clear in the entire section that Paul, as elsewhere in the Epistle, is enforcing his claim to apostolic authority, and that the first person plural is but an editorial "we" to introduce the subject in kindness and personal humility. With this in mind, we see that I Corinthians 2:13 is a clear declaration that the Apostle Paul was giving the very words of God. He claims that just as a man must reveal his own thoughts to another, so the thoughts of God cannot be discovered by human reason, but are matters of revelation. He claims that this revelation is by the Spirit of God, and that he, Paul, having been taught by the Holy Spirit, has given the Corinthian Christians this revelation. The verse is particularly significant because it claims that the very words have been given by the Holy Spirit. The final phrase of I Corinthians 2:13 is obscure, but it does not affect the clear teaching of the first part. Some have argued that the final phrase means that the apostle is joining spiritual things to spiritual words which would only reinforce the previous interpretation. Others would translate it "interpreting spiritual things to spiritual men," which would still be in line with the inspiration gift which the apostle claims. The words should be regarded as excellent evidence for the apostle's claim that his teaching was verbally inspired. Hodge remarks that "there is neither in the Bible, nor in the writings of men, a simpler or clearer statement of the doctrines of revelation and inspiration."[3] One point to which we must refer again is that in this passage the claim of inspiration is not merely for the apostle's writings, as in I Corinthians 14:37, but also for his speaking. What he claimed, he claimed for his teaching whether oral or written. The validity of his writing was the natural consequence of the validity of the authority of his spoken word. This authority is grounded in his claim to apostleship, as the verses in I Corinthians show. Cf. I Corinthians 9:1, 2, etc.

This conclusion that the apostle claimed that he spoke and wrote by inspiration is denied by some on the basis of I Corinthians 7, where three times he contrasts his speaking with the Lord's commandment (I Cor. 7:6, 10, 12). To adopt this view would make I Corinthians 7 contradict I Corinthians 14:37. And such an interpretation is quite unnecessary.[4] The passage simply means to say that on some points like divorce, Paul can quote a definite word of Christ — such as the one in Matthew 19:9. On certain other matters the apostle cannot quote the words of Christ in His earthly ministry, but gives his own commandment, or outlines for them action that may be permitted, but not required. His conclusion in verse 40 is certainly not to be taken to mean that he is dubious as to whether or not he has the Spirit of God. This would contradict his entire emphasis in these Epistles, as well as in his other writings. Clearly, verse 40 is to be taken ironically. The men who opposed him claimed to be extremely spiritual. Paul says that he, too, surely has the Spirit of God; and, therefore, his word is to be accepted. But notice that he claims to have the Spirit in a way that none of them could claim. He claimed it as an apostle and in 14:37 claimed that the mark of a spiritual man at Corinth was his acceptance of Paul's word as divine.

The claim of Paul in I Corinthians 2:13 is very much like that in I Thessalonians 2:13. Here his authority had not been questioned, but in this first letter, Paul's heart overflows with thankfulness that the Thessalonians had received him so well and accepted his message so readily. His commendation is that when they received the word of God at Paul's mouth they had received it as it truly was, the word of God and not the word of men. This statement, like I Corinthians 2:13, refers, be it noted, to the spoken message of the apostle. That it applies to the written word also there need be no doubt, but the reference is to his preaching. In harmony with that, he claims, when speaking to them concerning the coming of Christ, to say this "by the word of the Lord" (I Thess 4:15). This seems to be almost a New Testament equivalent for the Old Testament utterance "thus saith the Lord." First Thessalonians, the first Epistle written by Paul, closes with the charge that it be read publicly. This is exactly what we find the Early Church doing when the first evidence on the subject is available. They gathered to sing hymns and to read the writings of the apostles and the prophets. It is interesting to note how the actions of the Early Church can be shown to follow out the injunctions which the apostles left, both in receiving their words and in using them in the worship service. The second Epistle written by Paul, II Thessalonians, urges the brethren, in II Thessalonians 2:15, to hold inviolate the precepts ("traditions" hardly expresses the Greek) which Paul had taught them, and he specifically adds, "Whether by word, or our epistle" — note again the editorial "we." The note of authority reappears in II Thessalonians 3:6, 14, where he enjoins them to obey this, his Epistle, and to have no company with those who do not. The sixth verse of chapter 3 again refers to the precepts as received from "us," but they were clearly from Paul. Indeed, in II Thessalonians 3:17, he adopts the signature which he uses thereafter in all his Epistles. The purpose of this signature was to distinguish his writings from false epistles which evidently were already circulating (II Thess. 2:2). This signature may have been his own name written out, or it may have been his characteristic greeting "the grace of our Lord Jesus Christ be with you all." In either case, notice that the Epistles which often have the names of others associated with Paul in the salutation come specifically by the authority of the apostle.

The Book of Galatians is known as a book in which Paul spoke sharply to one of his churches that was in danger of going astray. The introduction is almost curt, verse 1: "Paul, an apostle, (not of men, neither by man, but by Jesus Christ, and God the Father, who raised him from the dead)." He insists in 1:8, 9 that the gospel which he had preached (note the "we" of verse 8, even though no one else is associated with Paul in writing Galatians) is so directly from heaven that it may not be contradicted even by an angel. He declares in verse 11 that the gospel which he had preached "is not after man. For I neither received it of man, neither was I taught it, but by the revelation of Jesus Christ." Even Galatians 2:2 declares that Paul's decision to go up to Jerusalem was by revelation. He thus appeals to a series of revelations in his work and teaching. It does not appear from 2:2 that he spoke to the apostles privately for fear his gospel should not be right. Rather, his mention of danger that he had run in vain would refer to whether or not his work would be hindered by any opposition by the brethren in Jerusalem. He had experienced that hindrance in Antioch, where he had withstood Peter to the face, not because he differed with Peter in doctrine, but because Peter's example was detrimental. Actually, he speaks of Peter in commendation as having the "apostleship of the Jews" (2:8). He does not deny the leadership of the other apostles, James, Peter, and John, but actually puts himself on a par with them as receiving revelations from God and giving the gospel in a God-appointed ministry.

The other main New Testament writings that deal with this subject of inspiration are Revelation and II Peter. In Revelation there is the well-known blessing for those who read and hear and keep the writings of this book (1:3). It is a book which John was commissioned to write (1:19), and at the conclusion there is a dreadful curse on anyone who would add to or take away from the words of this prophecy (22:10). It is doubtless true that some, by mistake, would think that these statements concerning Revelation refer to the whole of the New Testament. This thought, however, may well be justified as an application because the principles that led the Church to accept the Book of Revelation as apostolic, inspired, and divine are similar to those that would lead us to accept the remainder. But the primary reference of these verses is simply to the Book of Revelation itself, which, however, forms a fitting climax to the entire Bible. The second Epistle of Peter is, we know, not accepted by critics, and has less external evidence in its favor than do some of the other books.[5] However, there is no evidence that it is not by Peter, and eventually the ancient Church was convinced of its authorship. If it is not by Peter, it is certainly not worthy of a place within the canon because it so clearly claims to be Petrine. Indeed, the author plainly refers to experiences that he had on the mount of transfiguration and claims his work to be a "second" epistle and to be by an apostle. Scholars who believe II Peter to be a worthy part of the New Testament canon point out that the claims which are made are similar to those made in the other books, but they are more specific. Of great interest is II Peter 3:2, which puts the "commandment of us the apostles of the Lord and Saviour" on a strict parallel with "the words which were spoken before by the holy prophets." Again, notice that this claim of the equation of the New Testament teaching and the Old Testament writings is not limited to the written New Testament but is given for the apostolic commandment, however presented. That the written message of the apostles was regarded as inspired is certainly clear, also, in II Peter 3:15f., where Paul's letters are spoken of with the highest commendation and are actually classed with "the other scriptures." In this Epistle, then, there is a claim of inspiration by Peter for himself as one of the apostles and for Paul specifically in his Epistles. Another interesting case may be cited from Paul. In I Corinthians 9 he argues extensively from the Old Testament that it is proper to pay a minister. In his later Epistle, I Timothy 5:18, he returns to the same subject. This time, however, the Old Testament argument is compressed into two lines, and the matter is settled by a quotation of words of Christ which appear verbatim in Luke 10:7. The most natural conclusion is that Paul quoted it in the second instance and not the first, because Luke's Gospel had not then been written. The form of the sentence is "The scripture saith," followed by the Old Testament quotation and then immediately by the words of Christ as found in Luke. It is preferable, both from grammar and context, to believe that the words "The Scripture saith" apply to both quotations. According to this interpretation, we have here and in Jude 18 [6] the first quotation of the New Testament as Scripture, imbedded in apostolic writings.

It is important also to see how these claims of revelation are presented in the New Testament writings. We have already touched on the subject, but it should be emphasized that the authority which is claimed is apostolic authority. This fact received expression in II Peter 3:2. It is illustrated by the fact that of Paul's thirteen Epistles, nine begin with "Paul, an apostle of Jesus Christ" or some similar phrase. Only I and II Thessalonians, Philippians and Philemon are excepted.

We have noted the emphasis which Paul puts upon his apostleship in the Epistles, especially those to the Corinthians. The word "apostle" occurs especially in these two Epistles, and is actually emphasized more in the Pauline writings than elsewhere. This is probably for the simple reason that Paul's apostleship was questioned and was indeed of a special nature. If Luke and Acts be included, in the New Testament there are only ten instances of the use of this word outside of Pauline literature. The apostles were, under Christ, the foundation of the Christian Church (Eph. 2:20). (It may not be clear whether the apostles and prophets here referred to are the Old Testament and New Testament teachers, or the New Testament apostles and the prophets who were apparently local leaders in the New Testament congregations, but in any case, the apostles are emphasized.) In Ephesians 4:11 and I Corinthians 12:28 the first rank is held by the apostles, the second by the prophets. The gift of prophecy was one which all Christians were to desire; the apostolate came from God. The Lucan writings also magnify the other apostles. The election of Matthias is described in detail in Acts 1, which also emphasizes the requirement that an apostle must be one who was a witness of the resurrection, having had firsthand knowledge of the Lord Jesus and His ministry. In I Corinthians 15 Paul insists that he also is an apostle, though the least of them, by virtue of his supernatural vision of the risen Christ on the Damascus road. The history of the Book of Acts tells of the signs done by the apostles (2:43) and many later miracles, their holy boldness, and their leadership in the Church at Jerusalem. It was they who sent Peter and John that the Holy Ghost might be given to the Samaritan converts. It was they who questioned Peter about the conversion of Cornelius and who were satisfied with Peter's report. It was they who, with the elders, in the first council meeting in Jerusalem gave forth the decree that the Gentile converts were not under bondage to the Law (Acts 16:4). Paul, in advancing his apostleship, merely sets himself on a par with the others of the Twelve. It is true that there are five instances when the word "apostle" is used in broader sense than with reference to the Twelve. In the other seventy-six uses, the word denotes one of the Twelve. One of these five more general usages is John 13:16, where Jesus uses the term in its etymological significance, "he that is sent," with reference to His own sending forth of the apostles. In three instances the word is used to refer to people outside of the Twelve. In Acts 14:14 Barnabas and Paul together are called apostles. In Philippians 2:25 Epaphroditus is called the messenger of the Philippian Church, and in II Corinthians 8:23 those who assisted with the collection of the money sent to Jerusalem are called "your apostles" (messengers). Rather clearly, the etymological meaning is intended. In Romans 16:7 it is not clear whether Andronicus and Junia are of note among the apostles or are believers held in high esteem by the apostolic company. If it is the former meaning, we would have here another instance when men outside of the Twelve were called apostles. It is apparent that such a usage is extremely rare, though etymologically warranted. Regardless of the usage of the name itself, it is quite clear that there was no arrangement made in the Early Church for the office of the Twelve to be passed on to others as, on the contrary, arrangements were made for the eldership to be universal and perpetual. There is not the slightest New Testament evidence for an apostolic succession. When Paul calls himself an apostle, he does not use the term in a derived secondary or etymological sense. He is an apostle with a capital "A." Such was not true of Epaphroditus, Andronicus, Junia, or even Barnabas. Barnabas was given his surname by the apostles (Acts 4:36). He was sent by them to Antioch (Acts 11:22). In Acts 13:1 he is called one of the prophets and teachers. He is mentioned twenty-nine times in the New Testament. Only once is he called an apostle, and then rather clearly in a secondary sense. It seems plain that the New Testament recognized the office and the authority of the Twelve. Aside from the name "apostle," "the Twelve" are referred to in the Gospels some thirty-two times. It seems that the characteristic Gospel name for these men was "the Twelve," a name which, for obvious reasons, Paul could not adopt, being himself a thirteenth! The group is called "the eleven" six times after the defection of Judas. One interesting passage, Luke 24:33 says that the eleven were gathered together, and the parallel account in John indicates that Thomas was absent. In short, there was a group of men from which Judas fell and to which Matthias was added by vote and Paul by divine appointment. This group was chosen by Christ and ordained by Him to be with Him (Mark 3:14). He sent them forth to preach in the days of His flesh. He promised that they would sit on twelve thrones, judging the twelve tribes of Israel (Luke 22:30). Their names are engraved in the twelve foundations of the New Jerusalem (Rev. 21:14), and upon them is built the Christian Church (Eph. 2:20).

This well-nigh universal usage of the New Testament is fully borne out, as we shall see, in the patristic writings. Clement, Irenaeus, and Polycarp all clearly distinguished themselves from the apostles, and they named no other apostles than those within the circle of the Twelve. Though the word "apostle," of course, has an etymological meaning, it was used more specifically to designate a clearly defined group with special privilege and authority.

What led these men to feel that they had this special power? First of all, Christ had chosen them, and for three years they had companied with Him. During His last hours He had spoken to them extensively, as John's Gospel witnesses, and had promised them, among other things, the Holy Spirit. The verses in John 13-17 are usually taken by Christians to apply to the Church at large, and, truly, many of these verses are intended to apply to everyone in the new dispensation. The Comforter has come into the world on the basis of the finished work of Christ. We should not feel that John 16:7 implies that the Comforter can come only after Jesus leaves because the two persons somehow cannot work contemporaneously. Rather, as is clear from the context, Jesus means, "It is expedient for you that I go away," that is to say, "It is expedient for you that I die." Our Lord says, "I go away and I will come again." Jesus must go away, must go by the way of the Cross, in order to purchase redemption for us. On this basis, and on this basis alone, can the Comforter come. It was, however, to the eleven that Jesus made these promises of the Comforter, and He plainly had some promises for the eleven which are only indirectly passed on to Christians of succeeding ages.

This is clear from His high-priestly prayer, in which He prays for the Twelve, verses 6-19, whom the Father had given Him and from whom only the son of perdition had fallen, to which men He had given God's work and whom He had sent into the world. Following, in verse 20, he prays for succeeding generations who "shall believe on me through their word." And that the Holy Spirit was promised, in the first instance, for the apostles is clear from John 16:13, which declares that part of the Spirit of Truth's work is that "he will guide you into all truth . . . and he will shew you things to come." This is not a promise for Christians in general. It is a promise of revelations by the Holy Spirit. Again, John 14:26 declares that the Comforter is sent to "teach you all things, and bring all things to your remembrance, whatsoever I have said unto you." In this specific setting it is clear that the work of the Holy Spirit was to reveal truth to the apostles and also to remind them of things that Christ had already told them. This is a work of revelation, and is not applicable to Christians in general. That the Holy Spirit is given to Christians in general, we do not deny. Romans 8:9 makes clear that all Christians do have the Holy Spirit. Note, however, that Christ promised a special revelation work to the Twelve whom He had ordained to be the teachers and founders of His Church on earth. John 20:22 records that the resurrected Christ breathed on the apostles and said, "Receive ye the Holy Ghost." From the parallel account of this gathering in Luke 24:49 it is clear that Jesus did not mean to give the Holy Spirit to them at once, but His breathing was symbolic of the coming of the Holy Spirit upon them shortly, as they tarried in Jerusalem. This was fulfilled at Pentecost. At that time Peter gave his memorable sermon in the power of the Holy Spirit, and the apostles had begun their preaching, missionary, and revelation ministry.

We come to the conclusion that Paul and the apostles were conscious that they wrote as men inspired by God. This was not merely their own conviction, but was in full accord with the promises which Christ had given them that they would be ordained by the Holy Spirit for just such a work. The gift of the Holy Spirit in the matter of revelation was fully supported by other gifts of the Spirit for the extensive healing ministries of the apostles recorded in the New Testament. Acts 2:43 speaks of the wonders and signs which were done by the apostles. Acts 5:13 says that after the death of Ananias and Sapphira, the people magnified *them*, apparently, in the context, the apostles. It is true that the New Testament speaks of an occasional miracle done in the New Testament by those not of the Twelve, but very few. Also, there is an occasional prophecy of future events given by those not apostles, but, again, these are exceptions. The apostles were evidently the Spirit-ordained and recognized spokesmen of God. Is it any wonder that the apostle Paul can claim to speak in words taught of the Holy Spirit, and can require that his writings should be received as the commandments of the Lord?

It is true that all of the New Testament books do not make the apostolic claim explicit. This is not to be wondered at, and it will be considered shortly. We have remarked that Paul claimed apostolic authority mainly in relation to the church at Corinth, where it was most seriously questioned. As noted above,[7] Westcott argues that the Scripture was appealed to most explicitly by the heretics first because their agreement with Scripture was questioned. Among the orthodox leaders the same attitude toward Scripture is found, but the claims are much more natural and implicit in the writings. It is human, and to be expected, that the controverted points would be emphasized. Matthew need make no claims to apostleship, for his position was above question. As to the books which were possibly not written by apostles, namely, Mark, Luke, etc., we shall speak of them shortly. It is thus obvious that a test for inspiration is ready to hand in the New Testament age. The teaching of an apostle was received, and was intended to be received, simply because he was an apostle commissioned of Christ. As in the case of the Old Testament prophet, what he wrote was naturally as authoritative as what he spoke, and, therefore, any production of an apostle would at once be accepted as divine. It is this which the apostles in their writings command and expect. It is this which Jesus' commission to them would imply. We need speak of no strong intuition in the Early Church, as does Westcott,[8] whereby these holy writings were distinguished from others. It was not an intuition: it was simple obedience to the known commands of Christ and His apostles. This view would fully explain the sudden rise of the New Testament as an authoritative corpus of undoubted authority. As mentioned above, it was not a selection, but was a production. Undoubted letters and writings of the apostles were received, as far as we can tell, at once. Others were added to these books as it became known that they were in the same category of authorship. The New Testament canon at Corinth at first consisted of two Epistles; at Colosse, of one Epistle. But very soon the canon at Colosse grew in response to Paul's injunction of Colossians 4:16 that the Laodicean letter (and there is good reason to think that this is our letter called Ephesians) also be read so that the canon then included two Epistles. Very soon, by an exchange with the other Pauline churches, the canon included all of the Pauline Epistles and the Gospels as they were written and circulated. How long it took for all the inspired books to be circulated and established in any one church is difficult to say. By thirty years after the death of John virtually all of them were known and used in all the centers from which our evidence comes. Certain of the smaller books were still, in some quarters, questioned as to their authorship, and therefore as to their authority, for perhaps another fifty years.

Such a test of inspiration as is here indicated from the Scriptures would be in harmony with the Old Testament attitude toward a divinely inspired prophet and would at the same time provide a practical criterion for delimiting the New Testament writings. The Lord Jesus did not, in prophecy, give us a list of the twenty-seven New Testament books. He did, however, give us a list of the inspired authors. Upon them the Church of Christ is founded, and by them the Word was written. Two points remain to be considered before such a view can be established, however. The one is: was this, as a matter of fact, the test applied by the Early Church in the selection of the New Testament books, and, secondly, is this test really applicable in view of the question in regard to the authorship of six of the New Testament books, namely, Mark, Luke, Acts, Hebrews, James, and Jude? These questions we must consider in the following chapters.

CHAPTER 11

THE PATRISTIC TEST OF CANONICITY

We have reviewed (Part III, Ch. 9) the writings of the Early Church to 170 A.D. to determine when and where the canonical books were accepted. In connection with that study, references have emerged as to the importance of the apostolate in the estimation of the early Fathers. It may be helpful to draw these together and add further evidence as to the reason actually held by the Early Church for the acceptance of the New Testament. Again we shall start with Clement of Rome, the first witness, from 95 A.D. Clement, according to Irenaeus;[1] had seen the blessed apostles. His regard for them is extremely high. He writes, "The apostles received the Gospel for us from the Lord Jesus Christ. Jesus was sent forth from God, so then Christ is from God and the apostles from Christ."[2] They are "the greatest and most righteous pillars of the Church."[3] The apostles were even granted prophetic insight, says Clement, and he quotes from a detail of their writing to show this: "And our apostles knew, through our Lord Jesus Christ, that there would be strife over even the name of the bishop's office. For this cause therefore, having complete foreknowledge, he appointed the aforesaid persons."[4] We have already drawn attention to Clement's reference to I Corinthians. "Take up the Epistle of the blessed Paul the apostle," Clement writes, "what did he write to you at the time the Gospel began to be preached? Truly under the inspiration of the Spirit he wrote to you."[5] Clement continues with a reference to I Corinthians 3:3. The word is *pneumatikos,* which Lightfoot translates, "Of a truth he charged you *in the Spirit.*"[6] The word strongly reminds us of I Corinthians 2:14, where Paul, claiming inspiration, writes that spiritual things are *spiritually* discerned. Aside from the detail in this passage concerning the claim of inspiration for the apostles, note how exalted is the position he ascribes to the great Apostle to the Gentiles. Exactly in line is the witness of Ignatius of Antioch, who wrote in approximately 117 A.D. Ignatius' witness is the more instructive because he goes to great lengths to urge upon his readers obedience to their bishops as the basis of unity in the Church. He exalts his own office as a bishop (not necessarily to imply a superior type of clergy, however, for even in the New Testament the terms "bishop" and "elder" are synonymous, as witness Acts 20:17, 28, etc.). Ignatius' use of the New Testament we have outlined above, but the basis of his acceptance of these writings is also given by him. He frequently refers to the apostles as a distinct group: "As therefore the Lord did nothing without the Father united with Him, neither by Himself nor by the apostles, so neither do ye anything without the bishops and the presbyters."[7] Note that the apostles were a complete body of men who lived in the past and were in association with Christ. He deprecates himself as not being "competent for this, that being a convict, I should write you as though I were an apostle."[8] He names Peter and Paul as outside his own class. "I do not, as Peter and Paul, issue commandments unto you. They were apostles; I am but a condemned man."[9]

Polycarp, bishop of Smyrna, writing in the vicinity of 118 A.D., had a similar regard for the apostolate. Irenaeus declares that Polycarp had been instructed by the apostles and was indeed appointed bishop of the Church of Smyrna by apostles.[10] His extreme regard for Paul is shown in the following quotation: "For neither am I, nor is any other like unto me, able to follow the wisdom of the blessed and glorious Paul, who, when he came among you, taught face to face with the men of that day the word which

concerneth truth carefully and surely, who also, when he
was absent, wrote a letter unto you."[11] The emphasis on
Paul's teaching in truth is clear, and that the authority
derives from the apostolic office is clear further from the
following: "Let us therefore so serve Him with fear and
all reverence as He Himself gave commandment and the
apostles who preached the gospel to us and the prophets
who proclaimed beforehand the coming of our Lord."[12] The
apostles are here put on a par with the prophets of the
Old Testament, and are to be obeyed. In another place
this is explicit. He cites "these Scriptures" and proceeds
to quote both Psalm 4:4, "Be ye angry, and sin not," and
Ephesians 4:26, "Let not the sun go down upon your
wrath." The quotation certainly appears to be a citation
of the New Testament as on a par with the Old.[13] It may
indeed be a citation of Ephesians 4:26 alone, for the Psalm
(A.V., "Stand in awe, and sin not") is quoted in Ephesians.
In this case the New Testament itself is plainly called
"Scriptures."

The witness of Papias, from around 140 A.D., is of special
interest. He writes, "And again, on any occasion when a
person came in my way who had been a follower of the
elders, I would inquire about the discourses of the elders—
what was said by Andrew, or by Peter, or by Philip, or
by Thomas, or James, or by John, Matthew, or any other
of the Lord's disciples, or what Aristion and the Elder
John, the disciples of the Lord, say. For I did not think
that I could get so much from the contents of books as
from the utterances of the living and abiding voice."[14] This
interesting quotation divides between the first circle of the
apostles and some who are apparently second-generation
disciples, Aristion and Elder John. Some have equated the
Elder John with the apostle John, who calls himself an
elder, but the majority would think of a secondary disciple. It is not to be concluded that Papias did not regard
the apostles as superior, nor that he deprecated the New
Testament writings. On the contrary, as we have already
quoted, he wrote commentaries on the oracles of the Lord

and specifically mentions Matthew and Mark. Warfield argues at length that his word "oracles" here refers to our Gospel writings.[15] Actually, Papias is using all the traditions of the Lord which he can to illustrate the apostolic writings. He says immediately before our quotation, "For unlike the many, I did not take pleasure in those who have so very much to say but in those who teach the truth, nor in those who relate foreign commandments but in those [who record][16] such as were given from the Lord to the Faith and are derived from the Truth itself." The words "who record" as supplied by Lightfoot would better be "who relate," to parallel the previous statement. What Papias is interested in is the oral traditions concerning Christ. What modern commentator would not jump at such an opportunity!

Papias is largely remembered for his statements concerning Matthew and Mark. He says, "Matthew composed the oracles in Hebrew, and each one interpreted them as he was able."[17] Westcott remarks that when Papias wrote this, the Greek translation of Matthew was evidently already accessible. The "time" was then past when each one was his own "interpreter." Of Mark he says, "This also the Elder [John] used to say. Mark, having become Peter's interpreter, wrote accurately all that he remembered, though he did not [record] in order that which was either said or done by Christ. For he neither heard the Lord nor followed Him; but subsequently, as I said, [attached himself to] Peter, who used to frame his teaching to meet the [immediate] wants [of his hearers], and not as making a connected narrative of the Lord's discourses. So Mark committed no error as he wrote down some particulars just as he recalled them to mind. For he took heed to one thing — to omit none of the facts that he heard and to set nothing falsely in [his narrative of] them."[18] We must consider this statement more at length in connection with the problem of the authorship of the second Gospel, but for the present we will note that Papias explicitly states that the second Gospel is accepted because of Peter, not because of Mark. Mark's work was to write down accurately what Peter said. Mark made no mistake in writing the things he remembered. The main question in regard to Papias' doctrine is whether he exalted the oral utterance of the apostles above the written Gospels. The first quotation above would look in that direction, but in view of his emphasis upon the written Gospel of Matthew and Mark and his knowledge of John it seems clear that he trusted primarily the written records that had come down from the apostles themselves. In short, apostolicity was to him the criterion of authority, and the apostolic writings, including Mark, were thus authoritative, and, in his commentary, any other traditional word actually from the apostles was also at least of high regard and probably of authority. Some have argued that the authority of the apostles to Papias is only because he understood that they preserved the words of Christ and that the true authority was that of Christ. Of course, he did believe in the full authority of Christ, but that he set that over against the apostolic authority is not proved. We have referred above to Warfield's[19] discussion of the title of Papias' work, his *Exegesis of the Oracles of the Lord,* in which the word "oracles" is said by Warfield to refer to Scripture. His arguments are weighty. The word "oracles," *logion,* had been used by Philo in relation to the Old Testament Scriptures. Of more significance, it is so used by Paul in Romans 3:2. According to this view, the authoritative thing that Papias had before him was a book or books which, in effect, he calls Scripture, and which included the sayings of Jesus, but included much more. Some of critical bent have found in Papias' reference "Matthew composed the logia in the Hebrew (Aramaic) language" a reference not to our canonical Matthew but to a primitive source book of Jesus' sayings which is commonly denominated "Q." This view is considered at length by Zahn.[20] It seems highly artificial. There is no such source book referred to in all of the other patristic writing. If one ever existed — which is problematical — its memory had evidently been replaced by the second century. That Papias would refer to it in these terms when the canonical Matthew was already a well-known book, likely even translated into Syriac, and that he would not distinguish between the one and the other, would be impossible to believe. Furthermore, the reference to Mark is clearly to the canonical Gospel. Inasmuch as Papias says that Mark did not write the gospel story in order, some have argued that he must have been speaking of a proto-Mark rather than our canonical Gospel. Regarding this Westcott remarks, "In short, we must suppose that two different books were current under the same name in the times of Papias and Irenaeus — that in the interval, which was less than fifty years, the older document had passed entirely into oblivion, or at least wholly lost its first title — that this substitution of the one book for the other was so secret that there is not the slightest trace of the time, the motive, the mode of its accomplishment, and so complete that Irenaeus, Tertullian, Clement, Origen, and Eusebius applied to the later Gospel only what was true of that which it had replaced. And all this must be believed because it is assumed that John could not have spoken of our present Gospel as not arranged 'in order.' But it would surely be far more reasonable to conclude that he was mistaken in his criticism than to admit an explanation burdened with such a series of improbabilities."[21] Westcott continues to point out that Mark actually is not a chronological biography and would suit the description that Papias quotes from the Elder John. Westcott's argument should be allowed its full force, and the same argument is applicable to Papias' testimony concerning the canonical Matthew and the alleged Q.

Brief reference may be made to the Epistle to Diognetus mentioned above. The author claims to be a disciple of the apostles, and the chief interest is in the reference, already quoted in another connection, to "the fear of the Law . . . the grace of the Prophets . . . the faith of the Gospels . . . and the tradition of the apostles."[22] This word "tradition" — *paradosis* — does not convey merely the idea of tradition as we speak of ideas loosely handed down from generation to generation. Rather, its meaning, witnessed to in II Thessalonians 3:6, I Corinthians 11:2, etc., refers to a precept delivered, and it can be used of precepts transmitted in writing as well as of precepts transmitted orally. In the present quotation from the Epistle to Diognetus, when the Law, the Prophets, and the Gospels are mentioned, rather clearly the tradition of the apostles means the Epistles, which were by this time, of course, thoroughly established in the Christian Church. The Epistle of Barnabas, which we have seen was of interest because it quotes from Matthew and calls it Scripture, also gives us an indication as to why the author holds to such authority. He limits the number of the apostles to twelve[23] and declares that Jesus chose "His own apostles, who were to proclaim His gospel."[24] The fact that he disclaims apostleship is of special interest because it shows that in the mid-second century, when this epistle was composed, the one man outside of the Twelve clearly called an apostle in the New Testament was not really regarded as one of the Twelve. It evidently was held that Barnabas and any others would be apostles only in a derived sense.

The *Remains of the Elders* quoted by Irenaeus are, of course, very fragmentary, but their attitude is shown in the following quotations: "And again the apostle in the Epistle to the Thessalonians declares as follows . . ."; "And this again, he said, the apostle did most clearly point out, saying in the Epistle to the Corinthians . . . whereas therefore the apostle declares in a way which admits not of doubt or gainsaying . . ."[25] How much of this wording may possibly be the work of Irenaeus can be questioned, although the accuracy of the Church Fathers in their quotations is rather well admitted. It certainly shows that in the second century, and probably in the early part of it, Paul's authorship and apostolic authorship are in their writings as naturally interchangeable as in our references today. They were authoritative not merely because they were Paul's but because they were written by Paul the apostle.

When we turn to Justin Martyr, the evidence becomes more full. This man of God, who gave his life for the Faith within about seventy years of the death of John, makes many references to the apostles in a way that can only be said to be authoritative. We have pointed out how he refers to the Gospels as a corpus and ascribes them to apostles, "the apostles in the memoirs composed by them which are called Gospels."[26] The second Gospel was called Peter's. Justin refers to a passage peculiar to Mark, thus: "The mention of the fact that Christ changed the name of Peter, one of the apostles, and that the event has been written in his [Peter's] memoirs, together with his having changed the name of two other brethren who were sons of Zebedee to Boanerges, tended to signify that he was the same through whom the surname Israel was given to Jacob, and Joshua to Hoshea."[27] These points are found only in the Gospel of Mark, and the reference to Peter's authorship seems clear. Roberts and Donaldson interpret his memoirs to refer to Christ's memoirs,[28] but Zahn argues in the same vein as Westcott on the basis of Justin's regular usage.[29] At least it is evident that Mark's Gospel is attributed to an apostle, and Justin is very clear on the point that the term "apostles" refers only to the original men, "for from Jesus there went out into the world men, twelve in number, and these illiterate, of no ability in speaking; but by the power of God they proclaimed to every race of men that they were sent by Christ to teach all the word of God."[30] Later he identifies these men as apostles: "But the Gentiles, who had never heard anything about Christ until the apostles, set out from Jesus and preached concerning Him . . ."[31] Luke is also called apostolic by Justin. In the *Apology* he refers to the annunciation to the Virgin Mary and quotes from Luke 1 and Matthew 1.[32] Later in the *Apology* he quotes the institution of the Lord's Supper from Luke and says that "the apostles, in the memoirs composed by them which are called Gospels, have thus delivered unto us what was enjoined upon them."[33] Again he speaks of the "memoirs which I say were drawn up by His apostles and those who followed them [it is recorded] that His sweat fell like drops of blood."[34] This detail is found only in Luke. It is quite clear that Justin was fully aware of the details of the authorship of the Gospels, yet all of them are said to be by the apostles, and at the same time they are written by the apostles and those who followed them. It appears that Mark and Luke were not mere second-generation disciples who followed their masters in time and wrote what they pleased, but were disciples who followed the teachings of their masters in such a way that they presented the masters' teachings and their production had the masters' authority. The word *parakoloutheo* is defined by Thayer to mean "always at one's side, to accompany, always to be present, to examine thoroughly, to follow faithfully a standard and conform oneself to that standard." We are reminded of Tertullian's use of the phrase "apostolic men," referring to Mark and Luke. In both cases it should be noted that these are not mere companions but are, as it were, assistants, understudies, who reproduced their masters' teachings. Numerous other people were friends, companions, acquaintances of the apostles, but were not regarded in the Early Church as authoritative at all. Quite clearly Mark and Luke are not authoritative in their own right; rather, they are authoritative because of their adherence to their apostolic masters. We have already given the quotation from Justin in which he apparently equates the authority of the apostles of Christ and the Old Testament prophets[35] and his discussion of early worship, when the memoirs of the apostles and the writings of the prophets were read.[36]

We have thus considered again the authors of the Christian Church to about 170 A.D. The authors who are closest to the apostles make much of the fact that the apostles are far above them. There is no semblance of a claim by Papias, for instance, that because he had excellent traditions of what the apostles said that therefore his word should be received as authoritative. Likewise Clement, though he was a hearer of the apostles, insisted that he could not begin to approach to them. Ignatius and Polycarp are also strong in this direction. The apostles are linked to the Old Testament prophets. Their number is fixed, and their work is finished. Their Gospels and Epistles are quoted as the Word of God, and the Word of Christ. Papias sought the living voices of all of the apostles with equal industry; he names eight. Even the disputed Gospels of Mark and Luke are already called by the middle second century the work of apostles, meaning clearly not Mark and Luke but their masters, Peter and Paul. The later full and extensive witness from Irenaeus, Tertullian, Clement of Alexandria, and others only confirms the views of these early men. We shall therefore not continue our present summary but confine ourselves to the question as to how these books of irregular authorship are considered and for what reason they are received. In connection with this we can conveniently consider the books which were not so readily accepted into the canon, namely, Hebrews, II and III John, James, II Peter, Jude, and Revelation. We pass therefore to objections to the theory that apostolicity determines inspiration and shall consider particularly how these objections were faced and answered in the Early Church of approximately 200 A.D.

CHAPTER 12

THE LATER AUTHORS AND PROBLEM BOOKS

Irenaeus, the Bishop of Lyons, stands on the threshold of a new era. A native of Asia Minor, he traveled to Rome and eventually resided in Lyons, Gaul, where a flourishing church was already established. Jerome dates his work during the reign of Commodus, that is, in 180-192 A.D. Irenaeus tells us that he had heard Polycarp in his youth, and, therefore, is only one link removed from the apostle John, although three-fourths of a century had passed. He thus is not only the first writer of a new age, but is at the same time a most important link with the past. As Westcott observes, "Though the Fathers of the close of the second century are thus prominently distinguished from those who preceded them, it must not be forgotten that they were trained by that earlier generation which they surpassed. They inherited the doctrines which it was their task to arrange and harmonize. They make no claims to any discoveries in Christianity, but with simple and earnest zeal appealed to the testimony of the Apostolic Church to confirm the truth of their writings."[1] Sanday agrees: "To suppose that there was any great and sudden change between Justin and Irenaeus is to draw an inference from the writings of Justin which they certainly will not bear."[2] He shows that we have remaining only a portion of Justin's work, and that is a portion which is addressed to non-Christians where appeals to an authoritative Scripture are less expected. He adds very properly, "This absence of evidence must not be confused with negation of the fact for which evidence is sought."[3] As far as the evidence goes (and there is quite a little), Justin is in agreement with Irenaeus.

Irenaeus' doctrine of Scripture is clear. He refers to the "writings of evangelists and apostles" which the Gnostics twist as they do "the Law and the Prophets."[4] He clearly had a corpus of New Testament writings parallel to the Old Testament. Gregory observes that "he uses distinctly the four Gospels, the Books of Acts, First Peter, First John, all the Epistles of Paul save Philemon . . . and the Revelation."[5] He complains in his work "against heresies" about the Valentinians: "When, however, they are confuted from the Scriptures, they turn around and accuse these same Scriptures as if they were not correct nor of authority."[6] To Irenaeus they clearly were of authority. To him also we are indebted for the illustration that the Gospels are as unchangeable even in number as the four winds of heaven and the five zones of the world. In like manner the Creator has "given us the Gospels under four aspects but bound together by one Spirit."[7] The Scriptures are true, according to Irenaeus, because they are apostolic and therefore inspired. Naturally, Irenaeus regards Christ as ultimate authority: "Thus did the apostles, simply and without respect of persons, deliver to all what they had themselves learned from the Lord."[8] But although the apostles may be believed because they are accurate historians, that is not the only reason. Their authority, as Irenaeus understands it, is reflected in phrases of this sort: "The apostles, likewise being disciples of the truth, are above all falsehood."[9] "John, however, does himself put the matter beyond all controversy on our part, when he says . . ."[10] "For the apostles . . . certainly did not address them in accordance with their opinion at the time, but according to revealed truth."[11] "For it was unlawful to assert that they preached before they possessed perfect knowledge."[12] This apostolic authority is the result of their enduement with the Holy Spirit: "For after our Lord rose from the dead, [the apostles] were invested with power from on high when the Holy Spirit came down [upon them], were filled from all [His gifts], and had perfect knowledge: they departed to the ends of the earth preaching the glad tidings."[13] "Matthew might certainly have said, 'Now the birth of Jesus was on this wise,' but the Holy Ghost, foreseeing the corrupters . . . says by Matthew, 'But the birth of Christ was on this wise.'"[14] Paul's words are likewise attributed to the Holy Spirit.[15]

Furthermore, Irenaeus attributes the apostles' authority to Christ's appointment, and in virtue of this relation declares their words are equal to His: "For the Lord of all gave to His apostles the power of the Gospel, through whom also we have known the truth, that is, the doctrine of the Son of God, to whom also did the Lord declare: 'He that heareth you heareth Me, and he that despiseth you despiseth Me, and Him that sent Me.'"[16] Interestingly, Hodge, in his Systematic Theology, appeals to the same verse to establish the same doctrine that the word of apostles is per se authoritative, and thus their oral preaching is true and their writings canonical.[17]

It is worth noting that Irenaeus ascribes to the Holy Spirit the work of inspiring the apostles, not the work of testifying to the authority of their writings. An interesting case is his opposition to the Valentinians, who held to a Gospel of Truth. Irenaeus rejects this work because "it agrees in nothing with the Gospels of the apostles. . . . For if what they have published is the Gospel of Truth, and yet is totally unlike those which have been handed down to us from the apostles, any who please may learn . . . that that which is handed down from the apostles can no longer be reckoned the Gospel of Truth."[18] Actually there are in this quotation two tests of canonicity, one positive and one negative. Negatively, no writing can be canonical which contradicts previously revealed and well-authenticated truth. This test is as old as Deuteronomy 13:5 and is given with greater emphasis in Galatians 1:8. This negative test, however, is not enough — it would allow the multiplication table to be placed in Scripture! And it must be used with caution. It was this test which led Luther astray with respect to James. This test, however, is obvious enough. But it is quite overshadowed in Irenaeus' view by the positive test: "Is a writing apostolic?" If it is, it is true and will agree with previous revelation, for it is spoken by the same Spirit and prearranged by the same Christ.

How, then, does Irenaeus deal with the books of irregular authorship, Mark, Luke, and Acts? As we have shown above, Irenaeus accepts all four Gospels and Acts as of equal authority. Yet he is fully aware of the Marcan and Lucan authorship: "Matthew, among the Hebrews in their own dialect, brought out also a writing of a Gospel while Peter and Paul in Rome were preaching and founding the Church. After their death Mark, the disciple and interpreter of Peter, also himself committed to us inscripturated (ἐγγράφως) the things being preached by Peter. And Luke, the follower of Paul, the Gospel being preached by that one he put down in a book. Then John, the disciple of the Lord . . . also he gave out the Gospel while staying in Ephesus of Asia."[19] Again, "Wherefore also Mark, the interpreter and follower of Peter, does thus commence the narrative."[20] A problem for our view at once strikes us here. If Mark was written after Peter's death, how could it be properly ascribed to Peter? Yet Justin had already ascribed the Gospel to Peter, as mentioned above.[21]

A slightly earlier witness is that of Papias in the much-discussed fragments preserved for us in Eusebius. Papias says: "The elder [John] used to say, Mark, having become Peter's interpreter, wrote accurately all that he remembered; though he did not [record] in order that which was either said or done by Christ. For he neither heard the Lord nor followed Him; but subsequently, as I said, [attached himself to] Peter, who used to frame his teaching to meet the [immediate] wants [of his hearers]; and not as making a connected narrative of the Lord's discourses. So Mark committed no error, as he wrote down some particulars just as he recalled them to mind. For he took heed to one thing — to omit none of the facts that he heard, and to state nothing falsely in [his narrative of] them."[22] Zahn, in extensive comments upon the passage,[23] insists that the elder from whom Papias quotes is the apostle John himself. He argues that Mark is only said to have used the discourses of Peter for some of his writing, and that the lack of order with which Mark is charged is the natural consequence of the fact that Mark was a disciple of Peter and not of Christ, and an eyewitness like the apostle John could recognize the lack of order in the book. Further, he feels that the mention of recollecting Peter's discourses indicates that Mark wrote when Peter was not present or was already dead.[24] He feels that Irenaeus' language indicates knowledge of Papias' tradition and that his more explicit words confirm Zahn's interpretation of Papias.

Clement of Alexandria, on the other hand, clearly says that Mark wrote, or at least began to write, while Peter was alive. He says that while Peter was preaching in Rome some of those of equestrian rank at Rome who had heard Peter asked Mark to write down what Peter had spoken so that they might have it to keep. When Peter heard of this plan, he neither hindered nor encouraged Mark. Eusebius, quoting the tradition of Clement, says that Peter approved of the finished work. He adds that this is corroborated by Papias,[25] whose book, we may remark, was known by Eusebius as well as by Irenaeus. What we have remaining of Papias' work is due almost exclusively to Eusebius.

We have here two variant traditions. They may be harmonized, as Zahn does, by saying that Irenaeus is right, that Eusebius is wrong, that Clement refers only to a beginning of the writing during Peter's time, and that Papias should be interpreted accordingly. Another view actually suggested by Zahn[26] would be that Irenaeus' words are satisfied by the assumption that Mark began his work during Peter's lifetime but did not finish it or publish it (in a sense it was never finished as Mark 16:9ff. may well be a spurious addition!) until after his death. The words used by Irenaeus of Mark are ἐγγράφως ἡμῖν παραδέδωκεν, expressing it somewhat differently from Matthew and John. This would satisfy better the fact that Irenaeus is apparently the only ancient witness speaking of Mark's literary activity after Peter's death. Tertullian says only, but says repeatedly and emphatically, that Mark's Gospel is properly called Peter's.[27] We should realize that it is not absolutely necessary to harmonize all ancient tradition, though all should, of course, be seriously considered. Irenaeus may simply have been mistaken. Certainly the consistent voice of antiquity is to ascribe the Gospel by [or of] Mark to Peter, and even Irenaeus agrees with this.

It might be worth while to consider a fourth alternative. What was the relation of the Scripture authors to their amanuenses? What is meant by these terms of the Fathers — Mark, a "follower of Peter," or an "interpreter," or an "apostolic man," as Tertullian puts it? These terms do not indicate merely companions or disciples. The apostles had many hearers — Papias, Clement, Polycarp, Pothinus, and other unnamed elders are all recognized as such by the Fathers. Yet these men were not accorded any authority, nor did they claim any. But the apostles had certain helpers who are mentioned in the Scriptures as assisting in the writing. The indications are scanty, but they are clearly there. All know that Paul wrote Romans. Its authenticity is undoubted. Yet it concludes, "I Tertius, who wrote this epistle, salute you in the Lord" (Rom. 16: 22). First Peter likewise makes every claim to be the work of the great apostle. Yet it was written by Peter through Silas (I Pet. 5:12). Some have taken Galatians 6:11 to indicate that in this case Paul wrote the letter in his own hand — with large letters [28] because, perhaps, of poor vision — without an amanuensis. Zahn ably defends the genuineness of John 1:1 - 21:23, especially the last chapter,[29] but adds that verses 24 and 25 were added (still with John's approval) by the amanuensis.

We are led to conclude that the amanuensis was not a mere stenographer, but a trusted helper who could act as

research assistant, as private secretary, and companion in
the faith. Such a position would fit Mark well. The words
of the Gospel were Peter's, as Papias is careful to say.
Mark was careful not to omit anything or to state anything falsely. The first-century elder himself says that Mark
wrote with great accuracy. Yet the things he wrote were
not the words of Christ directly, for he was not Christ's
immediate disciple. He wrote Peter's words accurately, as
a capable amanuensis should. If it be insisted, as Zahn
does, that only some of the book was a reproduction of
Peter's teaching (though this is a large conclusion to hang
upon a single word indirectly reported), we may feel that
Mark supplemented the oral preaching with reference to
Matthew, for the uniform ancient tradition and usage indicates that Matthew was written first, modern Synoptic
criticism to the contrary.[30] Of course, any dependence of
Mark's Gospel upon Matthew's (and some interdependence
can hardly be denied) could be ascribed equally well to
Peter himself.

The further consideration of testimony to Mark is hardly
necessary as there is never any question of its canonicity,
nor serious question that Peter was in some way back of
Mark in the writing. Tertullian has numerous such references: "The same authority of the apostolic churches will
afford evidence to the other Gospels also, which we possess
equally through their means, and according to their usage
— I mean the Gospels of John and Matthew — whilst that
which Mark had published may be affirmed to be Peter's,
whose interpreter Mark was. For even Luke's form of the
Gospel men usually ascribe to Paul. And it may well seem
that the words which disciples publish belong to their
masters."[31] Note that Tertullian uses the ancient churches
for evidence, not authority. The authority stems from the
apostles. Again, "the evangelical Testament has apostles
for its authors, to whom was assigned by the Lord Himself this office of publishing the Gospel. Since, however,
there are apostolic men also, they are yet not alone, but
appear with apostles and after apostles; because the preach-

ing of apostles might be open to the suspicion of affecta-
tion of glory, if there did not accompany it the authority
of the masters, which means that of Christ, for it was that
which made the apostles their masters."[32] He speaks of
the company of the "Twelve" who had received the promised power of the Holy Spirit for the "gift of miracles and
of utterance."[33] With these he includes or equates Paul,
"who now should know better the marrow of the Scriptures than the school of Christ itself . . . To whom would
He rather have made known the veiled import of His own
language than to him to whom He disclosed the likeness
of His own glory — to Peter, John, and James, and afterwards to Paul?"[34] He equates the Old Testament with
the New Testament, and the terminology for the New is
the one form familiar from early days, "Gospels and
Apostles."[35] The truth of the writings is absolute: "What
man, then, of sound mind can possibly suppose that they
were ignorant of anything, whom the Lord ordained to
be masters? . . . Was anything withheld from Peter? . . .
Was anything concealed from John? . . . No doubt He
once said, 'I have yet many things to say unto you, but
ye cannot hear them now,' but even then He added, 'When
the Spirit of truth has come, He will lead you into all
truth.'"[36] "The apostles would never have taught things
which were self-contradictory, so the apostolic men could
not have inculcated teaching different from the apostles."[37]
"In the Lord's apostles we possess our authority, for even
they did not of themselves choose to introduce anything,
but faithfully delivered to the nations the doctrine which
they have received from Christ."[38]

Tertullian thus is explicit and quite in accord with the
views of the Fathers back to Clement, one hundred years
earlier, in so far as these men have spoken. He has a
corpus of Scripture of absolute authority equal to the Old
Testament. He refers by name or number to the four
Gospels, Acts, the thirteen Pauline Epistles, Hebrews, Jude,
and Revelation. He quotes also from I John and I Peter,
but omits reference to James, II and III John, and II Peter.[39]

The lack is not significant in view of the fact that there is less reason to quote these books. Jude is specifically quoted as authoritative and apostolic. Tertullian derives the authority of the books, even Mark and Luke, from apostles and declares that these men wrote under the inspiration of the Spirit and the commission of Christ. The books could have no contradiction, he emphasizes, and some of them could still be inspected in the churches founded by apostles.

At this point a few further ·remarks can be made regarding the Alexandrine doctrine, though Clement's view of Mark has already been given above. Clement of Alexandria was born in Greece about 150 A.D., and after his conversion he traveled to East and West. He finally settled in Alexandria at the school of Pantaenus, who himself was not far removed from the days of the apostles. Clement later became president of the school but had to flee the city under the persecution of Severus in 202 A.D. His witness is naturally of great value. Eusebius says that Clement used all the books of our New Testament except II Peter and II John.[40] Clement uses the phrase "Law and Prophets, and Gospels and apostles."[41] He ascribes full authority to the apostles: "We have as the source of the teaching, the Lord, both by the prophets, the Gospels, and the blessed apostles, 'in divers manners and at sundry times,' leading from the beginning of knowledge to the end. But if one should suppose that another origin was required, then no longer truly could an origin be preserved."[42] He speaks of the ministry of the apostles, including Paul, as ending with Nero.[43] Why he does not consider John's later work is not clear, but at least there is no thought of successors to the apostles. The apostles are limited to the original company: "After the Resurrection the Lord delivered the tradition of knowledge to James the Just, and John, and Peter, these delivered it to the other apostles, and the other apostles to the seventy, of whom also Barnabas was one."[44] Note the denial of apostolicity to Barnabas in spite of the broader usage of Acts 14:14. The fact is that Clement himself calls Barnabas an apostle once, but rather clearly in this broader sense.[45] Clement quotes noncanonical books occasionally, but evidently does not regard them as canonical. Charteris makes the comment that he is a litterateur rather than a theologian, a description which fits Clement's background and habits well.[46]

With the learned — but erratic — Origen we enter a later period (he died in 254 A.D.), and he is cited briefly here only because he possessed outstanding ability as a scholar and because he had in the library of his school a fund of information which we do not now have. His great work on the Old Testament text, the *Hexapla,* and his numerous commentaries and other writings are a study in themselves. His commentaries covered almost every book in both Testaments. He contrasts the "Divine Scriptures" of the "Old Testament" and the "New."[47] Westcott says that "he was acquainted with all the books which are received at present, and received as apostolic all those which were recognized by Clement. The others he used, but with a certain reserve and hesitation, arising from a want of information as to their history, rather than from any positive grounds of suspicion."[48] The authority of these books is, of course, the authority of Christ, but Origen is express in asserting that they are not merely accurate representations of Jesus' teaching. Actually the words of apostles *are* the words of Christ: "And by the words of Christ we do not mean those only which He spake when He became man and tabernacled in the flesh; for before that time, Christ, the Word of God, was in Moses and the prophets. . . . Moreover, that after His ascension into heaven He spake in His apostles, as shown by Paul in these words: 'Or do you seek a proof of Christ who speaketh in me?' "[49] Much more could be quoted from Origen, but this will suffice to show that the principle of canonicity is basically apostolic authorship. A few more details may be given in connection with the discussion of Hebrews.

We return to the other Gospel of irregular authorship, Luke, and its companion work, Acts. Many of the authorities quoted above in connection with the second Gospel also bear on Luke-Acts. The problem, moreover, is simpler in the present instance because the Lucan authorship is undisputed in antiquity, and the closeness of the author to Paul is plain for all to read in the "we sections" of Acts.[50]

Some of the very early witness which we possess for Matthew and Mark is lacking for Luke, though Westcott claims a parallel in I Clement to some of Christ's words recorded in Luke 6:36-38.[51] There is no reference in Ignatius to Luke-Acts, but Polycarp seems to use Acts 2:24.[52] Papias, it will be remembered, omits the Lucan writings completely. Still their antiquity is rendered certain by the fact that by 140 they were clearly referred to by heretic and orthodox alike. Justin refers to Luke as one of the unchangeable group of four Gospels, though he is aware, as in the case of Mark, that Luke wrote for Paul.[53] Marcion is of special interest here. It will be remembered that he refused to accept the writings of the Twelve as authoritative — though he knew of such works — but based all his teachings on Paul. Yet Marcion accepted the Gospel of Luke in mutilated form. He did not accept Acts, which, after all, devotes much time to Peter's ministry, but his acknowledgment of the abbreviated Gospel of Luke as Paul's is of special interest. The Muratorian Canon calls Luke "a disciple and fellow traveler of Paul."[54] Irenaeus says that he was "always attached to and inseparable from Paul" and "with him performed the work of an evangelist and was entrusted to hand down to us a Gospel."[55] Tertullian also called it Paul's Gospel written by Luke.[56] Clement of Alexandria says Luke composed Acts and translated Paul's Epistle to the Hebrews.[57] Origen uses a word similar to Irenaeus' and says that Luke "composed for Gentile converts . . . the Gospel commended by Paul."[58]

All the facts in the case are clear concerning Luke just as they are regarding Mark. Luke was, of course, a companion of Paul, but he was more. He was a follower, a helper, and an inseparable disciple. He was "entrusted" to write for Paul. Paul commended his work. The work may properly be called Paul's — even the heretics will admit as much. All the facts are explained if we regard Luke as an amanuensis in the free, first-century sense outlined above, that is, one who wrote down what Paul indicated he wanted. Nothing else will explain the plain testimony of both early and late antiquity that the number of the apostles was limited to the Twelve and that only apostolic writings were to be received as the Word of Christ, and yet Mark and Luke-Acts were received without question in all ancient and orthodox circles.

We turn now to the Books of Hebrews, James, II Peter, II and III John, Jude, and Revelation, whose apostolic authorship was sometimes denied and sometimes affirmed in antiquity. On what basis were they accepted into the canon?

The situation with regard to Revelation is rather clear. Widely accepted in the early days, it was later questioned, but soon regained its place and has been secure in orthodox circles since 400. The earliest writers, Clement, Ignatius, and Polycarp, do not mention it. This is not too surprising, as has already been noticed, for in Clement's day it had scarcely been written, and in Ignatius' time it was perhaps not yet well known in Antioch. Zahn argues similarly from the silence of Hermas and Didache.[59] Justin mentions the book by name and cites the doctrine that believers would dwell a thousand years in Jerusalem, which he ascribes to "John, one of the apostles of Christ."[60] The Muratorian Canon includes the Apocalypse and ascribes it to John.[61] Melito wrote a book on Revelation, but we are not told his views concerning its authorship.[62] A passage from Revelation 22:11 is quoted in the Epistle of the Churches of Vienne and Lyons, which tells of their persecution in 177 A.D., and is accompanied by the phrase "in order that the Scriptures may be fulfilled."[63] Irenaeus clearly accepts the book as from John the apostle and ascribes it to the end of Domitian's reign (96 A.D.).[64] Tertullian also quotes it frequently, saying it is by John the apostle.[65] Clement of Alexandria does the same.[66] As Zahn puts it: "In short, we have an unusually large number of

witnesses to the fact that between the years 100 and 180
Revelation was highly esteemed in the churches of Asia,
to which it was originally directed (Rev. 1:4, 11), and that
it was regarded as the work of John of Ephesus, who from
130 on, at the very latest, was generally held to be one
of the twelve apostles. Between 170 and 200 we find Revelation circulated and accepted in all parts of the Greek
and Latin Church as the work of the apostle and evangelist John."[67]

After this period however, Revelation suffered an eclipse.
Two influences came into play: the one was an increasing
departure from the premillennial expectations of the Early
Church, and the other was the influence of the Alogi. Anti-
Chiliastic tendencies appear in Egypt. Origen still accepted Revelation wholeheartedly as Scripture and from
the pen of the Apostle John,[68] but his pupil Dionysius the
Great (d. 264) argues that Revelation was by some other
author, though he still regards it as inspired. He knows
that others have opposed the book, but though he himself does not understand it, in view of the long sentiment
in its favor, he cannot set it aside. His arguments are
from diction and style rather than from any positive evidence against the ancient tradition. He has no new facts
beyond what we can observe ourselves today by comparing the Gospel and Revelation — and Alford remarks that
scholars today would disagree with Dionysius.[69]

Another voice against Revelation was, possibly, Caius,
of about 213 A.D. In debating with the Montanists, he
assigns to Cerinthus "revelations written, as he would have
us believe, by a great apostle" about an earthly kingdom
after Christ's return.[70] Stonehouse says that Caius ascribes
our Revelation to Cerinthus the heretic.[71] Westcott and
others declare that this is unlikely because Cerinthus' known
doctrine of Christ is not at all like that in Revelation.[70]
Westcott's view is that Caius referred to an imitation of
the Apocalypse. It may be pointed out, however, that
Caius might have ascribed the book to Cerinthus because
of the Chiliastic teaching and overlooked the book's ortho-

doxy in other respects. We know Cerinthus could not have written it, but perhaps Caius did not consider all angles of the problem.

At any rate, the view that Cerinthus wrote Revelation seems to have gained ground. Since in common tradition Revelation and the fourth Gospel were associated, the latter was also called Apocryphal. The Alogi heretics, as Epiphanius called them, ascribed all the Johannine writings (the Gospels, the first Epistle, and Revelation — all call Christ the *Logos*) to Cerinthus. "And so," remarks Westcott, drawing attention to the totally subjective nature of the argument, "this early essay in criticism was completed."[72] For us the point is that denial of the apostolic authorship carried with it denial of the book.

The Alogi were a little known and unimportant group. Revelation was soon accepted, in line with the universal tradition, by Hippolytus[73] in about 220 A.D. and by Victorinus of Pettau (d. 303), who wrote the oldest extant commentary on it.[74]

Eusebius (about 300 A.D.) vacillated on the subject. He acknowledged that the weight of tradition assigned the book to the Apostle John, but he believed Papias' remarks could be interpreted to refer to another John, not an apostle, so he questioned its apostolic authorship.[75] It is also worth while to observe that Eusebius was quite opposed to millennial teaching. Amphilocius of Iconium (about 390 A.D.) says, "The Apocalypse of John again some indeed receive, but most say that it is spurious."[76] This is the test. The anti-millennarians of later years, following poor criticism, had found an opportunity to deny its apostolic authorship and therefore expunged it. But Athanasius, in 367,[77] in his Festal Epistle, reverted to the older traditions of the Alexandrian canon and included Revelation in his list, where it has been ever since.

The only problem remaining is its omission from the Syriac Peshitto canon. History gives no answer. It is barely possible that the canon in Mesopotamia was formed before the Apocalypse reached it with competent evidence of its authorship, and thereafter it took centuries to establish itself. But where communication was easy and language was no barrier, the case was different. As Stonehouse says in his careful treatment, "It was the Church's conviction that the Apocalypse was apostolic in origin, and not its prophetic origin, which accounts for the high regard shown for the work. The question whether its prophecies were divine was settled once for all if the prophet was an apostle of Christ. And it is clear that apostolicity was the organizing principle of the New Testament of the Old Catholic Church in which the Apocalypse had a very secure place among 'the apostles.' "[78]

The minor Epistles are of less importance. External testimony to them is naturally more sparse. The question is: What is the nature of that testimony? Is II Peter by an apostle and was it received because it was so held? As to this Epistle, it is certainly clear that it was by Peter or it is a bold and clever lie. Its claim in 1:1, 1:14, 1:17, and 3:1 are quite clear. If it is to be believed at all, it is apostolic. External testimony for II Peter is weak. Polycarp may allude to it.[79] Origen refers to the second Epistle as disputed in his day, i.e., the authorship is disputed. Zahn admits that Origen was the first to refer to it and that through the fourth century doubts of its authorship and canonicity appear. He argues, however, that this is because it was sent to a different group of Jewish Christians and therefore had difficulty in establishing itself. He points to resemblances in wording, furthermore, to early writings: Hermas, I Clement, II Clement, and the Didache. And, finally, he insists that Jude, which was well established in an early time, definitely quotes II Peter, not only in Jude 17f., where it is called apostolic, but also in Jude 4. This should settle the matter, even though we cannot say why it was neglected in the early centuries.[80] The lack of clear testimony to its apostolic origin, however, was clearly the factor in the uncertainties of the fourth century.

The two last Epistles of John have sufficient testimony

to their genuineness, though it is not abundant. They are, after all, very short. The Muratorian Canon mentions two epistles of the Apostle John, and the context seems to indicate that the second and third are in view.[81] Clement of Alexandria does not mention II and III John but mentions the "greater" Epistle of John, implying that there was at least one other.[82] Origen speaks of the Epistles of John — the same as the author of the Apocalypse.[83] Thus the evidence is scanty, as we should expect, but it is all in the direction of a tradition of acknowledged apostolic authorship.

The problems connected with James and Jude are well known and may be discussed together. There are at least two Jameses and two Judes in the New Testament — possibly three of each. James the brother of John and son of Zebedee, and James the son of Alphaeus, are both repeatedly mentioned as apostles. Judas Iscariot also was one of the Twelve, and another Jude, called "the brother of James," is mentioned in Luke 6:16 and Acts 1:13.[84] Thus it appears that among the Twelve there were brothers named James and Jude. Also in Matthew 13:55 and Mark 6:3 a James and a Jude are mentioned among the "brethren of Jesus." For dogmatic reasons the Roman Catholic Church identified these two with the James and Jude who were among the Twelve. In any case, the father of the apostolic pair, Alphaeus, was married to Mary, the sister of Mary the mother of Jesus. At least comparison of John 19:25 with Mark 15:40 indicates that the two Marys, sisters, were at the Cross, and one is variously called the mother of James and the wife of Cleophas. It appears that Cleophas is to be identified with Alphaeus the father of James and Jude. So if there were half brothers of Jesus called James and Jude, they would have been cousins of the apostolic brothers James and Jude. This is the usual though not exclusive Protestant position.[85] The Roman Catholics hold that these pairs of brothers are one pair only, the sons of Alphaeus and Mary, the aunt of Jesus. The view held by the Roman Catholics presents no problem, for the Epistles James and Jude, if genuine, are clearly apostolic. We should remember that according to the usual Protestant view, these Epistles, if genuine, may very well still be apostolic, written by the sons of Alphaeus.

Ancient tradition is not too decisive, for it does not begin extremely early. Clement of Rome uses the Epistle of James, as does Hermas.[86] It is included in the Peshitto version. Jude is first mentioned in the Muratorian Canon; but James is there omitted. Westcott thinks that this omission is due to a possible hiatus.[87] Tertullian clearly (but only once) refers to the Epistle of Jude as authoritative and by "Jude the apostle."[88] That there is only this single reference in all of Tertullian's writings might teach us not to argue too heavily from silence in the earlier fragmentary witnesses. The witness of Clement of Alexandria is peculiar. Eusebius maintains that Clement commented on Jude, and his words could probably include James. Cassiodorus, of 575 A.D., remarks that Clement commented on the Epistle of St. James. But the Latin Adumbrations which we have include a work on Jude, not James, and he nowhere refers to James. Westcott concludes that Cassiodorus mistook Jude for James, but it also seems possible that Clement had a work on James now lost.[89] Origen includes both clearly in the canon[90] but gives no details as to his reasons.

Zahn insists that the Epistle of James was written by the half brother of the Lord.[91] He was clearly not the son of Zebedee, who was killed in 44 A.D. (Acts 12:2). This James is never mentioned without reference to his relationship to John or Zebedee. Zahn also notes that James the son of Alphaeus always has his relationship specified (Matt. 10:3; Mark 3:18; Luke 6:15; Acts 1:13). But there is a James mentioned repeatedly simply as James who held a position of leadership in the Jerusalem Church (Acts 12:17; 15:13-21; 21:18; Gal. 2:9). What Zahn does not notice is that all of the references which mention the name James in connection with a distinguishing relationship are from the time before the execution of the son of Zebedee (even including Gal. 1:19). In that period a distinguishing epithet would be helpful. After 44 A. D. the name James alone would be sufficient if there were only one left, or if the other were in a very minor position. Zahn cites the traditions, "partly legendary," of Clement of Alexandria, Hegesippus, etc., that there was such an eminent James, first bishop of Jerusalem, and brother of the Lord. It is just possible that this tradition is wrong, and that the pre-eminent James of Acts 12:17, etc. — or the only James — was the remaining apostle, brother of Jude. In this case also our Epistles would stand as apostolic if genuine.

However, even if Zahn is correct, it may yet be inferred that the half brothers of Christ, like Paul, were also inducted into the apostolic office as those born out of due time. First Corinthians 15:7 certainly tells of a resurrection appearance to an unspecified James whom we would suppose to be this eminent James, the son of Zebedee being dead when Paul wrote I Corinthians. Also Galatians 1:19 seems to include James, the Lord's brother — or cousin — with the apostles. It may well be that the complicated relationships of the different men called James is what resulted in some uncertainty as to the acceptance of these books. If the Roman Church is right, there is no uncertainty. If the usual Protestant view is right, the Epistles still may be by members of the Twelve. Or if they are by the half brothers of Jesus, these may have been counted as apostles in a special way. The New Testament certainly indicates that they could qualify. It is interesting that our first reference to the author of one of them by name — Tertullian — specifies that Jude was an apostle. We at least do not have enough information to deny the apostolic authorship of these two Epistles.

There remains only the much-discussed book of Hebrews. It is a question whether the many investigations have advanced beyond the conclusions of Origen of seventeen hundred years ago. Origen's remark is often quoted: "Who wrote the Epistle, in truth, God knows." It should be remembered, however, that the context of this remark argues that the Epistle is Pauline: "If I gave my opinion, I should say that the thoughts are those of the apostle, but the diction and phraseology are those of someone who remembered the apostolic teachings, and wrote down at his leisure what had been said by his teacher. Therefore if any church holds that this Epistle is by Paul, let it be commended for this. For not without reason have the ancients handed it down as Paul's. But who wrote the Epistle, in truth, God knows."[92]

This Epistle can claim an ancient pedigree, as it was referred to numerous times by Clement of Rome in 95 A.D., but not by name.[93] Justin Martyr does the same, quoting the unique designation of Christ as the "Son and apostle of God."[94] The early Ophite heretics, and Valentinus also, probably used Hebrews.[95] Early information on the authorship comes from Egypt. Eusebius quotes Clement as quoting Pantaenus to this effect: "And as the blessed presbyter [Pantaenus?] used to say, since the Lord, as being the apostle of the Almighty, was sent to the Hebrews, Paul through his modesty, inasmuch as he was sent to the Gentiles, does not inscribe himself apostle of the Hebrews, both on account of the honor due to the Lord, and because it was a work of supererogation that he addressed an Epistle to the Hebrews also, since he was herald and apostle of the Gentiles." Clement himself is quoted to say "that the Epistle to the Hebrews is Paul's," but that it was written to the Hebrews in the Hebrew dialect, and that Luke, having carefully translated it, published it for the use of the Greeks.[96] Westcott remarks, "The testimony to the Pauline origin of the Epistle to the Hebrews which is contained in this passage is evidently of the greatest value. There can be little doubt that the 'blessed presbyter' was Pantaenus; and thus the tradition is carried up almost to the apostolic age."[96] Origen, as we have quoted him above, accepts the same tradition, as do all the later Alexandrians.

Turning to the West, we find the viewpoint of Irenaeus is thus summarized by Westcott: "Some coincidences of language with the Epistle to the Hebrews are more striking;

and in a later chapter Eusebius states that in a book now lost Irenaeus 'mentions the Epistle to the Hebrews and the Wisdom of Solomon.' Agreeably with this, the Epistle to the Hebrews appears to be quoted in the second Pfaffian fragment as the work of St. Paul; but on the other hand, Photius classes Irenaeus with Hippolytus as denying the Pauline authorship of the Epistle. And this last statement leads the way to the most probable conclusion: Irenaeus was, I believe, acquainted with the Epistle, but he did not attribute it to St. Paul."[97] It should be noted, however, that the view that Irenaeus denied the Pauline authorship is late and not unanimous.

Tertullian is the first clear testimony from the West, and we must give his words in full: "The discipline of the apostles is thus clear and decisive . . . [he has been arguing in favor of his Montanism]. I wish, however, though it be superfluous, to bring forward also the testimony of a companion of the apostles, well fitted to confirm the discipline of his teachers on the point before us. For there is extant an Epistle to the Hebrews which bears the name of Barnabas. The writer has consequently adequate authority (*adeo satis auctoritati viri*) as being one whom St. Paul placed beside himself in the point of continence; and certainly the Epistle of Barnabas is more commonly received among the churches than the Apocryphal Shepherd of adulterers . . . [he then quotes Hebrews 6:4-8 and proceeds] one who had learnt from the apostles, and had taught with the apostles, knew this that a second repentance was never promised by the apostles to an adulterer or fornicator."[98]

Westcott concludes from this that Hebrews was not in the African canon or Tertullian would have emphasized the witness of Hebrews 6:4-8, which was directly in line with his argument, nor would he have compared it with the Shepherd. But he adds, "It is by this mark that Tertullian distinguishes between the Epistle of St. Jude and the Epistle (of Barnabas) to the Hebrews. The one was stamped with the mark of an apostle; the other was

neither that, nor yet supported by direct apostolic sanction."[99] Zahn comes to a similar conclusion.[100] The words
of Tertullian, however, do not clearly say this. He indeed
remarks that to add the witness from Hebrews is superfluous, and he adds it last. That might be, however, because the book was not always accepted by others. He
himself may well have received it. He seems to say that
the author has sufficient authority. He does not compare
Hebrews with Hermas except to the latter's detriment.
Actually Tertullian's words concerning Barnabas that he
was a "companion" of the apostles whom "St. Paul placed
beside himself . . . who had learnt from the apostles, and
had taught with the apostles," etc., elevate him far above
Hermas, which he calls "Apocryphal." These terms for
Barnabas are actually parallel to his designation of Mark
and Luke as "followers," "disciples," etc., of the apostles,
who therefore were "apostolic men" writing *for* the apostles.
It would seem possible to hold that Tertullian did actually
accept Hebrews and accepted it because it derived from
the apostles, specifically Paul.

Of course, if Hebrews is related to any apostle, it is
to Paul. This is shown not only because of viewpoint, his
relation with Timothy, etc., but also because it explicitly
claims to be written by a second-generation author (Heb.
2:3, 4). This passage at the beginning of the book bears
striking resemblance in viewpoint to Luke 1:2. No apostle
other than Paul is seriously mentioned in connection with
the writing of Hebrews.

The next witness in the West is Caius (about 213 A.D.),
who is reported by Eusebius as enumerating only "thirteen
Epistles of the holy apostle, not counting that to the Hebrews with the others. And unto our day there are some
among the Romans who do not consider this the work
of an apostle."[101] Hippolytus' (about 220 A.D.) testimony
comes to us second and third hand. Stephanus, of 600 A.D.,
claims that Hippolytus and Irenaeus do not say that the
Epistle to the Hebrews was by Paul.[102] Zahn remarks that
probably Stephanus gets his information about Irenaeus

through Hippolytus. Zahn believes that Irenaeus quoted Hebrews without naming the author.[103] It must be admitted that on such a questionable subject this evidence is very thin. We should like to know in context just what Hippolytus said. Perhaps he said no more than Tertullian, who urged that it was by Barnabas, a man joined to Paul, etc., which could be taken in either of two ways, depending on what we mean by the expression "by Paul."

Cyprian, Tertullian's pupil, does not use Hebrews, though he would be expected to do so since Hebrews 6:4-8 is so germane to the problem of the lapsed, those who had denied the faith under persecution. He further likens Paul's writing to seven churches, to the seven epistles of John in Revelation. The seven churches of Paul do not count Hebrews.[104] Again, however, this evidence is not explicit. The Epistle to the Hebrews is, in any event, not to a church any more than are four other of Paul's epistles. The same thought of seven churches addressed by Paul reappears in Victorinus of Pettau (d. 303). When we remember to what lengths commentators will go to find the number seven, we should not be surprised if Hebrews were excluded so as to make the correct number regardless of the opinion of its authority. More definite information is desired. Jerome, at about 400 A.D., does indeed give that opinion in his day. "The apostle Paul writes to seven churches, for this eighth Epistle to the Hebrews is by most excluded from the number."[105] Jerome, of course, included it in his translation. It was included in Athanasius' Festal Letter of 367. Eusebius of Antioch (270-340 A.D.) had said, "Of Paul the fourteen Epistles commonly received are at once manifest and clear. It is not, however, right to ignore the fact that some have rejected the Epistle to the Hebrews, asserting that it is gainsayed by the Church of Rome as not being Paul's."[106] He elsewhere remarks that Clement of Rome quotes it, and that it is therefore not recent and should be reckoned as by the apostle. He explains the differences from the Pauline Epistles as due to a translation and suggests Clement himself.[107] We note that according to Eusebius of Palestine the entire Church received Hebrews as Pauline except the West, and there the whole question revolved around the point of authorship.

The situation is that Hebrews was always received in the East and received as Pauline — though with a translator of some kind often mentioned. In the West the book was received early, though its authorship is not stated. Later there is some evidence — though the evidence actually is quite scanty and usually overdrawn — that the Pauline authorship was questioned, and therefore the Epistle's canonicity was questioned. The name of Barnabas is associated with the production in some way by Tertullian, but not as independent author. Indeed, Tertullian's testimony is not entirely clear. The Montanist controversies and problems about the lapsed probably made the Epistle a problem for the stricter party. Still the two Theodotians who were in Rome in the times of Hippolytus seem to have maintained the Pauline authorship.[108] This view so long held in the churches of Syria and Alexandria and the East in general finally prevailed, and thereafter discussion was only sporadic. The history of the Epistle is very instructive in its bearing on why books were accepted by the ancient Church. It was accepted as canonical in those places — and in only those places — where it was considered to be a genuine work of Paul. Appeal was not made to its antiquity nor to the testimony of the Holy Spirit nor to any other auxiliary reason. Authorship was what was decisive.

It is a further question as to whether the ancient churches were right. Can the contemporary Church accept Hebrews as Pauline? This is largely a study in special introduction and we can only outline the case. The same problems arise for us which troubled the ancients. The style of the Greek is not like that of the Pauline epistles. If we, with Zahn, deny that it could have been written in Hebrew and translated,[109] we are forced to accept the view that it is either not Pauline or that he used an amanuensis. Origen solved the problem simply by calling Luke or Clement the amanuensis. Attention was drawn to similarities in style with Luke. Now, if Luke-Acts be denied the adjective Pauline, the same must be true of Hebrews. But in view of the complete satisfaction in the second century with the idea that Mark, Luke, and Acts were by apostles using secondary authors, it would seem that we may be satisfied with respect to Hebrews also. Zahn acutely draws attention to the fact that the Old Testament quotation in Hebrews 10:30 departs from the Septuagint text in the same way that the same quotation in Romans 12:19 does.[110] The almost identical wording of the Habakkuk 2:4 quotation in Romans 1:17, Galatians 3:11, and Hebrews 10:38 could also be noted. These could be accounted for as quotations from the Pauline Epistles, but are perhaps more easily explained as being the product of the single mind behind both Hebrews and Paul's letters and the Hebrews quotation is longer than that in Romans and Galatians.

Zahn summarizes his conclusion thus: "It appears, therefore, from the above discussion, that there existed, between the years 180 and 260, three more or less widely diffused opinions regarding the authorship of Hebrews which stood over against each other — (1) Paul (held by the Alexandrians, and perhaps the Theodotians in Rome); (2) Barnabas (held by the Montanist Tertullian, evidently already by the Phrygian Montanists, and also by the Catholic churches of the province of Asia, as well as by the Novatians); (3) some unknown person (Irenaeus, Hippolytus, and probably still other Catholics of the West). The common source of the threefold tradition can only be the third view."[111] Some of the evidence Zahn refers to is slight indeed. But in any case his conclusion is not necessary. Instead of assuming that it was an anonymous writing which had attached to it two different names, it is easier to believe that it was a genuine Epistle of Paul using Barnabas as his secretary. This would at once explain the early unquestioned acceptance (no other anonymous work was so accepted), the variation in style from Paul's, the anonymity where the details of authorship were not known and only the style problem appeared, and the double tradition of authorship in other circles. The tradition of Barnabas' authorship is not too well established and another may have served; there would be no difference in principle.

Our conclusion is that the Early Church was not misled when it used the principle that that is inspired which is apostolic. They clearly included in their concept that which was prepared under direction of the apostles. The very sources which tell us of the Mark and Lucan authorship also tells us they were secondary authors. This concept of apostles and men commissioned by the apostles clearly includes all the New Testament except possibly Hebrews, James, and Jude. Scrutiny of the evidence shows that Hebrews will fit into the same category with Mark and Luke. James and Jude, on the other hand, can well be defended as by apostles — so they were understood in the second century.

The test of the Early Church is not arbitrary, nor was it arrived at long after, by intuition or the general leading of the Spirit. It is actually witnessed to within the apostolic period, and it is based on the promises of Christ and the injunctions of the apostles themselves. Indeed, the Early Church was conscious that the apostles held their position by virtue of the double relationship of Christ's commission and the Holy Spirit's enduement. No other men could claim this twofold authority, and none did. This authority extended to the ministry of the apostles to such an extent that all their words were regarded, and their writings preserved. We have no evidence whatever that there were writings of apostles which the Early Church refused, and no solid information that there were letters of the apostles which were not treasured and were therefore lost. It is a condition contrary to fact to argue that an apostle's writing which did not agree with established truth and previous revelation would be rejected. Of course it would. An angel from heaven could be rejected under similar circumstances. But the universal view of the Early Church and the Bible is that angels from heaven do not speak contrary to truth, and neither do apostles.[112] Their words and their writings are to be received without addition or subtraction upon pain of the curse of God (Rev. 22:18, 19).

CHAPTER 13

WAS THE LAW AND THE PROPHETS TWO-THIRDS OF THE OLD TESTAMENT CANON?[*]

A dozen times in the New Testament and about four times in the Dead Sea Scrolls, the expression is used, "The Law and the Prophets" or a very similar phrase. The most exalted things are said about these collections. They are of more striking witness than a resurrection from the dead — Luke 16:31. They are eternal as the heavens, not a jot or tittle shall fail — Matthew 5:17, 18. Such statements have caused many students to come to the conclusion that the Old Testament canon is regarded as fixed and immutable in the New Testament. It has been held that these expressions of a twofold canon are equal to the terminology of the threefold division in Luke 24:44. The Dead Sea Scrolls do not show a threefold division at all, but their contemporary, the prologue to Ecclesiasticus, evidences a threefold division in 132 B.C. as does Josephus at about A.D. 90.

What is the meaning of these varying expressions? Orthodox Protestant students have equated all of them as merely variant names for the Hebrew Old Testament canon of our 39 books. The writer has previously argued that the twofold terminology came first and the threefold developed from that.

Liberal scholars for many years have held a development view of the Old Testament canon. They base much on the threefold division as reported in the Talmud of the fourth century A.D. Their claim is that the Pentateuch was canonized in Ezra's time, about 400 B.C., the prophets soon after at about 200 and the Writings — eleven books in the Hebrew Bible — were not canonized until the Council of Jamnia in A.D. 90.

[*] Reprinted by permission from the Bulletin of the Evangelical Theological Society, Vol. 9, No. 4, Fall 1966.

An additional problem arises in that the Septuagint includes seven extra books and additional portions of others. How may this be explained? Orthodox Protestants have said that this usage was probably not original in the LXX and in any case was not accepted in the early church. Liberals have held that the more inclusive LXX canon was due to the practice of the Alexandrian Jews which the Christian Church uncritically took over. This is the so-called Alexandrian theory. The Roman Church, of course, accepts these apocryphal books on the basis of alleged tradition.

This whole field is now being seriously re-examined. The Dead Sea Scrolls do show that the division into two parts, the Law and the Prophets, is pre-Christian and requires explanation. There has also been an attack upon the significance and even historicity of the Council of Jamnia (by Jack Lewis of Harding College, "What do we mean by Jabneh?" *Journal of Bible and Religion*, Vol. 32, 1964, pp. 125-132). It will not do just lightly to by-pass this discussion and go on accepting a Council which is admittedly dubious. Also, as pointed out by Floyd Filson in his book *Which Books Belong in the Bible?* it is not careful scholarship to assume that the original LXX canon differed from the Hebrew canon merely because our LXX copies of the fourth century include extra books. The whole concept of a differing Alexandrian canon is being called in question, and rightly so.

In this situation a new theory is being advanced to explain the alleged difference between the Hebrew and Christian canon. It has been ably developed by Albert Sundberg, Jr. *(The Old Testament of the Early Church)* and in the writer's opinion will probably be the ruling view in critical circles in the foreseeable future. In brief the view accepts the threefold development view of the Jewish canon. First the Pentateuch was canonized at 400 B.C., then the Prophets at 200 B.C., finally the Writings were accepted at A.D. 90.

However, Sundberg makes much of the fact that the Christian Church split away from Judaism at around A.D. 70 when Jerusalem fell. He argues that this fact explains why the two groups share the same Law and Prophets. But the Christian

Church did not close its third division at the same time nor with the same books as did the Jews.

The Jews at A.D. 70 had a fixed canon of Law and a fixed Canon of Prophets. They also had an amorphous collection of other books that at Jamnia was settled as the eleven Writings. The Christians of A.D. 70 had the same Law and Prophetical books as the Jews. They also had an amorphous collection of other books that were more or less accepted and were finally adopted in the LXX copies and in the Council of Augustine's day to make the more inclusive canon of Catholicism. This view appears at first sight to explain neatly the difference between the LXX and Hebrew canon. Unfortunately it does not take into account all the facts and furthermore it builds on the threefold development view of the canon which is itself based on critical positions of the past. Some of these positions are now being abandoned leaving this view without adequate support in important points.

We should like to discuss this view with regard to three major points. First, what was the extent of the sections designated Law and Prophets in the first century? Second, did the early Christian Church in fact include an amorphous collection of books in its Old Testament canon? Third, is the threefold development theory of the Old Testament canon still justified in the light of new evidence? Our emphasis at present will be on the first two points as we have discussed the third at length elsewhere.

To begin with, we ask the question, what was the extent of the sections designated Law and Prophets in the New Testament? This question Sundberg does not specifically answer. He follows R. Pfeiffer and many others (op. cit. p. 38) in the assumption that the division of the Law, Prophets and Writings as held in our Hebrew Bibles today were the same in extent in the first century A.D. He offers no proof. No proof can be offered. The first list of the Old Testament books agreeing with the divisions of our Hebrew Bible is in the Talmud coming from about A.D. 400. The first list of the Old Testament books of any sort comes from Melito Bishop of Sardis at A.D. 170 and it departs widely from the Talmud order and division. It seems extremely odd that the majority of Old Testament critical scholars make the bold assumption that there was no shift in the order of the Hebrew books and their division from the first century to the fifth. Even more strange is their approach to the witness of Josephus.

Josephus does not give us a list, but he does give us the number of books in his three divisions — 5, 13, and 4. This is in sharp contrast to the later Talmud listing of 5, 8, and 11. Yet instead of adopting Josephus' witness for the first century situation or even facing Josephus' testimony, Sundberg virtually ignores it. He adequately presents Josephus' listing as including the Pentateuch in the first division; the books of Psalms, Proverbs, Ecclesiastes, and Song of Solomon in the last division and the others (with or without Esther) in the second division (op. cit. p.134). But his comment is "Even Josephus seems to reflect a tripartite division of the Scriptures, though his divisions are highly irregular" and "while the number of the books is the same, Josephus' order remains peculiar to him." Other authors of similar bent make the same astonishing assumption. The assumption is that Josephus of the first century exhibits an odd order because he does not follow the Talmud of the 5th century! We may not be able to tell why these two authorities differ, but it would seem to be poor methodology indeed to argue for the first century situation on the basis of the later Talmud listing and then castigate Josephus' contemporary listing as irregular and peculiar. Why not accept his listing as decisive when there is no contradicting evidence from the times?

Actually Josephus' listing is not as strange as it seems. Josephus assembles the 5 books of Moses and in another division Psalms, Proverbs, Ecclesiastes, and Song of Solomon, apparently. In Sundberg's presentation out of 22 early Christian lists, there are 16 that associate these four books, Psalms, Proverbs, Ecclesiastes, and Song of Solomon, together (pp. 58, 59). This would seem to argue that some principle associated these four books and that same principle may be evidenced in the listing Josephus followed. There is no warrant for by-passing Josephus' witness on the divisions of the Hebrew Bible.

But if Josephus' witness is followed, Sundberg's theory is seen to be highly questionable and the threefold development theory falls to the ground.

Consider the threefold development theory. Would any serious critical writer believe that Josephus' second division was canonized in 200 B.C.? That division according to Sundberg includes "Joshua, Judges, I-IV Kings, Isaiah, Jeremiah, Lamentations, Ezekiel, the Twelve, Ezra, Chronicles, Daniel, Job, Ruth (or if Josephus counted Esther, he may have counted Jeremiah and Lamentations as one work and thus exactly have paralleled the contents of the Jamnia canon)" (p. 134). Naturally orthodox scholars find no difficulty in the early canonization of these books (and also Psalms, Proverbs, Ecclesiastes, and Song of Solomon). But the hinge of the critical theory is the dating of Daniel after the second division was closed. To have Josephus' second division admitted as standard and canonized by 200 B.C. would put Daniel early and would be revolutionary indeed for criticism.

Furthermore, consider Sundberg's theory that the third division was not canonized until Jamnia. If Josephus' second division was already accepted why was Ezekiel questioned? Indeed this is a problem on either Sundberg's or Pfeiffer's view and the case of Ezekiel proves that Jamnia was not elaborating a canon but dealing with old problems as Christians and Jews both have done many times. Does Luther's questioning of James indicate that the Christian Church had no New Testament canon before the Reformation? Also why was Proverbs questioned at Jamnia? The New Testament evidence for Proverbs is clear and it is quoted with the formula "Scriptures saith" in the Zadokite document, portions of which were found in the Dead Sea Caves. The Psalms are surely quoted as authoritative in the New Testament and even the new scroll of Psalms, which includes some surprises, is taken by P. Skehan to be derived from our well-known Psalter (Patrick Skehan, "The Biblical Scrolls from Qumran and the Text of the Old Testament" BA XXVIII, No. 3 [Sept. 1965] p. 100). Sundberg cites Jamnia as refusing Sirach "and any books written after his time" (op. cit. p. 114). How does this fit with the inclusion of Daniel (written, according to the critics, after Sirach) and the exclusion of Tobit which is now thought by some to have been much earlier than Sirach? Clearly other factors entered into the original canonization of books than mere chonology. The scholars of Jamnia were actually rehashing old problems.

We should make a further point. Josephus was not a Jamnia scholar. Josephus first fought the Romans before A.D. 70, then turned about and became a friend of the Romans against the Jews. His witness given at A.D. 90 is hardly a synopsis of Jamnia. He speaks as if the 22 book canon were long established. "It is become natural to all Jews, immediately and from their very birth, to esteem these books to contain divine doctrines, and to persist in them, and, if occasion be, willingly to die for them" (Against Apion, 1-8). This he says just after enumerating the 22 books. In view of this evidence it seems impossible for Sundberg and others to maintain that there were 11 books of the Writings as listed by the Talmud which were uncertain in their canonicity as late as A.D. 70.

Furthermore, Sundberg gives no evidence from the Rabbis that a large group of other Jewish writings were clamoring for canonicity in the first century. His discussion of the Qumran material leaves something to be desired. He mentions the many non-canonical pieces found at Qumran. He says then that "it is not possible at the present state of investigation to state the exact relation of the extra-canonical works to those of the Hebrew canon" (p. 97). He quotes others — B. J. Roberts and J. Carmignac — to the effect that no line of canonization was clearly drawn (p. 98). The writer is not prepared to admit this. The Qumran scribes may well have used a wide literature, but only the canonical literature is quoted as authoritative or commented on. The opinion of Roberts and Carmignac may be questioned. That the Jews of the first century used many books is undoubtedly true. But that they had no limits to the third division of their canon before Jamnia is contradicted by Josephus' explicit testimony and is not proved by Qumran evidence. We turn now to Sundberg's second point: the early church also had an amorphous third division of its canon which was not closed for years and which at last included more than the 22 books of Jamnia.

The first point of interest is that actually the early church had no third division of any kind, amorphous or not! The only reference to a threefold division in Christian circles is in Luke 24:44, a reference quite in accord with Josephus and not usual to the New Testament or later usage. As mentioned above, Sundberg lists 22 early Christian listings from Melito to Augustine and none of them is divisible into three parts except one of Jerome's listings which *could* be divided like the contemporary Talmud listing of the Jews whom Jerome had come to know and appreciate. All the other Christian listings exclude a threefold division of the type of either Josephus' or the Talmud. Strange, then, that the Christians took over a fixed Law and Prophets and struggled to bring order out of an amorphous third division!

The second remarkable point is that the 22 Christian listings with few exceptions follow the number of the books in the Jewish canon of Josephus and the later Talmud. It just is not true that the early church was not interested in canon or had no definite Old Testament canon. The books are listed by many authors and frequently the number of the books is given as corroborative evidence. The authorities giving a larger canon like the later LXX copies are all 4th century. They are Pseudo Chrysostom, Augustine (though he speaks variously in various places) and the Councils of Rome, and Hippo which Augustine influenced. The others are largely earlier and they exclude the apocryphal books except that Jeremiah sometimes includes Baruch and the Epistle. Sometimes II Esdras is included which is in some cases merely a name for Nehemiah, sometimes a copy of Ezra-Nehemiah, with some additions. In view of these facts it seems hardly possible to claim that the early Christian Church had a canon differing from the canon of the Jews. The Church did indeed know and use other books and this doubtless becomes the basis for the larger Catholic canon based on tradition, but the early Christian authors are plain enough on these matters.

Sundberg is aware of these facts and presents them in handy

form. His excuse for not abiding by the natural conclusion is curious. He says all these early authors were under Jewish influence.

Melito of Sardis (A.D. 170) is admitted as presenting a 22 book canon probably under Jewish influence. Esther is omitted. Why we do not know. The old theory is that there are Greek additions to Esther at the beginning and therefore the Jews when queried would not recognize this book. It will be remembered that the Jews named their books by the first word of the book. Melito says he went to Palestine to get an authoritative opinion. It is of passing interest that a huge prominent Jewish synagogue has been excavated at Sardis dating from near Melito's time. Quite probably Melito and the Jewish community had many questions between them. One can hardly think that he was under undue Jewish influence. He seems to have had a mind of his own and a desire to investigate adequately.

Origen says, "But it should be known that there are 22 canonical books as the Hebrews have handed them down." Sundberg argues from various expressions of Origen's writing that he was merely stating the Hebrew opinion not his own. His arguments seem hardly convincing. The very wording of Origen's statement shows he was in agreement with the Jewish sources.

Athanasius also is said to show Jewish influence. His words are unequivocal. Actually the pervasive Jewish influence which Sundberg cites is good evidence against his conclusion. It just is not true that the Jews went one way and the Christians another after A.D. 70 without influence of the one group on the other. The Hebrew canon was known and held authoritative, Melito the first witness being explicit. The fact that Athanasius shows a looser usage in this manner of quotation should teach us not to depend too much on quotations by the Fathers. They did not have concordances, memory is faulty, and practice inconsistent. Sundberg strangely alleges that Athanasius was trying to bring the Church back from a broader view to the Jewish view. We wonder what Melito was trying to do two centuries earlier? Gregory of Nazianzus, Cyril of Jerusalem,

Epiphanius of Salamis also allege the Jewish canon. Tertullian, not mentioned by Sundberg, gives the number as held by the Jews.

Sundberg theorizes that these men used the Jewish listing of books, but in study used the LXX codices with their extra books. Origen and Epiphanius give both a transliterated Hebrew name and the Greek name of each book. We must note that Sundberg assumes that the early LXX codices included the apocryha as did the later ones. Actually the Chester Beatty manuscript did. We have no earlier evidence.

That the Church counted 22 books, Sundberg attributes partly to numerology. Twenty-two books are desired, there being 22 letters in the Hebrew alphabet. This number again is of Hebrew influence as was the variant 27 (counting the final forms of 5 letters extra). This alleged correlation of Jewish thought with Christian usage was not a flashback, but was the natural thing for a church which had adopted a Jewish book for its rule of faith.

Sundberg similarly treats the Western Fathers. Hilary of Poitiers, (died A.D. 368), is straightening out his earlier usage. Jerome is influenced by his Jewish teachers. Only Augustine gives us "the full description of the canon of the Old Testament of the church" (p. 157) — though Sundberg does not quote Augustine's variant usage where he denies Maccabees to be canonical. Rufinus first sided with Jerome then reacted and agreed with Augustine. This only shows that by the latter time a broader view was coming to prominence.

Sundberg can not prove his point with any more certainty than Roman theologians have been able to do. The Early Church did not have a flexible canon. It had the Jewish Canon, and the Jewish canon was not new with Jamnia. It was as old as the prophets that wrote it.

There are two further considerations I should like to add. First, Sundberg is at once both too loose and too free in his treatment of New Testament quotations. It is true that the church Fathers quote somewhat loosely and sometimes quote the apocrypha as inspired whereas they state elsewhere that they are not. We may learn from this that such expressions as "the Scripture (i.e. the Writing) saith" or "it is written" or "it saith" perhaps should not be overemphasized. But there are numerous New Testament statements ascribing the Old Testament writings to God or God's Spirit by the hand of the prophet. Such phrases are not used of the non-canonical books. That there are allusions to such books and that the history of such books is used does not mean that these books were semi-canonical, but only that they were considered profitable and in places true.

The most extreme case has been overemphasized — the quotation of Enoch in Jude. No list of any Church Father includes Enoch as canonical. Sundberg does not mention that the New Testament three times quotes Greek profane authors without in the slightest implying their canonicity. In Titus 1:12 a Cretan is quoted and actually called a prophet. Yet the quotation is obviously for illustration only. The same may be claimed of the treatment of Enoch in Jude 14. The phrase Enoch the Seventh from Adam occurs more than once in the book of Enoch; it is not an Old Testament phrase. It seems to identify the quotation as from the book of Enoch rather than from the historical patriarch Enoch. That the quotation is said to prophesy certain things need mean no more than Paul does when he cites a Cretan prophet. It is not a clear case of quoting Enoch as canonical in view of similar citations in Paul. We must not allow scholars to make too much of this word of Jude. At the same time we can admit that this quotation may have led some early Church Fathers to vacillate in their use of Enoch and make more of it than was necessary. In their careful treatment and sober listings Enoch was uniformly excluded.

The other addendum I would give is that the divisions of the so-called council of Jamnia are often quoted without noting the nature of the arguments. Why was Proverbs questioned? Obviously because it has an apparent contradiction in 26:4, 5. The book had been accepted as canonical, but how could it be with this problem? Likewise Ezekiel had a problem of a variant temple worship. Ecclesiastes and the Song of Solomon have a problem of the nature of their material. These are problems such as Luther found in James. And in the case of James the implication is that these books were already considered canonical. This must be admitted by all for Ezekiel. It should be admitted for the others. There is here therefore no place for a definitive action of a fictitious Council. The whole 22 books were accepted. But the rejection of Sirach by the men of Jamnia was on other grounds. They were recent (Sirach was well known to be 180 B.C.) and the implication is they were after the era of prophecy. All the valid Old Testament books were known to be early. The Dead Sea Scrolls give further evidence on this point.

The Dead Sea Scrolls have not decided all questions of canonicity, it is true, but they have added some new facts. Sundberg himself (p. 38) admits that Chronicles was written at 400 B.C. not 250 B.C. as critics long have thought. Why then was this book not included among the prophets like its counterparts Samuel-Kings? Ecclesiastes is now found in a copy of 150 B.C. Its editor (Muilenberg) dates the original as at least 250 B.C. Why was it still questioned by the Jamnia scholars when the Apocalyptic Daniel was not? And if Daniel was Maccabean and Enoch about contemporary why was one of these apocalyptic books accepted and the other rejected? Job is now found in a copy of 200 B.C. written in paleo Hebrew script and has a pre-Christian Targum. Why was it placed in the third division rather than the second if chronological considerations were decisive? These and other questions are raised by the Dead Sea material and the threefold development theory does not have the answers. The old orthodox view that the canon consisted of the books of prophets as I would hold or of prophets and men known to be inspired as some say, is still in line with all the facts although it does not fit the conclusions of destructive criticism.

As mentioned earlier, I have previously alleged that the "Law and the Prophets" of the Dead Sea Scrolls and the New Testament comprised the whole Old Testament in a twofold division. Dr. Allan A. MacRae suggests that the threefold division was possibly the consequence of liturgical factors. I am now not sure that the twofold division was earlier. After all, the prologue to Ecclesiasticus is contemporary with the Dead Sea Scrolls, and it shows the threefold usage. Critics say it is an inchoate third division. One can hardly prove that, if Josephus' third division comprising only 4 books is taken as a standard. But in any case I now feel it equally possible to hold that the twofold division was a variant practice followed by the Dead Sea community and by the Christian Church and the practice paralleled the Rabbinic practice of dividing into 3 sections, which practice eventually was solidified in the Talmud arrangement. None of the Early Christian witnesses suggest a threefold division. The New Testament uses the expression Law and Prophets yet cites material as authoritative from books appearing in the Talmudic third division. All is clear and all the facts are accounted for if we say that the Law and the other books listed by fathers of the Early Church were the "Law and the Prophets" of the New Testament and the "Law" and "books of the Prophets" of the Dead Sea Scrolls. The idea that Christ and the Apostles only held two thirds of the Old Testament to be canonical in the first century has many facts against it and no positive evidence in its favor.

CHAPTER 14

CONCLUSION

The view of the determining principle of the canon expressed previously may be summarized by saying that the canonicity of a book of the Bible depends upon its authorship. If the book was in the Old Testament, the people of the day accepted it because it was written by a prophet. If it was a part of the New Testament, it was recognized as inspired if it had been written by an apostle — either by himself or with the help of an understudy or amanuensis. A survey of the history of the early centuries of our era seems to indicate that this was the test actually used by the post-apostolic Church, and the evidence from ancient times, so far as it is available, seems to indicate that the Old Testament canon was similarly determined.

It is freely recognized that other views of the principle of canonicity have been held and that there are some problems connected with our thesis. The chief problem is that we cannot name with certainty all the authors of the Old Testament books and that the apostolic authorship of some of the New Testament books may be questioned. These points have been considered in the preceding pages, and the conclusion seems to fit the evidence that the authorship of the major parts of both Testaments is clear — discounting the higher critical views which throw almost the whole into doubt — and for the remaining portions where the authorship is less certain there is not positive evidence against, indeed, there is some evidence for, the authorship by prophets and apostles. It may be expected that in questions of this nature, asked of the remote past, absolute certainty may not be achieved on all points. Enough seems certain, however, to allow us safely to accept the rest on less conclusive evidence.

Such an answer does not satisfy some because it asks that Christians should be students of ancient history. Does it satisfy the needs of the humble as well as the minds of those who delight in historical research? Perhaps this objection forgets that in a real sense every Christian is indeed expected to be a historian. Christ was a historical figure. Our salvation is based upon a historical fact. We preach Christ crucified and argue for the historicity of the empty tomb. The New Testament begins with a family tree. The Gospel of Luke locates the birth of our Saviour in the reign of one Caesar and places the beginning of His ministry during the rule of five different rulers and officers of Rome and Palestine. The Old Testament is almost half history. The instructed believer of a century ago knew more about the ancient history of Egypt and Mesopotamia than all the unbelieving scholars combined. The Old Testament is still one of the most extensive sources of knowledge of the ancient world.

Moreover, the Bible gives us much of the history bearing upon the writing and acceptance of the canonical books. Indeed, our only direct source in the Old Testament field is the books of the Old Testament themselves. In the New Testament field the books support and explain one another so that anyone who reads them may know that, unless they are forgeries, the majority are apostolic. And it takes no great scholarship to see that the New Testament books are not forgeries, but bear the stamp of sincerity. Close scholarly scrutiny may check the arguments based on the Bible itself and may add information from other books where the Biblical evidence is slight. But the humble believer who has nothing but his English Bible does not need to feel himself to be without sufficient historical evidence of a very worthy kind as a basis for his views.

Although the Protestant churches have protested elevating allegedly apostolic tradition to a place of equality with Scripture, yet they have never minimized the use of historical evidences and traditions which assist in defining our faith and supporting our records. The Reformers were masters of the works of the Fathers. The Nicene Fathers themselves quote extensively from the earlier writings, and Tertullian, Origen, etc., lay great emphasis on information handed down to them from apostolic churches and the companions of the apostles. They do not use such traditions as a basis for faith but as evidences for the authenticity of the Biblical records. Much of this evidence has been preserved for us, as indicated in the preceding pages. Much more has been lost, but gives us its testimony second hand in the men of the second and third centuries. We have enough evidence, however, to give us confidence in the views expressed above.

It remains for us to survey other views of the principle of canonicity. Probably the chief competitor is Roman Catholicism. It says quite simply that the Church made the Bible, not the Bible the Church. We have maintained that God ordained the ancient authors as prophets and Christ Himself appointed the authors of the new volume. The entire responsibility for the giving of the Bible is, in our view, God's and not man's.

Of course, the main assumption of Roman Catholicism is the usual contention that the Church of the first three centuries was a Roman Catholic Church. If so, it was a strange one. No present-day Roman Catholic would have felt at home in it. There was no doctrine of purgatory, of confession, of the mass. Both elements of the Communion were given to the laity. The infallibility of the Roman pontiff was nowhere held, because never claimed. There was no rosary, no celibacy of the clergy, no doctrine of indulgences, no treasury of merit, no doctrine of the perpetual virginity of Mary or special adoration of her, no immaculate conception or bodily assumption of Mary. The fact is that the Church of those centuries would have passed very well for a Protestant Church, but a present-day Roman Catholic would scarcely have known he had been to church if he had attended a meeting in the catacombs! This was the Church which for three centuries was testing the evidences concerning the New Testament books and was within fifty years in full agreement on all but a handful of them. The remainder were accepted as the evidence was circulated and recognized. No church decree made them into Bible books.

Indeed, Roman Catholics themselves often forget that their own official standards insist that the authority of the books of the Bible does not stem from the Church, but from God. The Vatican Council of 1870 clearly says: "And these books of the Old and New Testaments are to be received as sacred and canonical, in their integrity, with all their parts, as they are enumerated in the decree of the said Council [of Trent], and are contained in the ancient Latin edition of the Vulgate. These the Church holds to be sacred and canonical, not because, having been carefully composed by mere human industry, they were afterwards approved by her authority, nor merely because they contain revelation, with no admixture of error; but because, having been written by the inspiration of the Holy Ghost, they have God for their Author, and have been delivered as such to the Church herself."[1]

At the most, it may be said that the Roman Church claims to authenticate the canonical books. In this, as has been shown, she has greatly erred, for Christ and the apostles have authenticated for us the thirty-nine Old Testament books and strictly avoided the seven Apocrypha. The Roman Church has contradicted this authentication by adding the Apocrypha to the sacred volume.

In connection with the question of the canon, the Reformers are noted for putting forward the principle of the inner testimony of the Holy Spirit. It may be debated just how this witness is appealed to. In the works of Calvin it does not seem to be really a test of canonicity; in certain of the Reformation creeds it does. Calvin's opponents were the Romanists who advanced the doctrine that the Church made the Bible. He quotes them thus: "It depends, therefore (say they), on the determination of the Church, to decide both what reverence is due to the Scripture and what books are to be comprised in its canon." His answer is: "For if the Christian Church has been from the beginning founded on the writings of the prophets and the preaching of the apostles, wherever that doctrine is found, the approbation of it has certainly preceded the formation of the Church, since without it the Church itself had never existed."[2] Calvin does not go on to argue the particular point of canonicity but does emphasize the inward testimony of the Holy Spirit to establish the "authority of Scripture." He gives rational arguments which he declares are sufficient to prove the authority of Scripture to any right-thinking man. But he rightly observes that unsaved men are not able to think rightly about heavenly things. "Those persons betray great folly who wish it to be demonstrated to infidels that the Scripture is the Word of God, which cannot be known without faith."[3] This testimony is rather a proof of inspiration, however, than a test of canonicity: "Religion appearing, to profane men, to consist wholly in opinion, in order that they may not believe anything on foolish or slight grounds, they wish and expect it to be proved by rational arguments, that Moses and the prophets spake by divine inspiration. But I reply that the testimony of the Spirit is superior to all reason. For, as God alone is a sufficient witness of Himself in His own Word, so also the Word will never gain credit in the hearts of men till it be confirmed by the internal testimony of the Spirit. It is necessary, therefore, that the same Spirit who spake by the mouths of the prophets should penetrate into our hearts, to convince us that they faithfully delivered the oracles which were divinely intrusted to them."[4] Again: "Let it be considered, then, as an undeniable truth, that they who have been inwardly taught by the Spirit feel an entire acquiescence in the Scripture, and that it is self-authenticated, carrying with it its own evidence, and ought not to be made the

subject of demonstration and arguments from reason; but
it obtains the credit which it deserves with us by the testimony of the Spirit."[5]

The French Confession of 1559, in which Calvin had a
large hand, goes beyond Calvin's expressions. It says, "We
know these books to be canonical, and the sure rule of
our faith, not so much by the common accord and consent
of the Church as by the testimony and inward illumination
of the Holy Spirit which enables us to distinguish them
from other ecclesiastical books."[6] The Belgic Confession
of 1561, used still among some of the Dutch churches in
this country, is less explicit. It speaks of God as having
"commanded His servants, the prophets and apostles, to
commit His revealed Word to writing,"[7] and refers to the
inner testimony of the Spirit which enables us to accept all
things contained in the holy and canonical books which are
accepted for this reason and not because the Church approves
them. The Scotch Confession of 1560, in the making of which
John Knox had a large hand, gives no test of canonicity
but affirms that the authority of Scripture comes from God
alone and in no way from the "Kirk." The Thirty-nine
Articles of the Church of England likewise give no principle for selecting the canon, nor does the Westminster Confession. The latter creed says that inspiration is the test
of canonicity, but gives no test for inspiration. It declares
that the authority of the Scripture "dependeth not upon
the testimony of any man or church, but wholly upon
God (who is truth itself), the Author thereof; and therefore it is to be received, because it is the Word of God."[8]
Yet it does not indicate a way to tell which books are
to be considered of divine origin. It mentions, indeed, the
inner testimony of the Holy Spirit, but in a different connection. It cites the testimony of the Church and the
various arguments evidencing the Scripture to be the Word
of God, "yet, notwithstanding, our full persuasion and assurance of the infallible truth, and divine authority thereof,
is from the inward work of the Holy Spirit, bearing witness by and with the Word in our hearts."[8] The Spirit

testifies to the truth of the Bible in general, but is not a direct test of canonicity according to this Confession, which holds a very high place among the Reformation creeds.

Among the individual authors of modern times, the work of S. R. L. Gaussen has probably been most widely received as representing the orthodox, conservative position. Dr. Gaussen, a colleague of Merle D'Aubigne at the theological school founded in Geneva in 1831, wrote his *Theopneusty, or the Plenary Inspiration of the Holy Scriptures* in the 1830's, and the first American edition appeared in 1842. It has appeared in many editions, and is a classic on the subject. In treating the subject of inspiration, Gaussen says much that bears upon the question of canonicity. He dismisses the statement of the French Confession, quoted above, that the testimony of the Holy Spirit is the ground of canonicity.[9] He admits the doctrine of the inner testimony as applied "to the whole collection of the sacred books" apparently as Calvin understood it. He allows the Church (Jewish and Christian) great weight in testifying to the Scriptural books, and argues that providence has led the Church catholic in the selection of our sixty-six books but gives no authority to the Church in this matter.[10] He adds to these arguments the fact that the authors of the Old Testament were all prophets,[11] and that the New Testament would surely not be on a lower plane. The New Testament, he says, was written largely by apostles who, in the exercise of their special gifts, were greater than the prophets.[12] The problem of Luke and Mark is solved by the assertion that they were prophets in any case and certainly greater than the Old Testament prophets. They may have been among the seventy disciples sent out by Christ, and were surely given the gifts which the apostles bestowed by the laying on of hands. "It is then, with the assent and under the prophetic government of those apostles commissioned to bind and to unbind, and to be, after Christ, the twelve foundations of the universal Church, that the *canon of the Scriptures was formed.*"[13] He holds that the New Testament canon was completed within the age of the apostles themselves.

Archibald Alexander, a professor at Princeton Seminary in the early days, is the author of another classic on inspiration and the canon. He first wrote a book on inspiration and then one concerning the canon. In the edition of the former which was printed in 1836, the latter work was incorporated in abridged form. Alexander settles the question of the canon of the Old Testament very simply by appealing to the historical fact of the testimony of Christ and His apostles.[14] As to the New Testament, he adopts the rule that we should receive the books which were universally received as inspired, by those who lived nearest to the times when they were published. The argument is that such people would have the complete picture upon which to base a judgment, whereas we have only fragments. But he goes further. "Their right to a place in the canon does not depend on the vote of any council, or the decision of any bishop, but upon the fact that they were given by inspiration; and this was known by the character of the men who wrote them. The appeal to testimony, therefore, is not to obtain the judgment of the Church that these books were canonical, but to ascertain the fact that they were indeed the productions of the apostles, to whom our Lord promised plenary inspiration."[15] As to the problem of Mark and Luke, he says, "Indeed, they [the ancients] seem to have esteemed the Gospel of Luke just as if it had been dictated by Paul, and that of Mark as if dictated by Peter."[16] This is the view for which we have argued.

A variation of this theme is given by B. B. Warfield in an all-too-brief article reprinted in his *Revelation and Inspiration*. Regarding Mark and Luke he argues that it is not apostolic authorship but the imposing of these books upon the Church by apostolic authority which guarantees canonicity. He cites Tertullian's name for the canon, *instrumentum*, as indicating apostolic regulation. He admits, however, the facts cited in our preceding pages, that "apostolic authorship was, indeed, early confounded with canonicity. There was doubt as to the apostolic authorship of Hebrews, in the West, and of James and Jude, apparently, which underlay the slowness of the inclusion of these books in the 'canon' of certain churches."[17] Actually, it is to be doubted if Tertullian's word *instrumentum* means that the early churches received the Old Testament by the apostles' imposing it on the churches. Surely in places where the synagogue was known at all, the Old Testament was readily received in its own right, without further apostolic decision; yet it, like the New Testament, is called an *instrumentum*.

A last witness on the subject may well be Charles Hodge, whose *Systematic Theology* has been well known and widely used in this country for three-quarters of a century. He treats the subject briefly — as happens all too frequently in this somewhat neglected field — in connection with the subject of inspiration. He argues that the question of the Old Testament canon is readily settled on the basis of the historical evidence of the approbation of Christ and His apostles. "The principle on which the canon of the New Testament is determined is equally simple. Those books, and those only which can be proved to have been written by the apostles, or to have received their sanction, are to be recognized as of divine authority. The reason of this rule is obvious. The apostles were the duly authenticated messengers of Christ; of whom He said, 'He that heareth you heareth me.' "[18]

In our conclusion that the principle of canonicity was inspiration and that the test of inspiration was authorship by prophets in the Old Testament and apostles in the New, we do not need to hold to an absolutely exclusive position. The authors mentioned above have touched upon auxiliary principles which we may readily grant. The testimony of the Holy Spirit is doubtless not a sufficient test to distinguish the Epistle of Jude from the Martyrdom of Polycarp. But it is sufficient to bear powerful witness to the heart and core of the Bible. To read the Apocryphal books and compare them, or, rather, contrast them, with the canonical Scriptures is enough for most discerning Christians. Internal evidence supports the external. And yet it is a remarkable fact that this inward testimony of which the Reformers made so much was never once mentioned in the ancient Church. Church authority fails, partly because the churches are now divided on the subject (of the Old Testament alone, of course) but also because the present-day Roman Catholic Church differs with its older expressions and more specifically with the witness of Christ and the apostles. Nevertheless, the unanimity of the entire Church of all branches with regard to the New Testament is remarkable, and the entire Early Church was also of one mind with regard to the Old Testament, as has been shown. The consent of the Church catholic, therefore, is a compelling argument, even if the authority of the Roman Catholic Church must be denied in this matter.

Furthermore, God's providence, which watched over the preservation as well as the preparation of these sacred books, was doubtless a factor. Although we have absolutely no record that any writing of any prophet or apostle was rejected knowingly by any part of the Church, it is possible that some of the writings of such men have been lost. Efforts to establish this as a fact have not been fully successful. But at least we may cheerfully concede that God in His providence saw to it that these books were preserved (together with satisfactory witness to them), and that they are a sufficient witness to the gospel of Jesus Christ. John assures us that much more could have been written, "but these are written, that ye might believe that Jesus is the Christ, the Son of God; and that believing ye might have life through his name" (John 20:31). Finally, it is also correct to say that agreement to truth already revealed is a proper test of canonicity. It does not militate against the value of apostolic authorship to say that if any writing does not agree with the Gospel, it cannot be received. Paul put agreement with the truth above his own or even above an angel's witness (Gal. 1:8). This only means, however, that no one should be drawn aside by error in the guise of an apostle. There was no danger that an angel from heaven would contradict Christ. Nor can we suppose that an apostle to whom Christ had given the gift of His Spirit would do so. On the contrary, the apostles were commissioned for the express purpose of giving out these truths.

We have thus come to the conclusion that historical study and Biblical evidence combine to give us a test of canonicity that is definite and which was readily applied by the early Christians. It can even be applied with confidence by us in spite of the lapse of centuries and the diminution of the evidence. The books did not become authoritative by Church decision or as a result of the veneration attaching to things of antiquity. They were authoritative when written because given by inspiration of God. They were recognized as authoritative, inspired, and canonical by the generations to which they were addressed because of the position of the authors as acknowledged spokesmen of God. In the ancient times the succession of writing prophets following Moses, the great prototype, gave us our Old Testament. In the times of the founding of the Christian Church the apostles were God's chosen instruments appointed expressly by Christ for the purpose and endued by Him with the Holy Spirit for their revelational activity. They were conscious of such a holy gift, and as they write to us the Word of God they attach to it a suitable blessing for all who receive it in faith and practice it: "Blessed is he that readeth, and they that hear the words of this prophecy, and keep those things which are written therein: for the time is at hand" (Rev. 1:3).

NOTES

Part I

CHAPTER 1 — INTRODUCTION (pp. 17-44)

[1] Hodge defines inspiration as "an influence of the Holy Spirit on the minds of certain select men, which rendered them the organs of God for the infallible communication of His mind and will. They were in such a sense the organs of God that what they said, God said." Charles Hodge, *Systematic Theology* (1872), Vol. I, p. 154.

Warfield makes the following statement regarding inspiration: "The Church, then, has held from the beginning that the Bible is the Word of God in such a sense that its words, though written by men and bearing indelibly impressed upon them the marks of their human origin, were written, nevertheless, under such an influence of the Holy Ghost as to be also the words of God, the adequate expression of His mind and will. It is always recognized that this conception of co-authorship implies that the Spirit's superintendence extends to the choice of the words by the human authors (verbal inspiration), and preserves its product from everything inconsistent with a divine authorship—thus securing, among other things, that entire truthfulness which is everywhere presupposed in and asserted for the Scriptures by the Biblical writers (inerrancy)." B. B. Warfield, *Revelation and Inspiration* (1927), p. 173 (from *Presby. and Ref. Review*, Vol. IV, 1893, pp. 177-221).

Gaussen in his classic work defines inspiration as "that inexplicable power which the Divine Spirit formerly exercised over the authors of the Holy Scriptures to guide them even in the employment of the words they were to use, and to preserve them from all error, as well as from every omission." S. R. L. Gaussen, *Theopneusty, or the Plenary Inspiration of the Holy Scripture*, 4th Amer. ed. (1853), p. 45.

These are definitions of plenary inspiration. The entire book of T. Engelder, *Scripture Cannot Be Broken* (1944), is in defense of such definitions, though he calls his view "verbal inspiration." He says, "No Christian can declare, in his sober mind, that God's Word contains errors," p. 30.

Machen, in *Christianity and Liberalism* (1930), still uses the term "plenary inspiration," making it identical in meaning with "verbal," p. 73ff.

[2] P. Schaff, *Creeds of Christendom* (1877), Vol. 2, p. 80.

[3] Schaff, *op. cit.*, Vol. 2, p. 242.

[4] J. Gresham Machen, *Christianity and Liberalism* (1930), p. 73.

[5] Theodore Engelder, *Scripture Cannot Be Broken* (1944), pp. 303-309. For the evidence from Barth, *vid. inf.* p. 74f.

[6] B. B. Warfield, *op. cit.*, p. 173 n.

[7] For a helpful survey of the history, see O. T. Allis, *The Five Books of Moses* (1949), p. 14ff. The book is a valuable defense of the traditional views.

[8] W. Sanday, *Inspiration* (1901), p. 414.

[9] This is the background of the remarks by R. H. Pfeiffer, *Introduction to the Old Testament* (1948), p. 170.

[10] Quotations are given extensively in O. T. Allis, *The Unity of Isaiah* (1950), to show that critical scholars postdate prophetic passages because to do otherwise would admit the supernatural. On the Cyrus passage, cf. Allis, p. 59ff.

[11] *Vid. inf.* p. 39ff.

[12] Cf. W. F. Albright, "The Bible After Twenty Years of Archaeology," *Religion in Life*, Vol. 21 (1952), p. 541f. Albright's own view is that the history preserved in epic poems for centuries was then written down in the early monarchy. In this way he allows for the substantial accuracy of the narrative and also for the alleged errors. However, the accuracy in small details is sometimes so remarkable that it is a question whether centuries of oral transmission can be allowed. For example, I Samuel 13:21 gives the enigmatic "pesirah (was) pim." Discovery of a weight marked "peh" and weighing a third of a shekel indicates that "pim" actually is a dual form meaning two-thirds of a shekel, the price of the sharpening of the instruments referred to. The entire situation pictured there at the start of the Iron Age was presumably misunderstood in later years in Israel; yet the transmission of the words was precise. (For the illustration I am indebted to Dr. E. A. Speiser of the University of Pennsylvania.)

[13] Nelson Glueck, *The Other Side of the Jordan* (1940), especially p. 89ff. Solomon appears as the ancient copper magnate.

[14] W. F. Albright, "The Bible After Twenty Years of Archaeology," *op. cit.*, p. 543f.

[15] W. F. Albright, *From the Stone Age to Christianity* (1940), p. 207.

[16] Albright, "The Bible After Twenty Years of Archaeology," *op. cit.*, p. 545, refers to "the total breakdown of Wellhausenism" today.

[17] Cf. the discussion of Belshazzar and Sargon below, pp. 149, 117f.

[18] His main assumption was that the genealogies in Genesis 5 and 11 are complete and, therefore, suitable bases for a chronology. Other genealogies in the Bible, however, are incomplete, and this should have warned Ussher not to press those in Genesis. Matthew 1:8 omits four links, as every Jew surely knew. Matthew 1:1 goes from Christ to Abraham in two steps. Compare the full discussion in John D. Davis, "Chronology," in *Bible Dictionary* (1st ed., 1898), *in loco.*

[19] Augustine, *Confessions,* Books XI, XII, and XIII, where he allegorizes somewhat the creative days.

[20] Bernard Ramm, *The Christian View of Science and Scripture* (1955), p. 256f., discusses the possibilities that life originated by chance and gives current differing views of biologists. Some believe the chances are so remote as to amount almost to an impossibility; others preserve a glimmer of hope. The fact is that the synthesis of organic compounds has gone on apace and now the synthesis of the complex protein molecules is being attacked. But is life merely a collection of protein molecules? Quite conceivably, the *matter* of life can be synthesized. But to assume that *life* can be synthesized is to deny that life is anything more than a collection of material compounds. It would seem to deny not only God as God, but also man as man.

[21] According to a report in "Newsfronts of the World," *Life* magazine, April 19, 1954.

[22] Richard Goldschmidt, *The Material Basis of Evolution* (1940), pp. 183, 212, 396.

[23] Franz Weidenreich presents two tables arranging human remains (a) as they are found according to the usual evolutionary dating and (b) as they ought to be found judging by their evolutionary progress. "Some Problems Dealing with Ancient Man," *American Anthropologist*, n.s., Vol. 3 (1940), p. 381. The tables are conveniently reproduced in *Modern Science and the Christian Faith* (2nd ed., 1950), pp. 165, 167. The striking thing is that the two tables differ widely. Modern types of men, like Swanscombe, occur very early. Carmel men are fairly early. Weidenreich concludes that evolution was "polycentric." He means that in one area evolution had progressed rapidly and

formed modern types 300,000 years ago. In other areas, evolution lagged. The human evolution that proceeded rapidly must then have been fairly advanced in the Pliocene Age — and we have no human fossils from the Pliocene Age. His data could more readily be interpreted by denying human evolution altogether. Such variation of human structure would then be due to racial differences, diets, differing longevity with differing ages of maturation, etc. The Carmel material is conveniently given in C. C. McCown, *The Ladder of Progress in Palestine* (1943), pp. 18-38.

Since the foregoing was written, an article reputed to give the latest information has appeared in the popular *Life* magazine, "The Epic of Man," Nov. 7, 1955. Three types are dated at 300,000 years ago: Swanscombe man, called "Europe's first true human" and full modern; Kanjera man, who is so like modern types that the remark is made, "He may have been an ancestral Caucasian"; and Peking man, who is said to have been chinless and to have had a small brain. The only remains said to be earlier than these are Pithecanthropus, who is said to be akin to Peking man ("550,000 to 200,000 years ago," "fully erect but half-brained") and the Kanam jaw of "true man" perhaps 650,000 years old. All that this gives is evidence of variation among human types, not of evolution from lower to higher forms.

[24] The C_{14} method of dating is explained in F. Zeuner, *Dating the Past* (3rd ed., 1952), pp. 341-346, and popularly in Ruth Moore, *Man, Time, and Fossils* (1953), chap. XVIII. Briefly, it proceeds upon the basis that cosmic rays bombarding nitrogen atoms in the atmosphere transmute them into C_{14}, a kind of carbon. This is absorbed by living matter, but is unstable, breaking down and losing half of its quantity every 5,000 years. Organisms, as long as they are alive, have the percentages of C_{14} to C_{12} (ordinary carbon) which exist in the air — about one in a trillion. After they die, that excess of C_{14} begins to break down and measurement of the amount that has broken down will indicate the time which has elapsed since the organism died. Since the amounts involved are small, measurements on material more than 20,000 years old are difficult, though refinements in method are workable to about 40,000 years. Errors are brought about if the organic material has been in contact with carbon of a different age. Too much reliance should not yet be placed on results unless they are carefully checked. *Science*, n.s., Vol. 113 (1951), pp. 111f. and 241ff., lists a number of determinations made up to that time. A count of the several hundred determinations shows that not many can be checked by independent criteria. Of those that can, fully 14 do not check with independent data or with duplicate determinations made from samples in the same horizons.

It should be noted that any variation in the proportions of atmospheric C_{12} and C_{14} in ancient days would upset the results. Since C_{14} production depends on cosmic ray intensity, the method assumes these rays have been relatively invariable. Since the above was written, a storm on the face of the sun equalling the explosion of a million hydrogen bombs has been reported in the public press (during March, 1955). Observations showed a temporary doubling of cosmic ray intensity. By the same token, if volcanic activity or any other cause should increase the amount of C_{12} in the atmosphere, the proportion of C_{14} to C_{12} in living matter would be changed and the method rendered invalid. The method is based on several assumptions. They may not all be valid. In any event, the method cannot be used in the times where our greatest interest lies.

[25] Emil Brunner, *Christianity and Civilization*, Pt. I, Foundations (1947), p. 68.

[26] The Auburn Affirmation is conveniently reprinted as an appendix in Edwin H. Rian, *The Presbyterian Conflict* (1940).

[27] George H. Betts, *The Beliefs of 700 Ministers* (1929).

[28] G. Bromley Oxnam, *Preaching in a Revolutionary Age* (1944), pp. 78f.

[29] Elmer G. Homrighausen, *Christianity in America, A Crisis* (1936), p. 121. In a personal letter Dr. Homrighausen indicates that he would no longer state the situation in the words of his book. He does indicate, however, that the quotation would apply if it were a question of the Bible being literally inerrant. In that case it could not be accepted. We have shown above that the doctrine of infallibility or verbal inspiration, or inerrancy is all one and the same under different terms through the history of the Church.

[30] Edwin C. Lewis, *A Philosophy of the Christian Revelation* (2nd ed., 1940), p. 40.

[31] John Sutherland Bonnell, "What Is a Presbyterian?" *Look* magazine, Mar. 23, 1954, pp. 86, 90, and 93.

[32] Reinhold Niebuhr, *Faith and History* (1949), p. 123.

[33] Ibid., p. 36. Cf. pp. 103, 106, 130, 131, etc., for similar denials.

[34] Ibid., p. 128.

[35] Reinhold Niebuhr, *Nature and Destiny of Man* (1949), Pt. II, p. 50. Speaking of Jesus' alleged view that the time would be short to the establishment of the kingdom of God, Niebuhr uses these words: "In this error He was followed both by St. Paul and the Early Church." It is of interest to note that most critical scholars would hold that the expectation of the Second Advent by Christ and the apostles was for an immediate future and tied in with the destruction of Jerusalem. But the chiliasm (premillennialism) of the Early Church seemed unaffected by the fact that He did not return in 70 A.D. or in the lifetime of the apostles. Their chiliasm persisted with a lively expectation of Christ's return — without setting dates — until it was lost due to an allegorizing exegesis which entered about the time of Origen, 250 A.D. Niebuhr misconstrues both the Biblical text and the history of the Early Church.

[36] Niebuhr, *Faith and History* (1949), p. 33f.

[37] Wilhelm Pauck, *Karl Barth, Prophet of a New Age* (1931), p. 212.

[38] Ibid., p. 219.

[39] Paul Tillich, "The World Situation," in *The Christian Answer*, ed. by H. P. Van Dusen (1945), p. 40.

[40] Shailer Mathews, *The Faith of Modernism* (1924), p. 38.

CHAPTER 2 — WHY WE BELIEVE THE BIBLE (pp. 45-71)

[1] For the following argument see the somewhat verbose but good treatment by Hugh McIntosh in a little-known book *Is Christ Infallible and the Bible True?* (2nd ed., 1901). Cf. also the valuable book giving the same argument, C. J. Ellicott, *Christus Comprobator* (1891), pp. 88-178.

[2] It is not intended necessarily to approve the view that Matthew and Luke are dependent upon an older source called Q, a collection of Jesus' sayings. But for those who hold that there was such a source, the genuineness of this saying is enhanced by its being found both in Matthew and Luke and hence in Q.

[3] *The Mishnah*, translated by Herbert Danby (1933), pp. 415, 418.

[4] This treatment of Matthew 5:21-48 was given by the author: "The Sermon on the Mount and Verbal Inspiration," in *The Reformation Review* (organ of the International Council of Christian Churches), Vol. 1, No. 4 (1954), pp. 21-32, and is reprinted here by kind permission.

[5] H. A. W. Meyer, *Commentary on Matthew, in loco.*

[6] *Vid. sup.* p. 27.

[7] It surely is not necessary to defend the Bible's calling a whale a fish. The Old Testament says that God prepared a great fish to swallow Jonah. Matthew

12:40 calls it a whale. Surely the English of the 1611 version need not be expected to use the modern biological classifications of animals. A whale is a fish in the popular terminology — a sea animal with a tail and finlike appendages. If one must get technical, the Bible does not refer to Jonah's host as either fish or whale, but in the Hebrew as *dagh* and in the Greek as *ketos*. These are names used indifferently of sea animals and would include sharks, porpoises, whales, etc. In any case, the fish was prepared by God for the role it played and was directed by Him.

8 Flavius Josephus, *Against Apion* (ed. by Whiston), i, 8.

9 A. T. Robertson, *A Grammar of the Greek New Testament in the Light of Historical Research* (1919), pp. 281, 667.

10 This interpretation is not given in most of the commentaries. The general sense of the passage is not affected by it, but this view would unify the subject matter of the verses nicely.

11 Charles Gore, H. L. Goudge, Alfred Guillaume, *A New Commentary on Holy Scripture* (1929), *in loco.*

12 *Vid. inf.* p. 227.

13 B. B. Warfield, *The Lord of Glory* (1907), pp. 226, 227n. Cf. I Cor. 12:5; Eph. 4:5, etc.

14 Frank M. Cross, Jr., "A New Qumran Biblical Fragment," BASOR, No. 132 (Dec., 1953), pp. 15-26, especially p. 25.

15 *Vid. inf.* p. 114.

16 C. H. Gordon, *Ugaritic Handbook* (1947), p. 81.

CHAPTER 3 — VERBAL INSPIRATION IN CHURCH HISTORY (pp. 72-84)

1 Point 1 of the Auburn Affirmation, conveniently found as an appendix in E. H. Rian, *The Presbyterian Conflict* (1940), p. 294.

2 B. B. Warfield, *The Westminster Assembly and Its Work* (1931), pp. 261-333. This section is a reprint of the article "The Doctrine of Inspiration of the Westminster Divines" in the *Presbyterian and Reformed Review*, Jan., 1893.

3 Quoted by Warfield, *op. cit.,* from a magazine, *The Independent,* July, 1893.

4 The antagonists of the early Church Fathers had pointed out a number which are still stock in trade for the objector, though most have long ago been satisfactorily dealt with. An interesting book with regard to the Old Testament is *The Conciliator* of R. Manasseh ben Israel (d. 1657), ed. by E. N. Lindo (1842), which in spite of its age deals quite well with many such problems.

5 Warfield, *op. cit.,* p. 266.

6 Ibid., p. 268.

7 Ibid., p. 273.

8 To the same effect are other creeds of the century previous to the Westminster divines. The Thirty-nine Articles of the Church of England, the Scotch Confession of 1560, and the Heidelberg Catechism of 1563 may be mentioned.

9 Karl Barth, *Doctrine of the Word of God* (1936), p. 126f.

10 Ibid., p. 128.

11 M. Reu, *Luther and the Scriptures* (1944).

12 Emil Brunner, *Christian Doctrine of God* (1950), p. 111.

13 Ibid., p. 107.

14 To the same effect, Alan Richardson, *A Preface to Bible Study* (1944), remarks that "from the second century to the eighteenth this theory (of verbal inspiration) was generally accepted as true," although Richardson finds that "few better educated Christians" hold to it any more (p. 25).

15 W. Sanday, *op. cit.,* especially pp. 28-42.

16 B. B. Warfield, *Revelation and Inspiration* (1927), p. 54. This section

is a reprint from *Bibliotheca Sacra,* Vol. 51 (1894). It is found in the reprint of Warfield's writings recently published by the Presbyterian and Reformed Publishing Co., *The Inspiration and Authority of the Bible,* chap. 2.

[17] S. R. L. Gaussen, *op. cit.,* p. 343.

[18] Clement (of Rome), chaps. 8, 13, 16, 22, etc. The epistle is conveniently found in ANF, Vol. 1.

[19] Ibid., chap. 45, p. 17.

[20] Ignatius, *Epistle to the Smyrneans,* chap. 5, ANF, Vol. 1, p. 88.

[21] Ibid., *to the Magnesians,* chap. 8, p. 62.

[22] Ibid., *to the Philadelphians,* chap. 5, p. 82.

[23] Ibid., *to the Philadelphians,* chap. 8, p. 84.

[24] Ibid., *to the Philippians,* chap. 7, p. 34.

[25] Ibid., *to the Philippians,* chap. 3, p. 33.

[26] Ibid., *to the Philippians,* chap. 6, p. 34.

[27] Ibid., *to the Philippians,* chap. 12, p. 35.

[28] Irenaeus, *Against Heresies,* iii, 2, 1, ANF, Vol. 1, p. 415.

[29] Ibid., iii, 14, 4, ANF., Vol. 1, p. 439.

[30] Ibid., iii, 16, 2, p. 441.

[31] Ibid., iii, 1, 1, p. 414.

[32] Ibid., ii, 28, 2, p. 399.

[33] Justin Martyr, *Hortatory Address to the Greeks,* chap. 8, ANF, Vol. 1, p. 276.

[34] Justin Martyr, *Dialogue with Trypho,* chap. 65, ANF, Vol. 1, p. 230.

[35] Justin Martyr, *First Apology,* chap. 31, ANF, Vol. 1, p. 173.

[36] Sanday, *op. cit.,* p. 38.

[37] *Epistle to Jerome,* 82, 3. Quoted by Warfield, *op. cit.,* p. 54.

[38] Sanday, *op. cit.,* p. 45.

[39] Cf. the remark by G. Ernest Wright in *Interpretation,* Vol. 3 (Jan., 1949), pp. 56f., where he says that the prevailing view of leaders of the World Council of Churches is that Fundamentalism holds a "mechanical inspiration" "analogous to the Mohammedan." For a denial of mechanical inspiration on the part of all leading theologians, *vid. sup.* p. 21f.

CHAPTER 4 — TEXTUAL CRITICISM AND INSPIRATION (pp. 85-103)

[1] Perhaps nowhere with more acumen than in Warfield's *Introduction to the Textual Criticism of the New Testament* (1886). A. T. Robertson's book on the subject, *Introduction to the Textual Criticism of the New Testament* (1925), which was intended to be somewhat of a revision of Warfield, seems to the writer to lack the insight of his predecessor, though he adds new material. A book including still later material and more popular in style is H. C. Thiessen, *Introduction to the New Testament* (1944).

[2] A. S. Lewis, *Light on the Four Gospels from the Sinai Palimpsest* (1913), p. 12, reveals this attitude. She holds, strangely enough, that the publication of the Revised Version in England killed the doctrine of verbal inspiration as it revealed variations among the manuscripts. As if this had not been known previously!

[3] An apparent exception is the publication of the Chester Beatty papyri, which, however, do not show any singular type of text and have not modified previous results appreciably. They have been confirmatory rather than otherwise.

[4] Quoted in W. H. Green, *General Introduction to the Old Testament, the Text* (1899), p. 127.

[5] B. B. Warfield, "The Westminster Divines on Inspiration," in *The Westminster Assembly and Its Work* (1931), p. 273.

[6] B. B. Warfield, *Introduction to the Textual Criticism of the New Testament* (1886), p. 10.

[7] Ibid., p. 160.

[8] Published and discussed with facsimile by C. H. Roberts, *An Unpublished Fragment of the Fourth Gospel in the John Rylands Library* (1935).

[9] Ibid., p. 16.

[10] It is of interest to note that the old Baur-Tuebingen school of New Testament criticism, fashionable in Germany about 1870, confidently asserted that the Gospel of John was not written until 170 A.D. Here is a fragment copied well before that time.

[11] B. F. Westcott and F. J. A. Hort, *The New Testament in the Original Greek* (1929), p. 565.

[12] A. S. Geden, *Outlines of Introduction to the Hebrew Bible* (1909), p. 55f.

[13] BA, XI (Sept., 1948), pp. 46-57; XII (May, 1949), pp. 26-31; J. L. Kelso, "The Archaeology of Qumran," JBL, LXXIV (1955), pp. 141-146.

[14] BA, XVII (1954), p. 8f.

[15] Frank M. Cross, "A New Qumran Fragment," BASOR, No. 132 (1955), pp. 15ff.

[16] Millar Burrows, ed., *The Dead Sea Scrolls of St. Mark's Monastery* (1950), Vol. 1.

[17] The Letter of Aristeas gives the tradition. It was quoted by Josephus and some of the Church Fathers. The Greek text is printed as an appendix and discussed by H. B. Swete, *Introduction to the Old Testament in Greek* (1902). It has been translated and re-edited recently by Moses Hadas, *Aristeas to Demetrius* (1951).

[18] W. F. Albright, "A Catalogue of Early Hebrew Lyric Poems," *Hebrew Union College Annual*, Vol. XXIII (1950-51), p. 4, argues that the Hebrew prototype of the Greek Isaiah must be third or even fourth century B. C. and the Greek Psalter was translated not later than mid-second century B. C.

[19] On the Samuel fragment and its relation to the Septuagint, cf. Frank M. Cross, *op. cit.*, especially p. 25. It has lately become apparent that a third type—that lying back of the Samaritan Pentateuch—is also witnessed by some of the scrolls. Cf. Patrick W. Skehan, "Exodus in the Samaritan Recension from Qumran," JBL, LXXIV (1955), p. 182f.

[20] The trend toward an earlier dating of books is shown in Albright's statement, "A rapidly increasing number of scholars today deny any Maccabean Psalms and doubt whether any part of the Psalter is later than the fourth or even fifth century B. C." "The Bible After Twenty Years of Archaeology," *op. cit.*, p. 544. If the Psalter is dated early, other books also must be pushed back.

[21] Robert Dick Wilson, *Scientific Investigation of the Old Testament* (1926), pp. 72-89.

[22] The evidence is given fully in Joseph P. Free, *Archaeology and Bible History* (1950), *in loco*.

CHAPTER 5 —

OBJECTIONS TO THE DOCTRINE OF VERBAL INSPIRATION (pp. 104-128)

[1] For the question of evolution and the Bible an elementary book of some years ago is still good, Floyd Hamilton, *The Basis of Evolutionary Faith* (1942, reprint). A more recent picture is given in *Modern Science and the Christian Faith*, ed. by F. A. Everest (2nd ed., 1950). For the higher criticism, cf. O. T. Allis, *The Five Books of Moses* (1949), as an introductory study, especially for the classic form of criticism of the past generation.

[2] The title of a useful little book by R. A. Torrey.

[3] For example, in Edward Robinson, *Harmony of the Four Gospels in Greek* (1879), p. 212ff.

[4] A. Dupont Sommer, *Sabbat et Parasceve a Elephantine* (1950), p. 3f.

[5] See John Lightfoot, *Horae Hebraicae et Talmudicae* (new ed., 1859), Vol. 3, p. 55.

[6] Frank M. Cross, "The Dead Sea Scrolls," *The Christian Century*, Aug. 10, 1955, p. 921. He also shows that the quotation in Hebrews 1:6 from the Septuagint is supported by the Scrolls.

[7] John W. Haley, *An Examination of the Alleged Discrepancies of the Bible* (1874), p. 313. It was reprinted by B. C. Goodpasture, Nashville, Tenn., in 1951. The book is scholarly, exhaustive, and reverent. The writings of prominent atheists here and abroad were first combed for objections worthy of a reply. The final paragraph of the preface is worth quoting: "Finally let it be remembered that the Bible is neither dependent upon nor affected by the success or failure of my book. Whatever may become of the latter, whatever may be the verdict passed upon it by an intelligent public, the *Bible* will stand. In the ages yet to be, when its present assailants and defenders are mouldering in the dust, and when their very names are forgotten, the sacred volume will be, as it has been during the centuries past, the guide and solace of unnumbered millions of our race." And so it has still proved to be. Andover Newton Seminary, where Haley wrote, has turned to a position of sharpest attack upon the Bible. Indeed, it has finally become defunct. But new seminaries have risen up in the defense, and multiplied millions are still loving and reading the Old Book regardless of the exceedingly bitter attacks of the last century. I have gratefully consulted Haley for most of the above discrepancies, though I have not followed his solutions in all points.

[8] *Op. cit.*

[9] *Op. cit.*

[10] Theodore Engelder, *Scripture Cannot Be Broken* (1944). A monument of industry and a mine of information, especially in quotations expressing the views of modern liberal theologians. He gives on pp. 97-107 a number of very helpful suggestions on the origin of these problems in skeptical minds and excellent principles of dealing with them.

[11] *Op. cit.*, pp. 10f., 79-84.

[12] R. P. Dougherty, Nabonidus and Belshazzar (1929).

[13] A friend, Professor John Whitcomb of Grace Seminary, Winona Lake, Indiana, has kindly let me see his unpublished thesis on Darius the Mede. His conclusion is that confusion among historians has arisen because of the similarity in names of an Ugbaru who died soon after the conquest of Babylon and a Gubaru (Gobryas) who continued for some time as a high officer under Cyrus. He makes the identification with Gobryas seem quite plausible. It is to be hoped that his material can be published.

[14] G. Bromley Oxnam, *op. cit.*, p. 78f.

[15] W. F. Albright, *From the Stone Age to Christianity* (1940), p. 214.

[16] C. H. Roberts, *Two Biblical Papyri in the John Rylands Library*, Manchester (1936).

[17] *Vid. sup.* pp. 55f.

[18] Charles Hodge, *Systematic Theology* (1872), Vol. 1, p. 170.

[19] Bernard Ramm, *The Christian View of Science and Scripture* (1955), p. 118.

PART II

CHAPTER 6 — HISTORY (pp. 131-153)

[1] Other standard books on the subject are: R. H. Pfeiffer, *Introduction to the Old Testament* (1941), and Frantz Buhl, *Canon and Text of the Old*

Testament (1892), from the critical point of view; and Edward J. Young, *Introduction to the Old Testament* (1949), and Merrill F. Unger, *An Introductory Guide to the Old Testament* (1951), of the orthodox persuasion. Not exactly on the question of the canon, but very helpful on related subjects, is R. B. Girdlestone, *The Building Up of the Old Testament.* (1912).

2 Emil Brunner, *Revelation and Reason* (1946), preface, makes quite a claim of discussing revelation and reason, whereas the usual order is reason and revelation.

3 Karl Barth, *op. cit.,* p. 125f., uses such terminology: "The Biblical witnesses point beyond themselves. If we regard them as witnesses — and only as witnesses do we regard them genuinely, i.e., in the way in which they themselves wished to be regarded . . ." "We do the Bible a poor honor and one unwelcome to itself when we directly identify it with this something else, with revelation itself."

4 *Vid. sup.* pp. 42f., 74f., and previous note, 3.

5 Green, *op. cit.,* p. 31.

6 P. Schaff, *op. cit.,* Vol. 2, p. 242.

7 *Vid. sup.* pp. 75f.

8 JBL, LXXIV (Sept., 1955). Several articles summarize both the archaeological and manuscript situation.

9 Ibid.

10 Additional finds from the first two post-Christian centuries have come from the Wadi Murabba'at region. Letters dated in 132 A.D. have been found. This cave has no direct relation to Qumran, apparently. Cf. BA, XVI (Feb., 1953), p. 18ff.

11 *Vid. sup.* pp. 98f.

12 J. Muilenberg, "A Qoheleth Scroll from Qumran," BASOR, No. 135 (Oct., 1954), pp. 20-28.

13 Frank M. Cross, "A New Qumran Biblical Fragment," BASOR, No. 132 (Dec. 1953), pp. 15-17, briefly referred to above, p. 68.

14 Solomon A. Birnbaum, "The Leviticus Fragments from the Cave," and S. Yeivin, "The Date . . . of the Leviticus Fragments," BASOR, No. 118 (Apr., 1950), pp. 20-30.

15 Frank M. Cross, "A Report on the Biblical Fragments," BASOR, No. 141 (Feb., 1956), p. 11.

16 William L. Reed, "The Qumran Cave Expedition of March, 1952," BASOR, No. 135 (Oct., 1954), pp. 8-20, mentions Jubilees. Unpublished reports mention Enoch. The Lamech scroll has now been unrolled and turns out to be a free Aramaic translation of Genesis; see BA, XIX (Feb., 1956), pp. 22f.

17 Published as DSO, "The Manual of Discipline," *Dead Sea Scrolls of St. Mark's Monastery,* Vol. 2. The War Scroll and Hodayoth (Thanksgiving Psalms) are so far completely published only in a Hebrew publication by Dr. E. L. Sukenik's son, Y. Yadin, but it seems difficult to secure it in this country as yet. The Hebrew title is *'wsr hmgylwt hgnwzwt* ("Treasure of the Geniza Scrolls"), Jerusalem, Bialik Foundation and Hebrew University (1954). Translations of much of the material is found in Millar Burrows, *The Dead Sea Scrolls* (1955). Sukenik's book is now available also in English.

18 Recently republished with introduction and notes by Chaim Rabin, *The Zadokite Documents* (1954). The preface, p. viii, mentions the find of fragments of the work in one of the caves.

19 J. Muilenberg, *op. cit.,* p. 23, remarks that the script of the work DSD and the Ecclesiastes fragment from 150 B.C. and the Isaiah Scroll, DSIs[a] are all similar.

20 DSD I, 3, and VIII, 15. Translated by W. H. Brownlee, "The Dead

Sea Manual of Discipline," BASOR, *Supplementary Studies*, Nos. 10-12 (1951), pp. 6, 32.

[21] DSD, V, VI, VIII, etc. Ibid., pp. 20, 22, 32, 34, etc.

[22] DSD, V, VII. Ibid., pp. 20, 30.

[23] CDC, V, 2; VII, 10; VII, 19; XI, 18; XI, 20; Rabin, *op. cit.*, pp. 18, 28, 30, 58, 58.

[24] CDC, XVI, 4; Rabin, *op. cit.*, pp. 74, 75n.

[25] Frants Buhl, *op. cit.*, and S. R. Driver, *op. cit.*, and others give the usual picture as it has been held among critical scholars.

[26] Green, *op. cit.*, pp. 34, 29.

[27] James A. Montgomery, *A Critical and Exegetical Commentary on the Book of Daniel, Int. Crit. Comment.* (1927), p. 96. S. R. Driver, *op. cit.*, p. 497, argues for the late date of Daniel on the basis of its position in the third division of the canon, the Writings.

[28] BASOR, No. 135 (Oct., 1954), p. 23f.

[29] *Vid sup.*, n. 23.

[30] For this discussion of the situation of Daniel, I am indebted to my instructor, former colleague, and friend, Dr. Allan A. MacRae, who has been giving such evidence in his classes in Old Testament introduction for twenty years. The data are published *in extensu* by Robert Dick Wilson in his *Studies in the Book of Daniel, Second Series* (1938), pp. 13-64.

[31] Tractate "Baba Bathra," *The Babylonian Talmud*, trans. by Michael L. Rodkinson (1916), Vol. 5, p. 44f.

[32] Josephus, *Against Apion*, i, 8.

[33] Ibid. (ed. by Whiston), p. 70.

[34] Green, *op. cit.*, pp. 160-175.

[35] Strangely, although this evidence of Wilson's has long been published, E. J. Young in his *Old Testament Introduction*, and Unger also (*op. cit.*), follow the old conservative view of Green (*op. cit.*, p. 85), that Daniel was not among the prophets because he had the "gift of a prophet," but not the "office of a prophet." This seems to be a thin and totally unwarranted distinction manufactured to explain why Daniel was not where it actually was! Green quotes Moses Stuart, who evidently correctly appreciated the facts long ago. But Green's argument has held the day in conservative circles.

[36] The fragments of Samuel (4Q Sam) are studied by Frank M. Cross, *op. cit.* He emphasizes that this fragment has some striking similarities with the text underlying the Septuagint. He treated it again in "The Oldest Manuscripts from Qumran," JBL, LXXIV (1955), pp. 147-172. On p. 164 he assigns it a "suitably conservative" date of the last quarter of the third century B.C.

[37] Details are given in R. D. Wilson, *op. cit.*, p. 22f.

[38] These finds come not from the Qumran district, but from the Wadi Murabba'at a bit farther south. They are from the first and second centuries A.D. and include mention of Bar Cochba, who led the Jewish revolt of 132 A.D. Some of the finds are published in BASOR, No. 131 (Oct., 1953), and following issues, and in *Revue Biblique*, 1953 and after. Scraps of the Greek are there given.

[39] Muilenburg, *op. cit.*, p. 24, cites older critics dating it from 100 B.C. to post-Christian times.

[40] *Vid sup.*, n. 23.

[41] I am indebted to Dr. Moshe Greenberg of the University of Pennsylvania for calling my attention to several of these in a private letter. He quotes from Ludwig Blau, *Studien zum Althebraischen Buchwesen* (Budapest, 1902), p. 63f., thus: "The two-part division of Biblical writings is older than the three-part. . . . The original two-part division is still reflected in the (Rabbinic) designations of the entire Bible under two names, such as *Torah* and

Kabbalah . . . Torah and *Nebi'im.* 'Guardians may sell houses, fields, and vineyards . . . in order to buy a *sefer tora unebi'im* (book of the Law and the Prophets) for orphans' (Tosefta Baba Bathra 8, 14; cf. New Testament 'Law and the Prophets'). . . . A controversy is indeed recorded in which Rabbi Meir permits the writing of 'Tora and Prophets' on one scroll; in this he is opposed by the majority who allow only the prophets and Hagiographa (Writings) to be united in one scroll (Jerusalem Talmud, Megilla 73a). R. Meir includes the Hagiographa in the Prophets, as is shown from a parallel in Talmud Baba Bathra 13b, where his opinion is recorded as 'One may unite Tora, Prophets, and Hagiographa in one scroll.'"

[42] As is now being done by Irwin, *The Problem of Ezekiel* (1943), and others.

[43] W. F. Albright, "The Bible After Twenty Years of Archaeology," *op. cit.,* p. 544f.

[44] R. D. Wilson, *op. cit.*

[45] Gesenius-Buhl, *Hebraisches und Aramaisches Handwoerterbuch ueber das alte Testament* (1915, reprint, 1949), *in loco.*

[46] Joseph P. Free, *op. cit.,* gives the evidence in a most interesting way. Ezra and Nehemiah are right. He quotes Albright as saying that Athenian silver money was almost international currency in the fifth century B.C.

[47] Franz Rosenthal, *Die aramaistische Forschungen* (1939), p. 62.

[48] *Vid. sup.* p. 118.

[49] *Vid. sup.* p. 119.

[50] E. J. Young, *The Prophecy of Daniel* (1949), gives a convenient summary, p. 213f.

[51] Ibid., p. 192f.

CHAPTER 7 — The Determining Principle of the Canon (pp. 154-179)

[1] Reported at the 1955 meeting of the American Oriental Society, Toronto.

[2] Though an adaptation of it was invented and used extensively on clay in Ugarit about 1400 B.C. and sporadically elsewhere.

[3] *Vid. sup.* p. 138.

[4] The Mishna, *op. cit.,* pp. 446-460.

[5] The claims of the Old Testament for itself are given extensively in Green, *op. cit.,* pp. 11-18 and 32ff.

[6] E. J. Young, *My Servants the Prophets* (1952), pp. 193-8, takes up extra-Biblical prophets, especially the references in the Mari literature.

[7] Frank M. Cross, "A Report on the Biblical Fragments," BASOR, No. 141 (Feb., 1956), p. 10f.

[8] R. B. Girdlestone, *The Building Up of the Old Testament* (1912), p. 26. It is not referred to by E. J. Young, *Introduction to the Old Testament,* nor by Unger, *op. cit.*

[9] DSD, IX, 11; W. H. Brownlee, *op. cit.,* pp. 35 n. and 50, argues that the prophet here expected is the Messiah, and the followers mentioned are the priests and laity. In any case, there is no consciousness of current prophetic activity.

[10] Josephus, *Against Apion,* i, 8.

[11] *Babylonian Talmud,* Tractate "Sanhedrin," Michael L. Rodkinson (1916), Vols. 7 and 8, p. 24.

[12] E. J. Young, *Introduction to the Old Testament* (1949), pp. 71, 73.

[13] DSD, I, 3; W. H. Brownlee, *op. cit.,* p. 6.

[14] DSD, VIII, 15; W. H. Brownlee, *op. cit.,* p. 32.

[15] DSD, V, 17; VIII, 14; and V, 15; W. H. Brownlee, *op. cit.,* pp. 20, 32, 20.

[16] CDC, V, 21f; Rabin, *op. cit.,* p. 20.

[17] CDC, VII, 15-17; Rabin, *op. cit.,* pp. 28, 30.

[18] CDC, III, 21; IV, 13; Rabin, *op. cit.,* pp. 12, 16.

19 CDC, V, 2; VII, 10; VII, 19; XI, 18; XI, 20; Rabin, *op. cit.,* pp. 18, 28. 30, 58, 58.

20 CDC, XVI, 4; Rabin, *op. cit.,* pp. 74, 75n.

21 DSD, II, 8-10; W. H. Brownlee, op. cit., p. 10.

22 Driver, *op. cit.,* p. 476ff.

CHAPTER 8 — THE EXTENT OF THE OLD TESTAMENT CANON (pp. 180-195)

1 Ecclesiasticus has been alleged to claim inspiration in chapter 50:27-29, but actually the author neither claims to have the Word of God or His Spirit. He claims only the "inspiration of understanding" and "wisdom."

2 *Op. cit.,* p. 195.

3 *Op. cit.,* p. 82f.

4 *Vid. sup.* p. 136. The "Lamech" Scroll has now been unrolled. While it was in the possession of the Syrian Archbishop, permission was not granted to unroll it. The scrolls first purchased by him have now been purchased at the fabulous price of more than a quarter of a million dollars by Israel. It had been named by the word "Lamech" tenuously identified on a fragment broken off. It is a free Aramaic translation of Genesis interwoven with legends of the patriarchs.

5 This is Green's conclusion (*op. cit.,* p. 143) and is fairly standard. Nestle's Greek Testament gives, in an index, a tabulation of the allusions to the Old Testament in the New Testament, marking with an asterisk those that are also express quotations. There are more than 600 allusions and about 250 strict quotations. He lists no strict quotations in the books of Judges-Ruth, Chronicles, Ezra-Nehemiah, Esther, Ecclesiastes, Song of Solomon, and Lamentations. Also there are none from Obadiah, Nahum, and Zephaniah, but these books were counted as part of the "Book of the Twelve," the Minor Prophets, which was quoted many times.

6 Green, *op. cit.,* pp. 146ff.

7 Ibid., p. 148.

8 *Vid. sup.* p. 141.

9 *Op. cit.,* p. 121.

10 *Op. cit.,* p. 126.

11 *Op. cit.,* p. 124.

12 *Vid. sup.* p. 144.

13 See the details in Robert Dick Wilson, *Studies in the Book of Daniel, Second Series,* referred to above, p. 224. Five copies of the Septuagint are examined and five differing orders are found. He adds listings from the other versions and Fathers, and finds that of 60 lists, no two exactly agree.

14 Preserved by Eusebius in *Ecclesiastical History,* iv, 26.

15 Ibid., vi, 25.

16 Quoted in Green, *op. cit.,* p. 166.

17 Ibid., p. 165.

18 Ibid., p. 165.

19 Ibid., p. 168 n.

20 Ibid., pp. 172f.

21 Augustine, *De Civitate Dei,* xviii, 36.

22 Ibid., xviii, 26.

23 Green, *op. cit.,* p.176.

24 Ibid., p. 177.

25 Schaff, *op. cit.,* Vol. 2, p. 81.

26 Green, *op. cit.,* p. 195.

PART III

CHAPTER 9 — INTRODUCTION (pp. 199-218)

[1] An effort had been made by C. C. Torrey in *The Four Gospels* (1933), and by others, to prove that all four Gospels were written in Aramaic. This would not change or solve the problem if it were true. Indeed, it would make it more strange that some Aramaic and some Greek documents were mingled in one volume. But Torrey's views can hardly be maintained. E. C. Colwell seems to have given an effective answer in *The Greek of the Fourth Gospel* (1931). The traditional view, maintained by Zahn, is still attractive to the author, namely, that Matthew wrote in Aramaic and the others in Greek, just as Papias asserts in the second century.

[2] *Vid. sup.* pp. 42f., 76.

[3] Brooke Foss Westcott, *A General Survey of the History of the Canon of the New Testament* (6th ed., 1889).

[4] We might mention the Rylands Fragment of John, C. H. Roberts, *An Unpublished Fragment of the Fourth Gospel* (1935); also, the Armenian manuscript of the Diatessaron, J. Hamlyn Hill, ed. *Earliest Life of Christ Ever Compiled from the Four Gospels* (1910); and the Chenoboskian scrolls of Gnostic writings, which are not yet available, but which are said to confirm the accounts of early heresies as given in the patristic writings. Cf. V. R. Gold, *The Gnostic Library of Chenoboskian*, BA, XV (Dec., 1952), pp. 70-88.

[5] Westcott notes that Clement of Alexandria and Jerome place him in the time of Hadrian (117-137) and quotes Eusebius to the effect that he lived "not long after the times of the apostles," *op. cit.*, p. 293.

[6] J. B. Lightfoot, *The Apostolic Fathers*, ed. by Harmer, Pt. I, Vol. 2 (1890), p. 143. Westcott, *op. cit.*, p. 48.

[7] Lightfoot, *op. cit.*, p. 112.

[8] Ibid., p. 52.

[9] Westcott, *op. cit.*, p. 52.

[10] E. J. Goodspeed, *The Apostolic Fathers* (1950), p. 205.

[11] Ignatius, *To the Ephesians*, chap. 12. Printed in ANF, Vol. 1, p. 55, where the translation differs slightly. I have usually followed Westcott's translations.

[12] C. R. Gregory, *Canon and Text of the New Testament* (1907), p. 72.

[13] Westcott, *op. cit.*, p. 53.

[14] Ignatius, *To the Philadelphians*, chap. 8. Discussed by B. B. Warfield, *Revelation and Inspiration* (1927), p. 453.

[15] Westcott, *op. cit.*, p. 55.

[16] Ibid., p. 40 n.

[17] Ibid., pp. 36f.

[18] Polycarp, *Epistle to the Philippians*, chap. 3, ANF, Vol. 1, p. 33.

[19] Westcott, *op. cit.*, pp. 49 n., 54 n.

[20] Westcott, *op. cit.*, p. 293, gives the evidence.

[21] *Vid. sup.* p. 202 n. 4.

[22] Hippolytus, *Against Heresies*, vii, 14; vii, 13; ANF, Vol. 5, pp. 107, 106.

[23] Westcott, *op. cit.*, pp. 292f.

[24] Ibid., pp. 282f.

[25] This well-known material is summarized with references, Ibid., pp. 40-46 and 51.

[26] J. B. Lightfoot, *The Apostolic Fathers*, ed. by Harmer, p. 293.

[27] Gregory, *op. cit.*, p. 78.

[28] Goodspeed, *op. cit.*, pp. 19f.

[29] Westcott, *op. cit.*, pp. 55f.

30 Ibid., p. 57.
31 Ibid., p. 312.
32 Ibid., pp. 312-319.
33 Ibid., p. 317.
34 Goodspeed, *op. cit.*, p. 261.
35 Westcott, *op. cit.*, p. 77.
36 Ibid., pp. 80f.
37 Ibid., pp. 86-93.
38 Westcott had written these words in his 2nd ed., p. 260. In his 6th ed., p. 299, he allows that there is some uncertainty as to whether all of this citation is to be ascribed to Valentinus. However, it seems at least to be ascribed to someone of his school.
39 Westcott, *op. cit.*, p. 305.
40 Details are found in Westcott, *op. cit.*, pp. 275-287.
41 Ibid., p. 99 n.
42 Ibid., p. 100.
43 Ibid., pp. 167f.
44 Justin Martyr, *First Apology*, chap. 66, ANF, Vol. 1, p. 185.
45 Justin Martyr, *Dialogue with Trypho*, chap. 103, ANF, Vol. 1, p. 251.
46 Ibid., chap. 106, p. 252.
47 Justin Martyr, *First. Apology*, chap. 61, ANF, Vol. 1, p. 183.
48 Ibid., chap. 33, p. 174.
49 Ibid., chap. 67, p. 186.
50 Justin Martyr, *Dialogue with Trypho*, chap. 119, ANF, Vol. 1, p. 259.
51 Westcott, *op. cit.*, p. 212.
52 Ibid., pp. 215f.
53 Ibid., p. 219.
54 Ibid., p. 210.
55 Novum Testamentum Graece, ed. by Eberhard Nestle, rev. by Erwin Nestle (21st ed., 1952), preface, p. 72.
56 Westcott, *op. cit.*, p. 246.
57 Ibid., p. 258.

CHAPTER 10 —
Determining Principles of the New Testament Canon (pp. 219-235)

1 Westcott, *op. cit.*, p. 55f. Quoted above, p. 209 in another connection.
2 C. H. Roberts, *An Unpublished Fragment of the Fourth Gospel in the John Rylands Library* (1935).
3 Hodge, *op. cit.*, p. 162.
4 *Vid. sup.* p. 66.
5 *Vid. sup.* p. 215. *Vid. inf.* p. 260.
6 *Vid. inf.* p. 260.
7 *Vid. sup.* p. 210.
8 *Vid. sup.* p. 209.

CHAPTER 11 — The Patristic Test of Canonicity (pp. 236-245)

1 Irenaeus, *Against. Heresies*, iii, 3; in ANF, Vol. 1, p. 416.
2 Clement, *To the Corinthians*, chap. 42, ANF, Vol. 1, p. 16. (The translations of ANF are not always followed in passages cited in succeeding notes if Westcott or Zahn comment on the passages in question.)
3 Ibid., chap. 5, p. 6.
4 Ibid., chap. 44, p. 17.
5 Ibid., chap. 47, p. 18.
6 J. B. Lightfoot, *op. cit.*, p. 143.
7 Ignatius, *To the Magnesians*, chap. 7, ANF, Vol. 1, p. 62.
8 Ibid., *To the Trallians*, chap. 3, p. 67.

[9] Ibid., *To the Romans,* chap. 4, p. 75.

[10] Irenaeus, *Against Heresies,* iii, 3, ANF, Vol. 1, p. 416.

[11] Polycarp, *To the Philippians,* chap. 3, ANF, Vol. 1, p. 33.

[12] Ibid., chap. 6, p. 34.

[13] Ibid., chap. 12, p. 35.

[14] Fragments of Papias, trans. by J. B. Lightfoot, *op. cit.,* p. 528.

[15] B. B. Warfield, *Revelation and Inspiration* (1927). pp. 375ff.

[16] Papias, in Lightfoot, *op. cit.,* pp. 527, 528.

[17] Westcott, *op. cit.,* p. 73.

[18] Ibid., pp. 74f.

[19] *Vid. sup.,* n. 15

[20] T. Zahn, *Introduction to the New Testament* (reprint, 1953), Vol. 2, pp. 509ff.

[21] Westcott, *op. cit.,* pp. 75f.

[22] Epistle to Diognetus, chap. 11, ANF, Vol. 1, p. 29.

[23] Epistle of Barnabas, chap. 8, ANF, Vol. 1, p. 142.

[24] Ibid., chap. 5, p. 139.

[25] Reliques of the Elders, in Lightfoot, *op. cit.,* p. 556f.

[26] Justin Martyr, *First Apology,* chap. 66, ANF, Vol. 1, p. 185.

[27] Justin Martyr, *Dialogue with Trypho,* chap. 106, as translated by Westcott, *op. cit.,* p. 114.

[28] Ibid., chap. 106, ANF, Vol. 1, p. 252.

[29] Zahn, *op. cit.,* Vol. 2, p. 451.

[30] Justin Martyr, *First Apology,* chap. 39, ANF, Vol. 1, p. 175.

[31] Ibid., chap. 49, p. 179.

[32] Ibid., chap. 33, p. 174.

[33] Ibid., chap. 66, p. 185.

[34] Justin Martyr, *Dialogue with Trypho,* chap. 103, ANF, Vol. 1, p. 251.

[35] Ibid., chap. 119, p. 259. *Vid. sup.* p. 214.

[36] Justin Martyr, *First Apology,* chap. 67, ANF, Vol. 1, p. 186. *Vid. sup.* p. 214.

CHAPTER 12 — THE LATER AUTHORS AND PROBLEM BOOKS (pp. 246-271)

[1] Westcott, *op. cit.,* p. 336.

[2] Sanday, *op. cit.,* p. 13.

[3] Ibid., p. 13.

[4] Irenaeus, *Against Heresies,* i, 3. Cf. also i, 8; ii, 2; ii, 35. ANF, Vol. 1, pp. 320, 326, 352, and 413.

[5] Gregory, *op. cit.,* p. 149.

[6] Irenaeus, *op. cit.,* iii, 2, 1, p. 415.

[7] Ibid., iii, 2, 8, p. 428.

[8] Ibid., iii, 14, 2, p. 438.

[9] Ibid., iii, 5, 1, p. 417.

[10] Ibid., iii, 11, 2, p. 426.

[11] Ibid., iii, 5, 2, p. 418.

[12] Ibid., iii, 1, 1, p. 414.

[13] Ibid., iii, 1, 1, p. 414.

[14] Ibid., iii, 16, 2, p. 441.

[15] Ibid., iii, 7, 2, p. 420.

[16] Ibid., iii, preface, p. 414.

[17] Hodge, *op. cit.,* Vol. 1, p. 153.

[18] Irenaeus, *op. cit.,* iii, 11, 9, p. 429.

[19] Ibid., iii, 1, 1, p. 414. Zahn, *op. cit.,* Vol. 2, p. 398f., shows conclusively that "after their exodus" can only mean "after their death." (The literal translation is from the Greek given in Zahn.)

[20] Irenaeus, op. cit., iii, 10, 5, p. 425.

[21] Vid. sup. p. 243. Zahn, op. cit., Vol. 2, pp. 450f., and Westcott, op. cit., p. 114, point out that the only proper antecedent of "his" memoirs is "Peter's."

[22] Eusebius, Ecclesiastical History, iii, 39. (Using the translation of Westcott, op. cit., pp. 74f.)

[23] Zahn, op. cit.. Vol. 2, pp. 438f.

[24] Zahn, op. cit., Vol. 2, p. 394.

[25] Ibid., Vol. 2, pp. 432 and 448, n. 9 and 10, quoting Clement of Alexandria, Hypotyposes, on I Pet. 5:13, and Eusebius, op. cit., vi, 14, 5.

[26] Zahn, op. cit., Vol. 2, pp. 433f.

[27] Vid. inf. pp. 252f.

[28] Thayer so defines grammasin of Gal. 6:11.

[29] Zahn, op. cit., Vol. 3, pp. 238ff.

[30] On this extensive subject the arguments of Zahn's Introduction are weighty. Graham Scroggie, in a most helpful book, A Guide to the Gospels, also defends the traditional views with great acumen.

[31] Tertullian, Against Marcion, iv, 5, ANF, Vol. 3, p. 350.

[32] Ibid., iv, 2, p. 347. The word "Testament" is Tertullian's favorite instrumentum, used of the Old Testament as well as of the New.

[33] Tertullian, Against Heretics, chap. 20, ANF, Vol. 3, p. 252.

[34] Tertullian, Against Scorpiace, chap. 12, ANF, Vol. 3, p. 645.

[35] Tertullian, Against Praxeas, chap. 15, ANF, Vol. 3, p. 610.

[36] Tertullian, Against Heretics, chap. 22, ANF, Vol. 3, p. 253.

[37] Ibid., chap. 6, p. 258.

[38] Ibid., chap. 6, 246.

[39] Westcott, op. cit., pp. 345-347. See p. 373 for Jude and p. 371 for Hebrews, where, however, Westcott argues that Hebrews was put on a lower plane than the Scriptures by Tertullian, and specifically because it was not apostolic.

[40] Westcott, op. cit., pp. 354ff.

[41] Clement, Stromata, vii, 1; also vii, 16, ANF, Vol. 2, pp. 523, 551.

[42] Ibid., vii, 16, p. 551.

[43] Ibid., vii, 17, p. 555. Note the inclusion by Clement of James the Just among the Apostles.

[44] Eusebius, op. cit., ii, 1, quoting Clement, Hypotyposes, vii.

[45] Clement, Stromata, iv, 17, ANF, Vol. 2, p. 428.

[46] A. H. Charteris, Canonicity (1880), p. lxxxii.

[47] Origen, De Princip., iv, 1. Quoted in Westcott, op. cit., p. 365.

[48] Westcott, op. cit., p. 364. Origen's remarks on II Peter and II and III John are found in his Commentary on St. John, 5:3.

[49] Origen, De Princip., preface, ANF, Vol. 4, p. 239.

[50] Even among the Fathers the argument from the "we" sections of Acts was appreciated.

[51] Westcott, op. cit., in his 2nd ed., p. 47. The parallel of words is not positive, and Westcott, with his usual caution, has dropped it in his 6th ed., p. 54.

[52] Ibid., p. 49.

[53] Vid. sup. pp. 213, 243f.

[54] Muratorian Fragment, in loco.

[55] Irenaeus, Against Heresies, iii, 14, ANF, Vol. 1, p. 438.

[56] Vid. sup. pp. 252ff.

[57] Westcott, op. cit., p. 357.

[58] Origen, Commentary on Matthew, preserved in Eusebius, op. cit., vi, 25. Cf. Zahn, op. cit., Vol. 2, p. 385.

[59] Zahn, op. cit., Vol. 3, p. 183.

[60] Justin Martyr, *Dialogue with Trypho,* chap. 81. Cf. Westcott, *op. cit.,* p. 121.

[61] Muratorian Fragment, *in loco.*

[62] Westcott, *op. cit.,* p. 222.

[63] Ibid., p. 340 n.

[64] Irenaeus, *Against Heresies,* iv, 20. Cf. iii, 1. ANF, Vol. 1, pp. 491, 414. For the date, cf. Eusebius. *op. cit.,* v, 8, 6.

[65] Tertullian, *Against Marcion,* iii, 14, "The apostle John in the Apocalypse..."

[66] Clement, *Paed.,* ii, 12, 119; *Stromata,* vi, 13, 107. Quoted in Westcott, *op. cit.,* p. 357.

[67] Zahn, *op. cit.,* Vol. 3, p. 182.

[68] Origen, *Commentary on the Gospel of John,* Book V. Quoted in Westcott, *op. cit.,* p. 359.

[69] H. Alford, *Greek New Testament* (1861), Vol. 4, pp. 213, 221.

[70] Eusebius, *op. cit.,* iii, 28. Westcott, *op. cit.,* p. 278 n., discusses this ambiguous fragment of Caius, arguing that it is not our genuine Apocalypse he is discussing.

[71] N. B. Stonehouse, *The Apocalypse in the Ancient Church* (1929), pp. 92, 99.

[72] Westcott, *op. cit.,* p. 279.

[73] Hippolytus, *Christ and Antichrist,* chap. 36. Westcott, *op. cit.,* p. 380.

[74] Westcott, *op. cit.,* p. 372.

[75] Eusebius, *op. cit.,* iii, 29; iii, 18. Quoted in Westcott, *op. cit.,* pp. 424f.

[76] Amphilochius of Iconium. Quoted in Westcott, *op. cit.,* p. 446.

[77] Westcott, *op. cit.,* p. 448.

[78] Stonehouse, *op. cit.,* pp. 4, 5.

[79] Westcott, *op. cit.,* p. 330 n.

[80] Charteris, *op. cit.,* pp. 313-318, cites more than fifteen quotations and allusions to II Peter between Clement of Rome and Eusebius, and on pp. 328-330 he gives ten allusions to II and III John in the same period.

[81] Westcott, *op. cit.,* p. 219 n.

[82] Ibid., p. 357.

[83] Ibid., p. 362.

[84] The Greek uses a mere genitive. AV translates it "the brother of" both times; RV, "the son of"; RSV says "the son of," footnote, "the brother of," in Luke 6:16, but "the son of" without footnote in Acts 1:13. It appears that the AV is more probable. It would be strange, though not impossible, if Alphaeus who married the sister of Mary the virgin had a son and a grandson among the Twelve.

[85] The Scofield Reference Bible adopts the alternative view, p. 999.

[86] Westcott, *op. cit.,* pp. 48f., 201.

[87] Ibid., pp. 218f.

[88] Tertullian, *De Hab. Muliebri,* chap. 3. Quoted in Westcott, *op. cit.,* p. 373.

[89] Westcott, *op. cit.,* pp. 357f.

[90] Ibid., p. 362.

[91] Zahn, *op. cit.,* Vol. 1, pp. 101f.

[92] Eusebius, *op. cit.,* vi, 25. Cf. Westcott, *op. cit.,* p. 360.

[93] Westcott, *op. cit.,* p. 49 n.

[94] Ibid., p. 170.

[95] Ibid., pp. 283, 299.

[96] Ibid., pp. 355, quoting Eusebius, *op. cit.,* vi, 14.

[97] Ibid., pp. 384f.

[98] Tertullian, *De Pudic.,* chap. 20. Westcott, *op. cit.,* gives the Latin text on p. 371 n. and a translation on pp. 260f.

[99] Westcott, *op. cit.,* p. 261.

[100] Zahn, *op. cit.,* Vol. 2, pp. 302f.

[101] Eusebius, *op. cit.*, vi, 20.   Partially quoted in Westcott, *op. cit.*, p. 378.
[102] Quoted in Zahn, *op. cit.*, Vol. 2, p. 310 n.
[103] Ibid., p. 310 n. Cf. Eusebius, *op. cit.*, v. 26.
[104] Westcott, *op. cit.*, p. 372.
[105] Quoted by Westcott, *op. cit.*, p. 373.
[106] Eusebius, *op. cit.*, iii, 3.   Westcott, *op. cit.*, p. 416.
[107] Westcott, *op. cit.*, p. 423.
[108] Eusebius, *op. cit.*, v, 26. Zahn, *op. cit.*, Vol. 2, pp. 301, 310 n.
[109] Zahn, *op. cit.*, Vol. 2, pp. 296ff.
[110] Ibid., Vol. 2, p. 365 n.
[111] Ibid., Vol. 2, pp. 303f.
[112] We have not considered Peter's error at Antioch reported in Galatians 2:11. He had not erred in teaching as far as the record shows, but in example. The apostles were not sinless. But even Peter's error — concerning eating with Gentiles — was not contrary to the Old Testament precept. It only confused an issue which Paul was anxious to give out in clarity. Peter agreed with Paul in the doctrine concerned, salvation by faith alone.

In summary of the evidence, Westcott remarks: "Something then may be learnt from this (the testimony of Serapion of Egypt) as to the authority and standard of the New Testament Scriptures at the close of the second century: the writings of the apostles were to be received as the words of Christ: and those only were to be acknowledged as such which were supported by a certain (clear) tradition," *op. cit.*, p. 391. To this we say, "Amen." Our principle of canonicity is exactly that of the Early Church.

Approaching the subject from a different angle, J. Norval Geldenhuys in his valuable book, *Supreme Authority* (1953), comes to very similar conclusions. His treatment is largely confined to the New Testament. There he concludes that in the Early Church the supreme authority was acknowledged as found in Christ as the Lord. The apostles were recognized as having been given by Him unique authority for the establishment of the Church, and the writings of these apostles were therefore accepted as authoritative (p. 120). Geldenhuys is particularly helpful in exposing the views of German criticism on these subjects.

CHAPTER 13 — CONCLUSION (pp. 272-282)

[1] *Dogmatic Decrees of the Vatican Council*, chap. 2. Schaff, *op. cit.*, Vol. 2, pp. 241f.
[2] John Calvin, *Institutes of the Christian Religion*, trans. by John Allen (6th Amer. ed., 1932), i, 7, 1, and i, 7, 2, pp. 75, 76.
[3] Ibid., i, 8, 13, pp. 90f.
[4] Ibid., i, 7, 4, p. 79.
[5] Ibid., i, 7, 5, pp. 79f.
[6] *The French Confession*, chap. 4, Schaff, op. cit., Vol. 3, p. 361.
[7] *The Belgic Confession*, Art. 2, Schaff, *op. cit.*, Vol. 3, p. 385.
[8] *The Westminster Confession of Faith*, chap. 1, Schaff, *op. cit.*, Vol. 3, p. 602.
[9] S. R. L. Gaussen, *op. cit.*, p. 319.
[10] Ibid., pp. 326ff.
[11] Ibid., pp. 355ff.
[12] Ibid., pp. 367ff.
[13] Ibid., p. 375 (italics his).
[14] Archibald Alexander, *Evidences of the Authenticity, Inspiration, and Canonical Authority of the Holy Scriptures* (1836), p. 258.
[15] Ibid., p. 267.
[16] Ibid., p. 277.
[17] B. B. Warfield, *Revelation and Inspiration* (1927), p. 455.
[18] Charles Hodge, *op. cit.*, Vol. 1, p. 153.

INDEX